THE KOREAN MISSIONARY MOVEMENT

THE KOREAN MISSIONARY MOVEMENT
Dynamics and Trends, 1988-2013

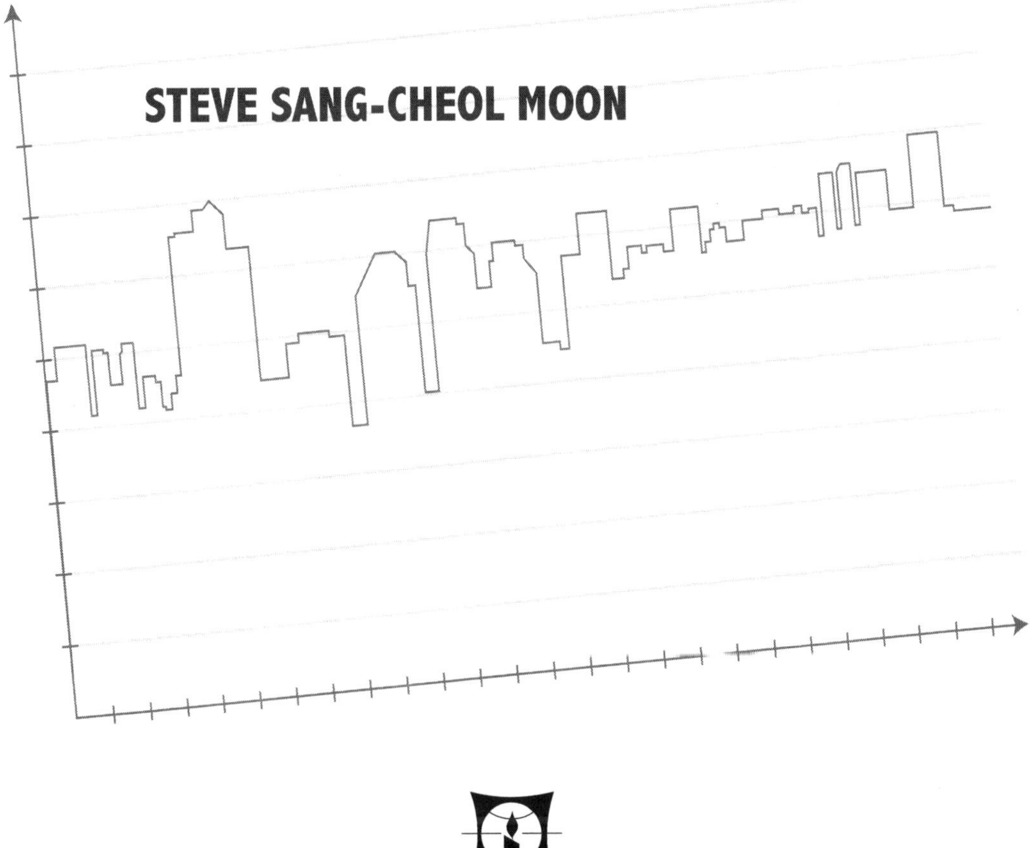

STEVE SANG-CHEOL MOON

WILLIAM CAREY
LIBRARY

The Korean Missionary Movement: Dynamics and Trends, 1988–2013

Copyright © 2016 by Steve Sang-Cheol Moon

No part of this work may be reproduced, stored in a retrieval system, or transmitted in any form or by any means—electronic, mechanical, photocopying, recording, or otherwise—without prior written permission of the publisher, except in brief quotes used in connection with reviews in magazines or newspapers.

Published by William Carey Library
1605 E. Elizabeth St.
Pasadena, CA 91104

Andrew Levin, editor
Josie Leung, graphic design
Rose Lee-Norman, indexer

William Carey Library is a ministry of
Frontier Ventures | www.frontierventures.org

Printed in the United States of America
20 19 18 17 16   5 4 3 2 1 BP400

Library of Congress Cataloging-in-Publication Data
Names: Moon, Sang-Cheol, author.
Title: The Korean missionary movement : dynamics and trends, 1988-2013 / Steve Sang-Cheol Moon.
Description: Pasadena, CA : William Carey Library, 2016. | "Some of the chapters are stand-alone studies and previously written essays." | Includes bibliographical references and index.
Identifiers: LCCN 2016000695 (print) | LCCN 2016001381 (ebook) | ISBN 9780878086306 (pbk.) | ISBN 0878086307 (pbk.) | ISBN 9780878088881 (eBook)
Subjects: LCSH: Missions, South Korean. | Protestant churches--Missions.
Classification: LCC BV2470.K6 M86 2016 (print) | LCC BV2470.K6 (ebook) | DDC 266/.0235195--dc23
LC record available at http://lccn.loc.gov/2016000695

CONTENTS

FOREWORD vii
    David Tai Woong Lee

FOREWORD xi
    William D. Taylor

PREFACE xvii
    Steve Sang-Cheol Moon

PART 1
A Record of the Progress

1   THE KOREAN MISSIONARY MOVEMENT: Dynamics and Trends, 1988–2013 3

2   MISSIONS FROM KOREA: Minitrends and Issues (2006–2013) 15

3   MISSIONS FROM KOREA 2013: Microtrends and Finance 37

4   THE KOREAN MISSIONARY MOVEMENT IN A GLOBAL AGE (2000) 43

5   THE RECENT KOREAN MISSIONARY MOVEMENT:
    A Record of Growth, and More Growth Needed 61

6   THE PROTESTANT MISSIONARY MOVEMENT IN KOREA:
    Current Growth and Development 77

7   THE KOREAN MISSIONARY MOVEMENT AND LEADERSHIP ISSUES (2008) 93

8   MISSIONS FROM KOREA 2012: Slowdown and Maturation 107

9   MISSIONS FROM KOREA 2014: Missionary Children 113

PART 2
Developmental Issues

10 MISSIONARY ATTRITION IN KOREA: Opinions of Agency Executives 121

11 GLOCALIZING KOREAN MISSIONS (2007). 143

12 THE PERFORMANCE LEVEL OF KOREAN MISSIONARIES IN TURKEY (2007) . . 153

13 THE LEADERSHIP STYLES OF KOREAN MISSIONARIES. 163

14 PARTNERSHIP IN KOREAN MISSIONS (2010) 173

15 MULTIFACETED GLOBAL PARTNERSHIP:
The Case of the Korea Research Institute for Mission 191

16 MISSIONAL ACCOUNTABILITY IN KOREAN CONTEXTS 203

17 THE PROMISE, LIMITATION, AND FUTURE
OF EMPIRICAL RESEARCH IN MISSIONS. 221

18 MISSIONARY FAMILIES AND KOREAN MISSION FINANCE:
Realities and Concerns. 231

19 THE KOREAN HOSTAGE INCIDENT: Seven Lessons Learned 243
David Tai Woong Lee and Steve Sang-Cheol Moon

20 THE PLACE AND FUNCTION OF RESEARCH IN CONTEXTS OF SUFFERING,
PERSECUTION, AND MARTYRDOM. 251

21 KOREAN MISSIONARY CHILDREN AND THEIR EDUCATIONAL NEEDS 259

22 KOREA AND THE MIDDLE EAST: Religious Encounters. 275

23 THE EDUCATIONAL MINISTRIES OF KOREAN MISSIONARIES. 281

CONCLUSION 301

BIBLIOGRAPHY. 303

INDEX 313

FOREWORD

The past thirty years have been a golden time for Korean missions. During this period the Korean missionary movement has witnessed phenomenal growth both in its magnitude and in its results. Whereas it took several centuries for a full-grown Protestant missionary movement to develop in the West, only three decades were required for the Korean mission movement to become one of the world's major missionary forces. Equipped with its own mission infrastructure and mission fields, the development of the Korean missionary supporting base has been a wholly Korean undertaking, accomplished without outside monetary aid and without being financed by the Western church. It is my pleasure and privilege to write a foreword to *The Korean Missionary Movement: Dynamics and Trends, 1988–2013*, written by Steve Sang-Cheol Moon. This volume is probably the best portrait available of what God has done through a young church, a church that itself was emerging from a series of national calamities: previous annexation by a neighboring nation; the devastation of war between the North and the South; a nation divided into two camps, resulting in more than 1,000 Christian martyrs; over 5 million war casualties in the South alone; and the whole nation turned into rubble.

A word about the author himself: It has been my joy to see the way Steve Moon has operated as a researcher during the past twenty-five years. His life as a missional researcher began with the founding of the Korea Research Institute for Mission (KRIM) in 1990, under the umbrella of the Global Missionary Fellowship (GMF). Moon became KRIM's founding director. Since 1990 his life as a researcher—his entire life, for that matter—has been intrinsically intertwined with this research center. The articles featured in this book are not only representative of his ministry during these years, but also they best tell the story of growth found in the Korean missionary movement during these formative years as it became a full partner within the global missionary force.

To put the present volume in its national context, hardly any reliable research on the Korean missionary movement done by Koreans is available for the years prior to the beginning of Moon's research ministry. As late as the 1980s, when reliable data on the Korean missionary movement was needed, we had to rely on research done by expatriates. The Korean church lacked experienced researchers as well as any means of structural support for conducting missional research. Financing of research was another obstacle that had to be overcome.

In contrast to the limited means available for research stood the growing need for research-based mission information, for about this time the Korean church and mission community had been gaining a missional conscience. The Korean missionary movement on a national scale followed. At least three areas required urgent development in order for the Korean missionary movement to be launched: the church had to be awakened to the missionary task, missionary candidates had to be trained, and mission fields needed to be pioneered. One could not dream of formulating effective strategies for developing these three essential areas without reliable research. Without the guidance provided by reliable research, the newly born movement could not grow as it should. The fledgling Korean missionary movement needed clear vision and direction. The research of Steve Moon and his companions at KRIM has had a definite role in this historical development. Moon's research products contained in the present work illuminate some of the Korean missionary movement's megatrends.

I am confident that the following three traits will become evident to readers. The first is clarity. Readers of the book cannot but see how the Korean missionary movement has progressed and where it stands currently. Second is Moon's integrity as a researcher. I have witnessed more than once that he has refused to give in to pressures for a popular or "easy" answer. Consequently, his research products are reliable. A case in point is the total number of Korean missionaries that he counts up every two years. His summary is usually conservative when compared to other higher figures that are based in part on questionable data. Third, though it is less evident, his work incorporates a global perspective. His early involvement with the global missional movement, such as the World Evangelical Alliance Mission Commission (WEA MC), and his participation in joint research projects with multinational missional leaders have borne fruit in his life and his work as a missional researcher.

The chapters, articles, and reports contained in this book are the result of hard labor exhibiting the three traits just mentioned. Often Moon's work was done from scratch, as missional research was still a rare commodity in Korea. In that sense he has captured the trends and the nature of the Korean mission movement as has no one else in Korea. His work is based on hard data and is planted on solid ground. The results of his research are a rare commodity, not only for English-speaking readers, but also for Korean nationals who until now have not had Moon's research products available in a single volume. These essays will be particularly helpful to those who are anticipating the rise of new missionary movements among latecomers to the global missionary force. New missionary movements from China and countries in Central Asia such as Kazakhstan and Kyrgyzstan are among potential beneficiaries. In light of these anticipations, I would like to express deep appreciation both to Steve Moon for writing this book and also to those who are responsible for publishing it.

David Tai Woong Lee
Director
Global Leadership Focus
Seoul, Korea

FOREWORD

God has done something unique and powerful through the mission vision of the Korean church as shown by the following salvo from this book's first chapter:

> The missionary movement in Korea recorded phenomenal growth for the period of 1988 through 2013. According to the *Korean Mission Handbook*, over these twenty-five years the total number of Korean missionaries burgeoned from 1,178 to 20,085 persons, a 1,705 percent increase. In 2013, these missionaries served with 166 mission agencies and worked in 171 countries. (3)

And by this comment from the concluding chapter:

> The striking dimension in Korea's experience of global missions is the country's swift turn from being a missionary-receiving country to being one of the foremost missionary-sending countries. As recently as the end of the 1970s, the number of foreign missionaries working in Korea was greater than the number of Korean missionaries working abroad. By the late 1980s that paradigm had been reversed. (301)

Nobody is more qualified than Steve Sang-Cheol Moon, executive director of the Korea Research Institute for Mission (KRIM; www.krim.org), to research and write this sweeping, seminal resource on the Korean mission movement. Korea now stands as the third largest missionary-sending nation (second largest "overseas" missionary-sending nation). As third largest, it follows the United States and India (most of India's missionaries serve within the borders of a nation with some 1.284 billion people).

KRIM is the research component of the Global Missionary Fellowship (GMF) network in Korea. "KRIM endeavors to provide information needed for intercultural ministry, to research and develop mission strategies, to consult on mission policies and programs, and to provide educational resources for churches, mission agencies, and missioners" (www.gmf.or.kr/category/ENGLISH).

Packed with statistics and numbers and percentages, trends and longitudinal studies and case studies, Moon's research boldly and creatively mines the Korean church and mission movement, driving shafts deep into its golden missiological heart. Moon and KRIM have produced the *Korean Mission Handbook* at regular intervals. In this new resource, which builds on the earlier Korean studies conducted by missionary researcher Marlin Nelson, Moon studies the twenty-five-year flow of Korea's mission movement, offering snapshots taken at discrete moments over the course of those years.

This work is a prime example of the maturity and competence of the Asian mission movement, and it stands out for the quality of its research and information. But the assembled research presented here is also the realization of a long-term dream and vision on the part of David Tai-woong Lee, founding chairman and senior mentor of GMF.

In chapter 14 we discover how David Lee launched the Global Missionary Training Center (GMTC) in 1986, but his broader dream was to create a Korean mission community to offer a full array of missionary services operated on a global standard. GMF now functions as an umbrella organization for nine ministries—three missionary sending agencies, two missionary training centers, one arm for research, one arm for educating missionary children, one arm for leadership training for experienced missionaries, and one arm for legal affairs and organizational coordination (see www.gmf.or.kr/category/ENGLISH).

Some of the chapters are stand-alone studies and previously written essays. Others focus on national case studies (e.g., chap. 11 on Koreans in Turkey). Some are more analytical or empirical, packed with numbers, while others provide trends and currents. Yet woven together they present a fascinating tapestry of the whole.

MY RELATIONSHIP WITH THE AUTHOR

I consider Steve Moon to be a long-term friend and am honored that he would call me a mentor. He is also a highly respected colleague on the Mission Commission of the World Evangelical Alliance, where he has played a central role in a number of our global studies on attrition and retention. He is a humble, competent, and bold cross-cultural servant with special gifting for creative empirical research balanced with a wide-angle missiological lens. To me he is the epitome of a reflective practitioner, one who asks thoughtful questions in the middle of mission praxis.

In chapter 10 he actually defines this creative term: "The notion of 'reflective practitioner' assumes the importance of combining reflection and practice in missions. Reflection without practice is irresponsible abstraction. Practice without reflection is naive activism. Putting reflection and practice together requires research; research enables practice and reflection to be combined" (251).

I was present years ago in Korea with David Lee and Steve Moon at the gathering of church and mission leaders when the Korean summary of the attrition project was presented.[1] It was a crucial moment of self-examination by all.

WHY YOU SHOULD READ THIS BOOK AND REFLECT ON ITS CONTENTS

This book is perhaps the most serious analysis of any national mission movement, providing a template for other nations, both Global North and South. Peruse the table of contents and consider the accessible richness of this book.

---

1. See William D. Taylor, ed., *Too Valuable to Lose: Exploring the Causes and Cures of Missionary Attrition* (Pasadena, Calif.: William Carey Library, 1997).

Bookend the introductory content of chapter 1 and the short concluding chapter and you have a meal—the first giving the panorama and the final one seminal lessons.

Early on, Moon lays out the structure of the book:

> Part 1 contains nine research reports showing the progress of the Korean missionary movement. The chapters seek to place the macrotrends, minitrends, and microtrends evident within Korean missions in perspective. Some chapters discuss issues that have arisen in the course of the movement's development. Part 2 contains fourteen research papers; they deal with specific issues ranging from missionary attrition to leadership development. (xxii)

Here you explore some of the singular realities of the Korean mission force. One example is their high educational level: 4.4 percent have completed a doctorate, 25.7 percent have a master's degree, 65.7 percent have an undergraduate degree, and 4.3 percent of Korean missionaries have completed only high school. At the same time, you learn of the small percentage of single women in long-term mission service, and discover why this is the case.

Chapter 14, which deals with partnership, is a gem. Moon first profiles six key Korean mission leaders, followed by crucial partnership lessons as seen through the perspective of these six.

The good news is balanced by the challenges:
- The disastrous and deadly results, generating national shame, of the twenty-three Korean short-termers who were held hostage in Afghanistan in 2007. Two were killed. The seven lessons provide a case study for us all (chap. 19).
- The pros and cons of a national surplus of seminary-trained people. With no room to serve in Korea, the vision of the surplus turns overseas. But this clouds the vision and obscures motives. Moon states, "Possibly more missionary candidates should go to business school instead

of seminary and so prepare for future ministry in creative access countries" (7).
- The downshift that started in 2006 in both Korean church growth and the Korean missions movement. This stagnation is cause for concern.
- Providing for Korea's aging mission force. What provision should be made for their retirement? In what ways are longer terms of field ministry being used as relief valves to counter retirement pressures?
- The challenge of the rising financial cost of Korean missions. Matters of concern include the growing number of Korean MKs (Moon's term is "hybrid-culture kids"), MKs' difficult return to their "passport country," the high cost of MKs' university training, the new horizon of retirement, and the growing cost of doing mission today.
- The issue of Korean-created and Korean-driven member care. Moon's observations on missionary accountability are astute.
- Ten strengths and ten weaknesses of Korean missionaries. Nobody writes with more courage than Steve Moon on this topic.

DRAWING TO A CLOSE

I love this thoughtful paragraph from chapter 8:

> In our mission work, do we rely more on "hard power" or on "soft power"? To depend inappropriately on hard power—military, material, financial, organizational, physical, and even mass media forces and equipment—may result in conveying worldviews that are non-Christian. The soft power of Christian love, in contrast, is unconditional, altruistic, nonnumerical, and immeasurable—but it transforms the world fundamentally. Only compassion for specific people motivates mission. Korean missionaries, especially

> mission leaders, need to check their actual worldviews and, as needed, change them to harness missional soft power. Short-termism, obsession with visible results, and exporting prosperity myths are a few expressions of secular worldviews. Only the practice of incarnational mission can bring about changes at a deep level. There is a growing awareness of the importance of incarnational humility among mission communities and practitioners from Korea. (110)

Moon's evocative word picture, "Toward a Theology of Ivy," is found in chapter 15. He observes:

> The life of the ivy lies in the fact that as a creeping plant its leaves and branches can grow to cover the walls of a whole building. Like ivy, we need to cover our fragmented and compartmentalized missions, churches, theologies, and lives according to the biblical image of the holy community described in Revelation 5 and 7. (196)

Writing into and from the perspective of a peninsular nation, and from the primarily monocultural and monolingual Korean realities, brings advantages and disadvantages. Moon has given us a treasure to study and from which to learn. With no reservations I commend this book to you.

William D. Taylor
Senior Mentor, Mission Commission
World Evangelical Alliance
Austin, Texas

PREFACE

In 1907, the Korean church decided to begin sending out missionaries. The first presbytery resolved that one of seven newly ordained pastors, Ki-poong Lee, would be sent to Jeju Island with full support. In 1908, the presbytery decided to send Suk-Jin Han, another of the seven who had been ordained in 1907, to Japan as a foreign missionary.[1] Since then, the Korean church has continued to send forth missionaries.

Marlin Nelson, an American who served as a missionary in Korea for forty years, saw the need for research on the status of Korean missions. In 1979 he edited the first directory of Korean missionaries and mission agencies, which served as the launching point for research on the status of Korean missions. By 1989 he had conducted three more research projects on Korean missions.[2]

In the development of the Korean missionary movement, the year 1988 stands out as especially significant. That summer Seoul hosted the Summer Olympics, a step that propelled the country to open itself to the world. The changes in policy made traveling to and from Korea easier, and transactions by Koreans in foreign currencies became more convenient. As the wait for passports became shorter, the number of Korean missionaries rose to 1,000.

---

1. For more details, see Yong Kyu Park, "Historical Overview of Korean Missions," in *Accountability in Missions: Korean and Western Case Studies*, ed. Jonathan J. Bonk (Eugene, Ore.: Wipf & Stock, 2011), 6.

2. Marlin L. Nelson, ed., *Directory of Korean Missionaries and Mission Societies* (Seoul: Asian Center for Theological Studies and Mission, 1979, 1982, 1986); Marlin L. Nelson, ed., *Directory of Korean Mission Societies, Mission Training Institutes, and Missionaries* (Seoul: Basilae, 1989).

Korea's first student mission convention, called Mission Korea, was held that same year. The convention's 664 students and young adults gathered in Seoul; 427 of them, nearly two-thirds of the participants, committed themselves to serve as missionaries in another country. The convention continues to be held every two years, sponsored by a coalition of missionary-sending agencies and campus-ministry organizations. Korean missions' systemization as a movement can be dated from 1988.

For these reasons, the year 1988 was foundational for the subsequent emergence of the missionary movement in Korea as a massive movement incorporating the participation of student ministries, sending agencies, and local churches. This book is a record and analysis of the progress of the Korean missionary movement from 1988 through 2013—a period spanning a quarter century. I have been privileged to observe and report on the progress of the movement since 1990, the year the Korea Research Institute for Mission (KRIM) began. Until 2008, my colleagues at KRIM and I completed a research project every two years. Following a gap between 2008 and 2011, KRIM has carried out research projects each year.

KRIM's operational definition of "missionary" is conservative. That definition does not include independent missionaries who do not belong to any mission agency or pastors of diaspora churches who do not belong to agencies. People who work with migrant workers in Korea are not included, either. Korean missionaries sent by diaspora churches are not counted in our numbers, although we know that there are many such missionaries. The above criteria have been applied consistently for the past twenty-five years in our research, making our identification of trends all the more valid.

RECORD OF THE KOREAN MISSIONARY MOVEMENT

Marlin Nelson's research on Korean missionaries and mission agencies resulted in four reports on the status of Korean missions, issued in 1979, 1982, 1986, and 1989. See table 0.1.

From 1979 to 1989, the span of a decade, the number of Korean missionaries grew from 93 to 1,178, marking growth of 1,266 percent. During that decade the number of Korean missionaries increased at an average annual growth rate of 29.8 percent. Stimulated by such explosive growth, some Korean church leaders at the time dreamed of someday being able to send out 10,000 missionaries. Both churches and individuals considered doing missions to be a privilege. International mission agencies served as the primary channel for sending missionaries, since indigenous mission agencies and denominations were inexperienced and lacked expertise.

Year	Missionaries	Mission Agencies	Countries of Service
1979	93[A]	21	26
1982	323	47	37
1986	511	65	47
1989	1,178	66	72

[A] In his 1979 report, Nelson did not include the number of missionary wives, although he included single missionaries of both genders. Missionary wives were included from 1982 onward.

Table 0.1. Status of Korean missions, 1979–1989

In 1990 Marlin Nelson passed the baton of research related to Korean missions to me, and I began to update the numbers from then on. Table 0.2 gives a summary for the years 1990–2000, during which period the Korean missions workforce enlarged at an average annual growth rate of 17.2 percent.

Year	Missionaries	Mission Agencies	Countries of Service
1990	1,645	74	87
1992	2,576	90	105
1994	3,272	113	119
1996	4,402	113	138
1998	5,948	127	145
2000	8,103	136	162

Table 0.2. Status of Korean missions, 1990–2000

The second Mission Korea convention, held in 1990, differed from the first by providing participants with resource materials about the unfinished task. The strategic agenda themes the convention addressed were heavily influenced by American missiology and mission strategies. During the 1990s the Korean missionary movement was further shaped and molded by efforts to strategize and systematize. Indigenous Korean mission agencies grew rapidly in their capacity to recruit new missionaries and mobilize resources for missions.

Factors that contributed to the explosive growth of Korean missions in the 1980s and 1990s included the rapid growth of the Korean church up into the 1970s, the churches' conservative theological orientation, a culture of sacrificial giving and support for missionaries, government policies that allowed for unrestricted travel and stays overseas, and a surplus of seminary graduates, who could not find ministry opportunities in Korea.

In the 2000s the total number of Korean missionaries continued to grow, but the rate of increase fell. The average annual growth rate for the decade was 10.5 percent. See table 0.3.

Year	Missionaries	Mission	Countries of Service
2002	10,422	163	164
2004	12,874	165	160
2006	14,905	174	168
2008	18,035	190	177
2011	19,373	168	177
2012	19,798	167	175
2013	20,085	166	171

Table 0.3. Status of Korean missions, 2002–2013

Though the rate of growth decreased, much progress was made in several key areas of the Korean missionary movement. Efforts to address the need for member care increased significantly, attempts were made to contextualize field strategies, discussions related to networking and partnership became more realistic, leadership transitions occurred smoothly in many mission agencies, and Korean mission leaders began to play more extensive roles within international mission agencies and missions circles. The Korean missionary movement matured phenomenally during this period.

The number of Korean missionaries reached 100 in 1980, 1,000 in 1989, 10,000 in 2002, and 20,000 in 2012. For the quarter century between 1988 and 2013, the number of missionaries from Korea increased approximately eighteenfold, and the Korean church emerged as a leading missionary-sending force. In character, the Korean way of doing missions more or less followed the Western style and was not typical of the Majority World. Because the preponderance of Majority World cross-cultural missionaries work within their own national boundaries, they do not need rigorous sending structures. One reason that partially accounts for Korean missions' Western style is that Korean missionaries have understood doing missions to mean going overseas. Since going to live and work overseas is expensive, mission agencies have felt constrained to adopt Western policies for organizing their field ministries.

The chapters in this volume offer further analyses to explain various details of the progress made by Korean missions and significant issues that have emerged along the way.

RESEARCH REPORTS AND METHODOLOGIES

Most of the chapters in this book are based on empirical research projects that utilized either questionnaire surveys or qualitative interviews. Most of the chapters were not written for this book but were reports issued over a number of years. They give snapshots of the state of the Korean mission movement at particular points along its trajectory and identify some of the issues of special concern to it at different points of its maturation. Some chapters—the articles from the *International Bulletin of Missionary Research* plus articles and chapters that have appeared in several other journals and books—have previously been published in English. A number of research reports are available here in English for the first time. All are reprinted with permission and have received various levels of editing during preparation of this volume. The data in the chapters reflect the date of the chapters' original publication or presentation. Though the chapters have received copyediting in preparation for inclusion in this volume, they have not been revised or had the information in them updated. They remain snapshots of the Korean mission movement as it appeared at particular points in time. Each chapter includes a note indicating the venue of original publication or, if an unpublished report, original presentation.

Part 1 contains nine research reports showing the progress of the Korean missionary movement. The chapters seek to place the macrotrends, minitrends, and microtrends evident within Korean missions in perspective. Some chapters discuss issues that have arisen in the course of the movement's development. Part 2 contains fourteen research papers; they deal with specific issues ranging from missionary attrition to leadership development. David Taiwoong Lee is coauthor of the chapter that discusses the 2007 incident in which Korean Christians were taken hostage in Afghanistan.

As noted, the research methodologies employed in gathering data were either quantitative using a questionnaire survey or qualitative based on interviews and direct observation. Some research projects combined the two methods. At times, quantitative research projects experienced problems in sampling, both in terms of size and representativeness and also as a result of a low response rate. Therefore, in many cases statistical analysis has been confined to descriptive statistics. In most cases, the research population was too small for a sample to represent it well, and therefore regression analysis or other rigorous statistical analyses were not possible. The qualitative research projects faced problems in using Qualitative Data Analysis (QDA) software, which is not available in Korean. I attempted to code manually, a process that took much more time for encoding and analysis and was less effective.

Although I have been responsible for conducting the research processes as a whole and for writing the reports, the numbers in this book are the result of teamwork on the part of the KRIM staff. To report the numbers correctly, the team has patiently checked and verified the original reports from mission agencies and other sources over the years.

ACKNOWLEDGMENTS

I am indebted to many people in my life and ministry. Even this book would not be possible without investment, encouragement, and support from many people around the world.

I want to express my deepest gratitude to David Taiwoong Lee, founding chairman of the Global Missionary Fellowship (GMF), Moon Gap Doh, Dong Hwa Kim, and other leaders of GMF for their special care and mentoring over the past twenty-five years. My sincere gratitude is due to Jung Kil Hong, my long-time pastor, and other pastors and lay leaders who ministered to me. My big thanks go to Jonathan J. Bonk and William D. Taylor for their encouragement, advice, and example in spirituality and leadership. I wish also to express my appreciation for my professors, especially to Paul G. Hiebert and Ted Ward for their precious teaching in research methods and also their lasting spiritual influence in my life and ministry. I humbly thank Nelson Jennings, executive director of the Overseas Ministries Study Center (OMSC), for his encouragement and partnership, and Dwight Baker and OMSC's editorial team for their efforts in copyediting this book. Eunjin Lee checked the style of some chapters, for which I am grateful. I am also grateful to Jeff Minard, manager at William Carey Library, for his encouragement and effort for this book. I thank my colleagues at KRIM for their faithfulness, understanding, and diligent work behind the scenes. I also thank my wife, Mary Hee-Joo, my daughter, Lottie Cho-Eun, and my son, Chris Nam-Eun, for their sacrifice for our ministry over the years.

Most of all, God deserves my praise and adoration and worship. I praise the name of the Lord God for his grace and peace that have sustained me on my pilgrimage!

This book is not without faults and shortcomings. I am solely responsible for all the weaknesses; they should be attributed to me alone. I hope that this book will be of help to missionaries, students of missions, mission researchers, and other mission-minded people around the world. My prayer is that many leaders of the emerging missionary movements in the Majority World will be encouraged as they read about the Korean case. Our God can do the same in other nations in the future. Amen.

Steve Sang-Cheol Moon
Executive Director
Korea Research Institute for Mission
Seoul, Korea

PART 1 A Record of the Progress

1

THE KOREAN MISSIONARY MOVEMENT: Dynamics and Trends, 1988–2013

The missionary movement in Korea recorded phenomenal growth for the period of 1988 through 2013. According to the *Korean Mission Handbook*, over these twenty-five years the total number of Korean missionaries burgeoned from 1,178 to 20,085 persons, a 1,705 percent increase.[1]

Written for the present volume, this chapter is published here for the first time.

1. The title and coverage of the *Korean Mission Handbook* has evolved over the years. It first appeared as Marlin L. Nelson, ed., *Directory of Korean Missionaries and Mission Societies* (Seoul: Asian Center for Theological Studies and Mission, 1979). Nelson prepared revised editions, published by ACTS, in 1982 and 1986. His fourth and final edition, *Directory of Korean Mission Societies, Mission Training Institutes, and Missionaries*, was published by Basilae in 1989. As requested by Nelson, Steve Sang-Cheol Moon and the staff of KRIM have—since KRIM's founding in 1990—continued the work of research on the status of the Korean missionary movement that he inaugurated.

The first edition of the directory prepared by KRIM was David Taiwoong Lee and Steve Sang-Cheol Moon, eds., *Directory of Korean Missionaries and Mission Societies* (Seoul: Basilae, 1990). From 1992 through 1998 KRIM issued an updated directory—titled *Korean Mission Handbook*—every two years, showing the development of the Korean missionary movement. These handbooks were published by GMF Press, the publishing arm of KRIM. For the years 2000–2008, only electronic editions of the handbook were issued; these also appeared biennially. Since 2010, for security and other reasons, KRIM has published only the final reports. Beginning in 2012, KRIM changed to a yearly research cycle; an English language report appears in the April issue of the *International Bulletin of Missionary Research* each year.

KRIM's operational definition of "missionary" does not encompass independent missionaries who are sent directly by local churches and do not belong to a mission agency; pastors of diaspora churches who do not belong to a mission agency;

In 2013, these missionaries served with 166 mission agencies and worked in 171 countries.[2]

More than half of Korean missionaries were serving in Asia (52.9 percent) and more than a quarter in countries with a Muslim majority (26.9 percent). A large majority of Korean missionaries (81.3 percent) were involved in traditional soul-winning ministries, including Bible translation, church planting, discipleship training, educational ministry, itinerant evangelism, and theological education.[3]

More Korean missionaries were:[4]

- married (86.2 percent) rather than single (13.8 percent)
- ordained pastors or spouses of pastors (70.4 percent) rather than lay people (29.6 percent)
- full-time (92.5 percent) rather than bivocational or tent-makers (7.5 percent)
- members of a Korean agency (88.1 percent) rather than of an international agency (11.9 percent)
- serving in regular missions (65.0 percent) rather than in frontier missions (35.0 percent)
- women (53.7 percent) than men (46.3 percent)
- members of interdenominational agencies (51.5 percent) rather than of denominational agencies (48.5 percent)

---

people who work with migrant workers in Korea (although we know that there are some); or Korean missionaries sent by diaspora churches (having emigrated, they are no longer Korean citizens). The number 20,085 is thus conservative.

Consistent application of our operational definition increases the validity of KRIM's analyses of trends in Korean missions. The statistical data and reports on Korean missionaries for the period 1979 through 1989 are drawn from Marlin L. Nelson's research. The other time periods are analyzed using data gathered by KRIM staff.

2. Steve Sang-Cheol Moon, "Missions from Korea 2014: Missionary Children," *International Bulletin of Missionary Research* 38, no. 2 (2014): 84.

3. Steve Sang-Cheol Moon, "Missions from Korea 2013: Microtrends and Finance," *International Bulletin of Missionary Research* 37, no. 2 (2013): 96.

4. Ibid., 97.

Most Korean missionaries were:
- in their forties (42.2 percent) or fifties (28.4 percent); combined 70.6 percent
- university graduates (96.2 percent); more than a third (37.5 percent) have a postgraduate degree (master's, 33.3 percent, and doctorate, 4.2 percent).

The number of Korean missionary kids (MKs) was estimated at 17,675, which nearly equaled the total number of missionaries (88.0 percent as many MKs as missionaries). Though the Korean mission movement was so young, already over one-third of Korean MKs were either university students (29.1 percent) or graduates (4.9 percent). The rest were divided among preschoolers (16.8 percent), elementary students (22.9 percent), middle-school students (13.4 percent), and high-school students (12.9 percent). Korean MKs of elementary through high school age were educated in local schools (35.9 percent), international schools (28.6 percent), schools in Korea (14.6 percent), home schooling (9.0 percent), MK schools (8.9 percent), and others (3.0 percent).[5] Many mission leaders wish to know the percentage of Korean MKs who have themselves become involved in an intercultural ministry after finishing their formal education. According to a survey carried out by the Korea Research Institute for Mission (KRIM) in 2012, only 2.3 percent of the total number of Korean MKs are serving as missionaries.[6] This percentage is very small, but the great majority of Korean MKs are still enrolled in school or university.[7]

For the year 2012 an estimated US$363 million was channeled through mission agencies for Korean missionaries. The sources for this

---

5. The figure of 8.9 percent includes students enrolled in either international MK schools or Korean MK schools.

6. This percentage does not consider the breakdown of age groups and the number of job seekers (or the employable MK population). It is simply the proportion of MKs who are already doing missionary service as a career, out of the entire MK population of all age groups.

7. Steve Sang-Cheol Moon, "Korean Missionary Children and Their Educational Needs," in *Family Accountability in Missions: Korean and Western Case Studies*, ed. Jonathan J. Bonk (New Haven, Conn.: OMSC Publications, 2013), 245–46.

income were local churches (41.6 percent), individual supporters (34.9 percent), organizations (9.8 percent), and others (13.7 percent). Mission finances were expended for missionaries' living costs (41.9 percent), field ministries (23.9 percent), home office costs (13.2 percent), organizational projects (2.8 percent), and other general purposes (18.2 percent).[8] The average monthly allocation for living costs for a four-person missionary family with two children was US$1,518. The average educational allowance for the two children of the four-person family was US$556. The average ministry fund (that is, funds provided to missionaries to cover ministry expenses) was US$812.[9]

DYNAMICS AND TRENDS

A diachronic yet descriptive analysis will enable us to look into the deeper realities of the Korean missionary movement. Dynamic factors and trends (macro, mini, and micro) related to the unprecedentedly rapid growth of the Korean mission movement are highlighted below.

Dynamic factors. What lies behind the phenomenal growth of the Korean missionary movement over the past twenty-five years? Long-term observation brings to light five factors that have contributed to the rapid advance of this movement.

First, the Korean churches' conservative theological orientation laid a good foundation for the growth of missions over the years. Without a solid theological foundation, missions can easily become too vague to practice and bear fruit. Since 1988 the conferences and related activities of Korea's equivalent to the U.S. Urbana Mission Convention, the Mission Korea movement, have orchestrated the efforts of all campus ministries and missionary-sending agencies that are evangelical in theological orientation.

Second, the explosive growth of the church in Korea in the 1960s and 1970s affected the growth of missions beginning in the 1980s. In

---

8. Moon, "Missions from Korea 2013: Microtrends and Finance," 96–97. The amount shown for "other general purposes" appears rather high because some agencies place project funds in that category.

9. Ibid.

the case of Korea as elsewhere, the missionary movement followed as the child of church revival.[10]

Third, the globalization of Korean society had an enabling impact on the missionary movement. Government policies, including unrestricted travel and overseas residence, have facilitated the missionary movement.[11]

Fourth, sacrificial giving by Korean Christians propelled the Korean missionary movement. Many Christians and churches prioritized missions budgets and mission giving over other financial needs and purposes. With the active participation and financial contributions of supporters, missionaries can survive and their ministries be sustained in their countries of service.

Fifth, the surplus of seminary graduates helps to explain the increase in expatriate Christian workers from Korea. Many young Christians who commit themselves wholeheartedly to the cause of God's kingdom enroll in seminary and then, as there are insufficient ministry positions within Korea for all seminary graduates, turn overseas for their future ministry. This phenomenon has both positive and negative consequences.[12] Positively, more workers go overseas as missionaries, but negatively, a problem arises of wrong motivation in considering missionary service. Possibly more missionary candidates should go to business school instead of seminary and so prepare for future ministry in creative access countries.

Trends: macro, mini, and micro. The Korean missionary movement has recorded explosive growth since 1988. As we have seen, the number of Korean missionaries grew from 1,178 in 1989, the year for which we have a count, to 20,085 in 2013. In the same period the number of mission agencies increased from 92 to 166, and the number of hosting countries for Korean missionaries grew from 72 to 171. The following data, based on the different editions of the *Korean Mission Handbook*

---

10. Andrew F. Walls, *The Missionary Movement in Christian History: Studies in the Transmission of Faith* (Maryknoll, N.Y.: Orbis Books, 2000), 160; Steve Sang-Cheol Moon, "The Protestant Missionary Movement in Korea: Current Growth and Development," *International Bulletin of Missionary Research* 32, no. 2 (2008): 60.

11. Walls, *Missionary Movement*, 221–40; Moon, "Protestant Missionary Movement in Korea," 60.

12. See Moon, "Protestant Missionary Movement in Korea," 60.

and related surveys (1979–2013), indicate macrotrends evident in Korean missions for this period.[13]

- The number of Korean missionaries reached 100 persons in 1980, 1,000 persons in 1989, 10,000 persons in 2002, and 20,000 persons in 2013.
- The decadal rate of increase has dropped each decade, from 29.8 percent in the 1980s, to 17.2 percent in the 1990s, 10.5 percent in the 2000s, and 1.8 percent in the 2010s.
- The annual rate of growth decreased significantly over the macro time span, from 32.10 percent in 1989 to 25.14 percent (1992), 12.70 percent (1994), 15.99 percent (1996), 16.24 percent (1998), 16.72 percent (2000), 13.41 percent (2002), 11.14 percent (2004), 7.60 percent (2006), 10.00 percent (2008), 2.41 percent (2011), 2.19 percent (2012), and 1.43 percent (2013).

The slowdown noticeable in recent years seems to be related to the negative impact of a hostage incident involving twenty-three Korean Christians in Afghanistan in 2007 as well as to the economic recession and to stagnation in church growth, among other factors.

Minitrends apparent in Korean missions for the period 2000 through 2006 include the following:[14]

- The proportion of Korean missionaries working in Asia has grown, increasing slightly from 45.3 percent in 2000 to 47.3 percent in 2006.

---

13. In the mission movement, a microtrend can be defined as one that extends for less than four years, a minitrend for four to eight years, a macrotrend for eight to twenty-five years, and a megatrend for over twenty-five years. In the technology world, the suggested time spans are different, covering much shorter periods; see John H. Vanston, *Minitrends: How Innovators and Entrepreneurs Discover and Profit from Business and Technology Trends* (Austin, Tex.: Technology Futures, 2010), xxi.

14. See Steve Sang-Cheol Moon, "The Recent Korean Missionary Movement: A Record of Growth, and More Growth Needed," *International Bulletin of Missionary Research* 27, no. 1 (2003): 11–17; Moon, "Protestant Missionary Movement in Korea," 59–64. A separate analysis of the minitrends between 2006 and 2013 is provided in chapter 2 of this book.

- Korean missionaries working in Eurasia or the former USSR increased from 10.3 percent to 14.6 percent. Korean missionaries noted the similarities between the languages and cultures of the Central Asian republics and those of Korea, and went to the region to serve as missionaries.
- Difficult situations in Islamic countries led to a decrease from 29.0 percent to 24.1 percent in missionary deployment to those countries. Analysis of more recent microtrends, however, shows that the percentage is increasing again.
- Missionaries pursuing soul-winning ministries decreased significantly from 92.0 percent to 82.1 percent; conversely, missionaries pursuing holistic ministries increased from 8.0 percent to 17.9 percent, reflecting a missiological emphasis on the need for holistic approaches such as community development and business missions.
- Single missionaries decreased from 12.7 percent to 11.3 percent. Separate and specialized means should be designed for the care of single missionaries.
- The composition of the missionary population by ministry experience has changed. Korean missionaries with over twelve years of ministry experience increased sharply from 8.0 percent in 2000 to 23.5 percent in 2006. The opportunity for theorizing and for seasoned missionaries to share their accumulated experiential knowledge is increasingly evident.

A number of significant microtrends are evident within the Korean missionary movement during the four-year span of 2008 through 2012.[15]

- The slight increase in the proportion of Korean missionaries working in Western Europe, from 3.9 percent to 5.0 percent, reflects recent challenges faced by missionaries engaged in re-evangelizing Europe.

---

15. Moon, "Missions from Korea 2013," 96–97.

- Missionaries pursuing holistic ministries increased significantly from 9.3 percent to 18.7 percent, partly reflecting the recent shift in strategic emphasis.[16]
- Ordained clergy (including spouses) have increased from 64.0 percent to 70.4 percent. This trend shows the need for greater emphasis to be on tentmaking and Business As Mission.
- The proportion of missionaries working with Korean agencies (rather than with international agencies) increased significantly, from 78.2 percent to 88.1 percent. International mission agencies need to find ways to make minority members feel at home in their organizational culture.
- Missionaries working for "regular missions" (rather than for "frontier missions") grew significantly, from 59.0 percent to 65.0 percent. This trend indicates a rebalancing of Korean missions after a time of heavy emphasis on frontier missions. Korean missionaries have become more concerned than before about receptivity to the Gospel and its spread in the field.
- The composition of the missionary population by age group has changed significantly. Korean missionaries aged fifty or older have grown from 24.4 percent in 2008 to 35.6 percent in 2012, pointing to increased need for retirement plans and preparation for retirement.
- A continuing increase in missionaries' educational level is noticeable. Missionaries with an undergraduate or higher degree increased from 95.5 percent to 97.2 percent. Missionaries with a master's as their highest degree increased from 27.3 percent to 33.3 percent over these years. Here we see too much emphasis on formal education. More attention needs to be given to nonformal and informal modes of education.

---

16. The decrease in the ratio of Korea missionaries pursuing holistic ministries from 17.1 percent in 2006 to 9.3 percent in 2008 seems to be related to the incident in Afghanistan in 2007 in which twenty-three Korean Christians were taken hostage. Sorrowful reflections on martyrdom and suffering may have affected mission agencies' reports on the purpose and nature of their members' ministries.

The Korean missionary movement recorded explosive growth for the twenty-five year period following 1988, especially up to 2006. Such rapid growth in such a short period of time has brought both positive and negative results. The recent slowdown in the rate of growth reminds us of the need to address the growing pains of the Korean missionary movement.

ISSUES AND CONCERNS

The missionary movement in Korea is not without problems and concerns. Its short history has provided little time for preparation and follow-up, and Korean churches and mission agencies have not fully understood what it takes to do missions well. If the issues are addressed properly, however, the current slowdown will be an opportunity for qualitative growth and maturation.[17] If we ask the right questions, paths to further growth will open up.

The first question is "How can we care for missionaries well?" In the 2007 survey conducted by KRIM, one open-ended question directed to Korean mission executives asked about the most urgent developmental issue faced by Korean missions. Fully one-quarter of the respondents (25.0 percent) identified member care for missionaries as the most urgent issue. Further, virtually one out of ten respondents (9.8 percent) pointed to the issue of MK education. Combining these two closely related issues shows that more than a third of the mission executives responding to the survey (34.8 percent) saw a need for increased care for missionary families. The urgency of this need is shown by a 2013 survey: out of 7,044 MKs identified, 61 (or 0.87 percent of the total) were reported to have serious problems in adjusting to their school environments.[18] Further, according to the assessment of mission executives, 0.6 percent of Korean MKs needed professional counseling or mental health

---

17. Steve Sang-Cheol Moon, "Missions from Korea 2012: Slowdown and Maturation," *International Bulletin of Missionary Research* 36, no. 2 (2012): 84.

18. There seem to be many more cases of adjustment problems than are officially reported here. Quite probably many mission executives and even staff members assisting with MK education lack detailed information about the situations of individual missionary families.

treatment.[19] Other issues highlighted by respondents to the 2007 survey were leadership (21.4 percent), research and development (18.8 percent), missionary training (16.1 percent), and support systems (8.9 percent).[20] Support systems are administrative functions carried out by home office staff, but as they have a vital relationship to member well-being they have a relation to member care as well.

The second question is "How can we facilitate leadership development for Korean missions?" The rapid increase in the number of missionaries in the field requires good leadership at different levels and in different contexts. Team leaders, country coordinators, area directors, and field directors need to be prepared for both field ministry and member care. Conscious efforts and systematic plans for leadership development need to be made both at the home base and at the international level. One of the most serious problems is that many mission agencies find it hard to form quality leadership teams because those missionaries who return home to take up leadership roles do not feel well received and supported by their commissioning churches.[21]

The third question is "How can we meet the escalating financial needs of Korean missions?" The mission agencies do not have long-term plans in place for the care and support of mission families who may be entrusted or assigned to them. Although mission agencies use most of their financial resources for missionaries' life and ministry in the field, current resources are insufficient to support the present missionary force, let alone to think of adding additional new missionaries to the harvest force. The net growth in the missionary force in 2012, which was 425 persons, indicated that additional financial support equivalent to US$7.8 million per year would be required. Calculations also suggest that within ten years over 7,000 Korean MKs would be of university age. Retirement is not a distant reality for many Korean missionaries—over 1,400 missionaries will enter retirement within the decade 2013–23

---

19. Moon, "Korean Missionary Children," 245–46.
20. Moon, "Protestant Missionary Movement in Korea," 61–62.
21. Steve Sang-Cheol Moon, "Missionary Families and Korean Mission Finance: Realities and Concerns," in *Family Accountability in Missions: Korean and Western Case Studies*, ed. Jonathan J. Bonk (New Haven, Conn.: OMSC Publications, 2013), 147.

and a total of 7,000 missionaries by 2033. Korean mission agencies do not have the financial surplus or reserves to meet these future needs.[22] Disparities in the monthly allowances paid to Korean missionaries are another urgent problem.[23]

The fourth question is "How can Korean missions best undertake self-missiologizing?" My own understanding is that self-missiologizing means to do missiology with both the local and the global interdependently in view, not independently. In Korea the level of self-theologizing, a foundation for self-missiologizing, is not at all satisfactory. Without a good foundation in self-theologizing and self-missiologizing, a missionary movement can easily fall into activism, repeating the trials and errors of the past. Integration of what we have learned through experience into the accumulated missiological knowledge base seems to be a core answer to this question.

The fifth question is "How can we participate in and facilitate well-functioning partnerships in missions?" Unity is the norm of the global churches in this ever-globalizing world. Korean churches need to make conscious effort to advance partnerships across the boundaries of cultures, traditions, and organizations. In response to a 2007 survey conducted at KRIM, a majority of Korean mission leaders projected that Korea (51.9 percent) and China (36.8 percent) would be the two leading missionary-sending countries during the twenty-first century.[24] Many other countries and streams also contribute to the global missionary movement. We cannot know for certain the future shape or contours of God's global mission, but we do know that all members of the body of Christ must work together synergistically.

SUMMARY AND CONCLUSION

The twenty-five year span, 1988–2013, saw dramatic turnarounds for the Korean church, from being a missionary-receiving church to becoming

---

22. Moon, "Missionary Families," 139–40, 143.

23. The monthly expenditure for living costs for a four-person missionary family ranges from a minimum of US$376 to a maximum of US$2,352, according to KRIM's 2013 survey (Moon, "Missions from Korea 2013," 97).

24. Moon, "Protestant Missionary Movement in Korea," 62.

a missionary-sending church. Numbers help us determine the outlines of the Korean missionary movement. A "thick description," however, would bring greater detail to that picture, allowing us to perceive the sweat, blood, and sacrificial commitment made by Korean missionaries, the driving force provided by Korean church leaders, and the contribution of Korean Christians who prayed and supported missionaries.[25] Further, behind the scenes of the Korean missionary movement that so catch the eye and receive so much attention in missionary reports stands an important and often insufficiently recognized factor: God's humble people who provide support.

Above the multiple levels of numbers, data, trends, dynamics, and movements is an all-encompassing worldview. The missionary movement is a corporate expression of the Christian worldview. At the core of the Christian worldview lies the sovereignty of God, who transformed traditional Korean worldviews into a Christian worldview, a transformation from the local to the global. Transforming worldviews, as Paul G. Hiebert succinctly states, is the central task of the Christian missionary movement in the twenty-first century.[26]

The Korean missionary movement is only one stream of many in God's global mission throughout the history of humankind. My conclusion of 2003 is still valid for Korean missions: "The phenomenal growth of the Korean missionary movement has been an unexpected expression of God's providential work, which works through the foolish and the weak" (1 Cor. 1:27–28).[27] The Triune God is the Creator and Lord of the global missionary movement, and we are all part of his harvest force.

---

25. The term "thick description" comes from Clifford Geertz, *The Interpretation of Cultures* (New York: Basic Books, 1973), 6–10.

26. Paul G. Hiebert, *Transforming Worldviews: An Anthropological Understanding of How People Change* (Grand Rapids: Baker Academic, 2008), 12.

27. Moon, "Recent Korean Missionary Movement," 17.

2
MISSIONS FROM KOREA:
Minitrends and Issues (2006–2013)

For periods of less than four years, shifts within a missionary movement can be categorized as microtrends, for periods between four and eight years as minitrends, for periods between eight and twenty-five years as macrotrends, and for over twenty-five years as megatrends.[1] This analytical report deals with minitrends in the Korean missionary movement for the seven-year period between 2006 and 2013.

MINITRENDS IN KOREAN MISSIONS

The following analysis of minitrends in Korean missions focuses on four topics: number of missionaries, deployment by religiocultural bloc, ministry types, and personnel composition.

Trends in the number of missionaries. The number of Korean missionaries continues to grow. The total number reached 14,905 in 2006, 18,035 in 2008, 19,373 in 2011, 19,798 in 2012, and 20,085 in 2013, according to surveys of Korean mission agencies conducted by the Korea Research

---

Originally delivered in Korean as a report at the Korean Missions R&D Forum, Seoul, June 13, 2014, this chapter appears in English for the first time in this book; translated, edited, and reprinted by permission.

1. This categorization is different from that adopted for technology, where a minitrend is defined as covering 2 to 5 years; a microtrend covers a time period of less than 2 years; and a macrotrend a period of over 5 years (see John H. Vanston, *Minitrends: How Innovators and Entrepreneurs Discover and Profit from Business and Technology Trends* [Austin, Tex.: Technology Futures Inc., 2010], xxi). For analysis of a missionary movement, longer time periods are desirable because the speed of change is much slower in missions than in technology.

Institute for Mission (KRIM). The number of Korean missionaries is becoming larger year by year, but the number is not growing at the same rate as in the past. Overall, from 2006 to 2013 the number of Korean missionaries grew by 5.19 percent annually, but a finer grained analysis focusing on the annual rate of increase makes the decline in the rate of growth clear: 13.11 percent for the period 2006–2008, 2.41 percent for 2008–11, 2.19 percent for 2011–12, and only 1.44 percent for 2012–13.

Several factors help to account for this noticeable decrease in the growth rate. In the summer of 2007, twenty-three Christians on a short-term vision trip to Afghanistan were taken hostage. This incident gave Christian missions a negative public image, intimidated Christians who might have been inclined to make a commitment to missions, and caused local churches to be more cautious in doing missions. Additionally, a long-term perspective suggests that the stagnation of church growth in Korea, which became noticeable in the 1990s, has significantly inhibited the growth of missions from 2008. The weakening of the mission support base is undermining the missionary movement. This minitrend is evident in young adults' pessimistic opinions about missions as well as in the decreasing number of participants and volunteers at mission conventions, of applicants for missionary training programs, and of new recruits in missionary sending agencies.

Trends in deployment. The years 2006–13 have seen only minor shifts in the proportion of missionaries serving in particular areas. The percentage of Korean missionaries working in Christian blocs decreased from 29.1 percent in 2006 to 27.5 percent in 2012. In the same period, Korean missionaries working in Islamic blocs increased from 24.1 percent to 26.9 percent. No significant changes were observed in Communist, Buddhist, and other religious blocs. The percentage of Korean missionaries working in animistic blocs decreased from 4.1 percent to 2.7 percent, but the percentage of Korean missionaries in Hindu blocs grew from 3.8 percent to 4.1 percent.

The increase during this period in the number of Korean missionaries serving within Islamic and Hindu blocs indicates that the Korean missionary movement is driven more by frontier missions (outreach to unreached people groups) than by regular missions (missions in reached areas). The momentum behind Korean involvement in the frontier missions movement, which began in the early 1990s, continued into the next decade. During the years 2006–13, the proportion of the Korean mission force as a whole active in frontier missions increased significantly from 29.6 percent to 35.0 percent. The conservative theological orientation of the mainline churches, their leaders' evangelical understanding of mission, and the volunteers' eschatological vision of mission gave strong support to the enterprising spirit of Korean missions.

Trends in ministry type. Several minitrends in ministry type can be observed in the period 2006–13: an increase in church-planting ministry, from 39.1 percent to 45.3 percent; a decrease in discipleship training, from 21.5 percent to 16.1 percent; a slight increase in educational ministries, from 9.2 percent to 10.4 percent; a slight increase in theological education, from 5.0 percent to 6.6 percent; a significant decrease in itinerant evangelism, from 4.4 percent to 1.5 percent; a slight decrease in social work, from 4.3 percent to 3.9 percent; no significant change in community development, from 4.0 percent to 4.2 percent; a significant decrease in medical service, from 3.5 percent to 1.5 percent; a significant increase in missional business, from 3.4 percent to 9.2 percent; and a decrease in Bible translation, from 2.9 percent to 1.4 percent.

Overall, ministries directly related to winning souls recorded a slight decrease, from 72.9 percent to 70.9 percent. Conversely, the proportion of holistic ministries is slowly increasing. These changes do not reflect a fundamental change in missionary vision, but can be understood as a complementary effort to be more effective and strategic in field ministries.

The increase in church-planting ministries reflects the goal of frontier missions to plant a viable indigenous church within each of the world's unreached people groups. The increase in educational ministries and theological education has come from the need for development of spiritual leadership on the various mission fields. Increases in community development and missional business have arisen with the adoption of a holistic understanding of missions, since indirect approaches to ministry are often more effective as means of evangelization. Missional businesses in particular create opportunities for access to and for living and ministering in many areas.

Changes in the harvest force. During the period 2006 to 2013 the percentage of female missionaries increased from 50.3 percent to 53.7 percent, while the proportion of single missionaries grew from 11.3 percent to 13.8 percent. This trend reflects the increasing leadership by women and unmarried individuals in Korean society. Such significant changes in the sociocultural climate of Korea affect the Korean church and Korean missions as well.

The percentage of missionaries in their 20s decreased from 7.4 percent to 4.4 percent, and of missionaries in their 30s from 32.0 percent to 17.9 percent. In the same period, Korean missionaries in their 40s increased slightly, from 39.8 percent to 42.2 percent; those in their 50s rose sharply, from 17.0 percent to 28.4 percent; and those in their 60s grew from 3.8 percent to 7.2 percent. The aging of the Korean mission force is evident as the proportion of missionaries 50 and over advanced from 20.8 percent to 35.6 percent over this seven-year period. Korean missionaries who have spent the prime of their lives in the mission field are now turning gray. Also, many people are joining the harvest force after spending the first half of their lives in a secular field. The sharply increasing number of missionaries who will be facing retirement within ten years makes the issues surrounding missionary retirement of considerable importance.

Between 2006 and 2013 the Korean mission force matured in terms of length of ministry experience. At the low end of the scale, the proportion of missionaries with less than four years of experience decreased, from 29.0 percent to 25.2 percent. Those with four to eight years' experience grew slightly, from 25.2 percent to 28.2 percent, but the proportion of missionaries with eight to twelve years' experience fell, from 22.3 percent to 15.3 percent; those with twelve to sixteen years' experience also fell, from 15.2 percent to 12.8 percent. The proportion of missionaries with over sixteen years' experience, however, climbed dramatically, from 8.3 percent to 18.6 percent. These figures show that the Korean missionary movement is gaining on-the-mission-field experience as it shifts from being a new sending force into a more mature sending force.

Analysis of Korean missionaries' final academic degrees also indicates maturing of the missionary force. During this period the proportion of missionaries with only a high school diploma decreased from 4.3 percent to 2.8 percent, and holders of undergraduate degrees as their highest degree declined from 65.7 percent to 59.6 percent. Missionaries with master's degrees increased significantly from 25.7 percent to 33.3 percent, while those with doctoral degrees decreased slightly from 4.4 percent to 4.2 percent. Many volunteers for missionary service enter seminary to prepare for ministry abroad. A large majority of Korean missionaries now go to the field after finishing a master of divinity program, hence the increase just noted in the percentage of missionaries with master's degrees. A related observation is that 70.4 percent of Korean missionaries are ordained pastors or the spouses of ordained pastors. Whether this tendency reflects the needs found on the mission fields merits thorough discussion.

From 2006 to 2013 the percentage of Korean missionaries serving with international mission agencies dropped, from 18.6 percent to 11.9 percent. Conversely, the percentage of missionaries who are members of domestic agencies increased significantly, from 81.4 percent to 88.1 percent. Reasons for the shift include the higher level of support required by international mission agencies, the burden of learning English as an intra-agency lingua franca, the international agencies' unfamiliar organizational culture, and the longer and more subtle screening procedures utilized by international agencies. Korean missionaries find domestic mission agencies to be more receptive to their specific needs: they are more culturally sensitive, form Korean teams that share Korean sentiments, and are stronger in their ties with Korean denominations and local churches.

The percentage of tentmakers or bivocational missionaries has dropped steeply, from 33.5 percent in 2006 to 24.2 percent in 2008 and to 7.5 percent in 2012. This huge change represents a diminishing role for tentmaker-sending agencies such as University Bible Fellowship and Campus Ministry International as well as the failure of other mission agencies to develop good models of tentmaking ministries. Theories of tentmaking ministry were introduced within Korean mission circles from the early 1980s, but successful examples were not cultivated and were not shared effectively. Attempts in greater number are now being made to create missional businesses, but cases of self-support through business are still underreported. The vision of Business As Mission is an excellent example for missional businesses and ministries to follow as they prepare for field ministry.

ISSUES WITHIN KOREAN MISSIONS

The analyses that follow draw on data gathered by means of surveys, questionnaires, visits, and structured interviews carried out by KRIM. They report on the perceptions of Korean mission leaders during the period from 2006 to 2013 regarding mission strategizing, leadership, accountability, finance, care of missionary kids (MKs), and educational ministries. The respondents were asked to select one answer from a pre-established range of possibilities in the surveys, and the percentages indicate the proportion of respondents who ranked that answer in first place.

Strategizing. In KRIM's 2006 survey questionnaire, the strengths of Korean missions checked by the mission leaders include, in decreasing order, rich personnel resources (75.0 percent), technological expertise including IT (11.5 percent), know-how in missions (8.7 percent), and rich financial supply (4.8 percent). What some saw as strengths, others saw as points of weakness. Concerns were identified as weak support system (45.0 percent), lack of know-how (25.2 percent), lack of expertise and experts (24.3 percent), and lack of applicability of high technology such as IT (5.4 percent).[2] As ways for consolidating bases of support, respondents ranked introducing good ministry models (46.3 percent), raising awareness levels among local churches (38.9 percent), regulating the number of missionaries (11.1 percent), and mobilizing support from individuals and organizations (3.7 percent).

The percentage of mission executives who highlighted each issue as most significant was: member care (25.0 percent), leadership development (21.4 percent), missionary training (16.1 percent), research and development (18.8 percent), education of MKs (9.8 percent), and

---

2. The 2006 dataset, based on a forty-question survey conducted at the end of December 2006 and completed by mission administrators, was analyzed along with the issue of strategizing in Steve Sang-Cheol Moon, "The Protestant Missionary Movement in Korea: Current Growth and Development," *International Bulletin of Missionary Research* 32, no. 2 (2008): 59–64.

consolidating support bases (8.9 percent). These executives expect that providers of member care will be experts (that is, professional counselors and others with similar expertise) (44.9 percent), fellow missionaries (22.4 percent), agency leaders (20.6 percent), and leaders of supporting churches (12.1 percent). For the education of MKs, approximately half of the respondents checked the issue of MKs' establishing their cultural identity (47.3 percent).

In the area of research and development (R&D), urgent tasks ranked were research about mission strategies (45.7 percent), mission fields (26.7 percent), mission personnel (23.8 percent), and mission history (3.8 percent). The strong desire expressed by the executives for R&D related to mission strategy gives evidence of a pragmatic orientation. As for innovations in mission strategy, respondents saw the use of mass media as important for missions, including the Internet (55.0 percent), satellite broadcasting (27.5 percent), printing (9.2 percent), and on-air broadcasting (8.3 percent).

According to the mission leaders the areas of missionary training in most need of being reinforced are character formation (43.5 percent), communal living (32.4 percent), and study of mission fields during pre-field training (20.4 percent). Only 3.7 percent listed missiological knowledge as an area receiving inadequate attention during missionary training. Stability and maturity in personality along with spirituality (53.7 percent) are considered essential in leadership development, more so than knowledge, experience, or managerial capability.

The mission executives' forecasts regarding the future growth of the Korean missionary movement varied considerably. They projected that by 2030 the number of Korean missionaries would grow by 15,000–20,000 (10.1 percent), 20,001–30,000 (24.7 percent), 30,001–50,000 (18.0 percent), 50,001–80,000 (24.7 percent), 80,001–100,000 (11.2 percent), and over 100,000 (11.2 percent). Those who supplied an estimate of 50,000 or less (52.9 percent) were nearly equaled by those who thought the figure would be more than 50,000 (47.1 percent).

The high value mission leaders gave to strategizing highlights their realistic awareness of and conservative views about human nature and leadership, but also discloses that they rank the massive size of the movement over its qualitative maturation.

Leadership. In responding to a survey conducted by KRIM in 2008, Korean mission leaders (92.2 percent) overwhelming agree on the importance of leadership in missions, with more than half (51.9 percent) considering leadership very important and another 40.3 percent considering it important.[3] Only a small number of respondents (3.9 percent) replied that leadership is not important, while 2.6 percent were not certain.

Virtually all the survey respondents (93.5 percent) considered the concept of servant leadership to be appropriate, with very appropriate selected by 36.4 percent and appropriate by 57.1 percent; inappropriate was selected by only 3.9 percent, very inappropriate by 0.0 percent, and others by 1.3 percent. Positive evaluations of field missionaries' willingness to practice servant leadership totaled 88.3 percent, combining very positive (14.3 percent) and positive evaluations (74.0 percent). Only 5.2 percent of respondents evaluated that willingness negatively, indicating negative (3.9 percent) and very negative (1.3 percent). A small number of respondents (5.2 percent) were uncertain.

When asked who has the greatest influence on missionaries' learning about and growing in servant leadership, respondents identified agency leaders (32.5 percent), missionary trainers (27.3 percent), and fellow missionaries (26.0 percent). The role of home church leaders (11.7 percent), seminary professors (1.3 percent), and other leaders (6.5 percent) received much less emphasis. To the question of which stage of leadership training should receive particular focus and be reinforced, respondents identified pre-field training (50.6 percent), churches and student fellowships (23.4 percent), continuing education for missionaries (13.0 percent), seminaries (5.2 percent), and others (6.5 percent).

A majority of respondents (77.9 percent) highlighted the need for missionary leadership to be adaptable, with more than half asserting that leadership should be very different depending on the situation (57.1 percent) and one in five stating that it should be somewhat different depending on the situation (20.8 percent). Only a minority asserted that the

---

3. An unpublished report based on the 2008 dataset drawn from the forty-question survey highlights the issue of leadership with responses from Korean mission executives. See Steve Sang-Cheol Moon, "The Korean Missionary Movement and Leadership Issues (2000–2020)" (unpublished paper, 2009).

nature of missional leadership is fixed, stating either that it will vary little in different situations (15.6 percent) or that it is not related to differences of circumstances at all (5.2 percent). To the question, "What situational factors should missionaries consider when they exercise leadership?" half of the respondents pointed to the cultural context of the field (50.6 percent). Other factors identified were leadership of the churches in the field (19.5 percent), the missionaries' gifts (18.2 percent), the status of evangelization (9.1 percent), and other responses (1.3 percent).

A large majority of mission leaders (84.4 percent) agreed that within the community of mission personnel in the field, horizontal, not hierarchical, leadership structures need to be set up, with 24.7 percent very positive and 59.7 percent positive. The remainder of the respondents, a small minority, did not agree. Nearly as many respondents (79.2 percent) considered Western models of leadership structure to be irrelevant for Korean mission teams and organizations (irrelevant, 72.7 percent, and very irrelevant, 6.5 percent). Only 18.2 percent thought them to be either relevant (14.3 percent) or very relevant (3.9 percent). Respondents indicated that field leaders (57.1 percent) should take the initiative for forming leadership structures for the mission personnel in the field, followed by field members (28.6 percent), home leaders (9.1 percent), leaders of supporting churches (1.3 percent), and others (2.6 percent).

Virtually all respondents affirmed that leadership structure and organizational culture are interrelated, with 72.7 percent confirmative and 19.5 percent very confirmative, leaving only 1.3 percent denying that they are linked, another 1.3 percent strongly denying the correlation, and 3.9 percent not expressing an opinion. Elements influencing the organizational culture of missionary teams include Korean church culture (33.8 percent), the local culture of the receiving countries (31.2 percent), Korean secular culture (15.6 percent), theological orientation (14.3 percent), and others (3.9 percent). A majority (67.5 percent) viewed the influx of younger missionaries as a cause of incremental changes in the organizational culture of missions, with 64.9 percent confirmative and 2.6 percent strongly confirmative. Those who disagreed were divided between 20.8 percent negative and 2.6 percent strongly negative. The remaining 7.8 percent were neutral.

The most frequent answer to the question, "How long has your mission's executive been in the position of CEO?" was less than five years (37.7 percent), followed by five to ten years (26.0 percent), ten to fifteen years (7.8 percent), fifteen to twenty years (14.3 percent), and over twenty years (13.0 percent). A majority of present mission leaders have been serving as CEO for less than ten years (63.7 percent). For the question, "What is a desirable term of service for mission executives?," the largest number of respondents chose five to ten years (46.8 percent), followed by fifteen to twenty years (24.7 percent), over twenty years (11.7 percent), fifteen to twenty years (10.4 percent), and less than five years (5.2 percent). Qualifications seen as important for mission leaders include character and spirituality (75.3 percent), ministry experience abroad (11.7 percent), educational and training experience (5.2 percent), fund-raising ability (5.2 percent), and other (1.3 percent).

Korean mission leaders generally support the ideal of servant leadership, yet they seek to avoid naivety in applying it to missionary service. The leaders favor adaptability as situations may require, approve of horizontal organizational cultures for missionary teams and organizations, are aware of the diverse cultural dynamics that surround organizational cultures, and prefer shorter terms in office for CEOs. These preferences show a stabilizing tendency within Korean missions' leadership as Korean missions pass beyond their early entrepreneurial stage.

Accountability. In answering KRIM's 2011 survey, the sixty-one Korean mission executives who filled out the questionnaire were nearly unanimous (57.4 percent very important and 39.3 percent important) in asserting that accountability is an important issue for Korean mission agencies.[4] Only 3.3 percent denied the issue's importance. Problem areas the respondents identified as needing greater accountability were ministry (47.8 percent), finance (22.4 percent), strategy (14.9 percent), property ownership (3.0 percent), and others (11.9 percent).

---

4. This survey, on accountability, was conducted at the end of 2011. Sixty-one mission executives participated by answering eight questions. Related key-informant interviews were completed by July 2012. The results of the analysis were published as Steve Sang-Cheol Moon, "The Missional Accountability in Korean Contexts," *Hapshin Theological Review* 1 (November 2012): 137–49.

Nearly two out of five Korean mission organizations (37.7 percent) utilize nonprofessional accountants to handle financial audits. An equal number engage certified professional accountants (24.6 percent) or external auditing organizations (11.5 percent), but one in twelve (8.2 percent) conducts no audit and 18.0 percent follow some other procedure. Audits are carried out at varying frequencies: once a year (52.5 percent), twice a year (30.5 percent), four times a year (5.1 percent), non-periodically (5.1 percent), or other (6.8 percent).

Sixty-one mission agencies reported a total of forty-four cases of dispute about property ownership. The top decision-makers regarding property ownership were reported to be the home board (56.7 percent), the missionaries involved (11.7 percent), field entities representing missionaries (10.0 percent), related stakeholders including representatives of supporting churches (5.0 percent), and others (16.7 percent). These practices contrast with the desires that respondents expressed as to what entity should be responsible for making final decisions about property ownership; their preferences were home boards (56.9 percent), field entities representing missionaries (19.6 percent), related stakeholders including representatives of supporting churches (19.6 percent), and the missionaries involved (3.9 percent).

Responsibility for overseeing ministerial and strategic accountability was seen as falling to the home director and administrative team (35.9 percent), field systems and entities (21.9 percent), home boards (17.2 percent), and others (18.8 percent). Some respondents (6.3 percent) did not see a need for such oversight.

Factors affecting missionaries' level of accountability include pre-field training, minimal structures and policies (relying on the voluntary spirit of individual missionaries), practicing biblical principles, using an accountability checklist, setting periodical reporting systems, and sharing positive cases as models for accountability.

A series of key informant interviews conducted by the author, in July 2012, with ten mission administrators and missionaries brought important insights on accountability to light. Analysis of the interviews identified both different perspectives and common ground and also offered practical solutions for some issues. Field missionaries approach the matter of accountability holistically and relationally, whereas mission administrators understand the issue from the perspective of policies and regulations. Mission administrators tend to think in terms of bounded sets, whereas field missionaries tend to think in terms of centered sets.[5] Outwardly, bounded-set people would appear to be more thorough in pursuing accountability, but at a deeper level centered-set people tend to practice accountability voluntarily. In its essence, accountability is related to one's spiritual attitude.

For many mission executives accountability is a sign of maturity. Improvement of accountability structures is important, but voluntary pursuit of rectitude in one's conduct and relationships is a matter of personal integrity. The *coram Deo* spirit, living one's life in the presence of God, should be the foundation of accountability. Common wisdom, based on spirituality, commends prioritizing well.

Practically speaking, the boards of mission agencies need to function effectively, and from time to time their character and functions should be redefined. To avoid being overpowered by a dominant individual or being relationally oriented, boards need to be reinforced with expertise. Large-scale projects need to be checked and double-checked for their relevance in the field. Team structures and ministries need to be built up within field structures. In order to harmonize specific needs in the field and the overarching perspectives at home, leaders need to communicate well. Clear terms and conditions for property ownership need

---

5. The cognitive category of bounded sets points to clear boundaries demarcating homogeneous groups. Bounded-set thinking, a cultural orientation characteristic of Westerners, can emphasize integrity but at the same time raises the potential for problems of legalism. Orientation of life and outlook by reference to a central value or person, which defines the cognitive category of centered sets, characterizes the cultural orientation of many Asian peoples, including the Korean people. People with a centered-set outlook tend to emphasize relationships. For the Korean people the concept of a boundary is not absent, but a person's relationship with the center has overriding importance. These cultural differences should be neither exaggerated nor underestimated. Both outlooks have strengths and weaknesses. Awareness of the important distinction between bounded sets and centered sets for missiological thinking is especially indebted to Paul Hiebert. See his *Anthropological Reflections on Missiological Issues* (Grand Rapids: Baker Books, 1994), 130–31.

to be defined and agreed on prior to purchasing properties in the field. Good accountability requires the development of leadership at various levels.

Finance. KRIM's 2012 survey of sixty-six major mission agencies highlighted the issue of finance. For 2012 the total income of Korean mission agencies came to Korean won 385,874,403,850 (equivalent to US$363,005,083).⁶ In 2011, missions income per missionary was ₩18,809,194 (US$17,694), a figure that grew to ₩19,490,575 (US$18,335) in 2012.

In 2012, sources of financial income for mission agencies were local churches (41.6 percent), individuals (34.9 percent), institutions/organizations (9.8 percent), and others (13.7 percent). Expenditures were made for missionaries' living expenses (41.9 percent), ministry expenses (23.9 percent), home ministries and managerial costs (13.2 percent), projects at the organizational level (2.8 percent), and general funds and others (18.2 percent).⁷

The average monthly living cost for a four-person missionary family was ₩1,614,358 (or US$1,518), ranging from a low of ₩400,000 to a high of ₩2,500,000.⁸ The monthly educational cost for the four-person family's two children spanned from ₩200,000 to ₩1,000,000, with an average of ₩591,082 (US$556). The average family's ministry expenditure was ₩863,933 (US$812), with a minimum of ₩300,000 and maximum of ₩2,000,000.

---

6. KRIM's annual survey conducted at the end of 2012 focused on the issues of MK education and finance. Sixty-one mission executives participated. The survey results were reported in Steve Sang-Cheol Moon, "Missions from Korea 2013: Microtrends and Finance," *International Bulletin of Missionary Research* 37, no. 2 (2013): 96–97. The figure shown does not include financial support channeled directly from local churches, which is hard to calculate. The exchange rate between Korean won and U.S. dollars was US$1=₩1,063 as of December 31, 2012.

7. Many mission agencies categorize the cost for field projects under "general funds." Some agencies also included funds for member care within the category "others."

8. We need to note the disparity in living expenses for missionaries. What does it mean to relate to another missionary incarnationally in the light of a financial gap? See Jonathan J. Bonk, *Missions and Money: Affluence as a Missionary Problem Revisited*, rev. ed. (Maryknoll, N.Y.: Orbis Books, 2006), 172–79, 182–88.

The Korean missionary movement is inhibited both qualitatively and quantitatively by insufficient funding. Both new and seasoned missionaries experience financial shortage. Only 47.8 percent of missionaries have sufficient financial support. The actual financial supply comes to only 62.3 percent of the desired level of support. Many Korean missionaries (42.9 percent) have experienced a decrease in their financial support since their departure for the field. Although overall mission income for the period 2008 to 2012 has grown at a faster rate (4.29 percent) than the increase of personnel (2.36 percent), the financial allocations over which missionaries have control and that they can use for their own purposes are not increasing as needed. Creative and innovative means of fund-raising need to be developed for the sake of continual quantitative growth as well as qualitative maturation of the Korean missionary movement.

Missionary kids. In 2012 KRIM carried out research on the education of Korean missionary kids (MKs). This research project involved a questionnaire circulated among mission agencies at the end of 2012 and field-based interviews conducted in nine countries from October 2012 through April 2013. As of December 2012, there were 19,798 Korean missionaries; they had 17,432 children.[9] By educational level, the children were younger than school age (16.8 percent), or attend elementary

---

9. The questionnaire survey for this research was conducted at the end of December 2012, and the field-based research was conducted from October 2012 through April 2013 in 9 countries, interviewing 176 members of the Korean missions circle (70 missionaries, 76 MKs, 30 MK educators). After transcription, interview notes were prepared for qualitative data analysis. The survey of Korean missions with special attention to MKs was published as Steve Sang-Cheol Moon, "Missions from Korea 2014: Missionary Children," *International Bulletin of Missionary Research* 38, no. 2 (2014): 84–85. A more detailed report, also in English, was published as Steve Sang-Cheol Moon, "Korean Missionary Children and Their Educational Needs," in *Family Accountability in Missions: Korean and Western Case Studies*, ed. Jonathan J. Bonk (New Haven, Conn.: OMSC, 2013), 243–58. A fuller report in Korean was published subsequently as a booklet entitled *Hankuk Seonkyosa Janeodeuleu Kyoyukjeok Pilyo* [The educational needs of Korean missionary children] (Seoul: GMF Press, 2013), for presentation at a consultation on MK education.

school (22.9 percent), middle school (13.4 percent), high school (12.9 percent), or university (29.1 percent), or are post-school jobseekers (4.9 percent). At the elementary, middle, and high school levels, the children attended local schools in the host country (35.9 percent), international schools (28.6 percent), Korean schools in Korea (14.6 percent), home-schools (9.0 percent), MK schools (8.9 percent), and Korean schools abroad or others (3.0 percent). According to the field study, each of these types of school presented certain strengths and weaknesses.

In order to improve the education of MKs, more effort needs to be given to understanding their psychological condition before they leave for the field so as to help consolidate their relationship with God and with their parents, to help them to learn the language needed for education in their field, to encourage them in learning how to initiate and develop meaningful friendships with other students, and to help them preserve their cultural identity.

Parents and others need to prepare financially for their children's education rather than to choose a course of education based on naive fideism. They need to check carefully the real conditions and costs for educational programs. Considering the financial limitations of Korean churches and missions, that the parents pursue the best option the family can afford in light of its own financial realities seems to be a good guideline when they make decisions about their children's education.

For their part, MKs need to be helped to understand the realities of their lives and education as well as to accept the givens of their circumstances with a grateful heart. An MK's spiritual, cultural, and relational assets are rich, which can create opportunities for him or her later in life. If MKs internalize their identity and develop sound coping strategies, they may strengthen their psychological and emotional stability and thus be prepared to adjust well in unfamiliar situations in the future.

Successful MK educators can help MKs to belong to both their home culture "A" and their host culture "B," which practically speaking means that they belong to a hybrid culture "AB." My suggestion, based on empirical study, is to replace the old term "third culture kid" with "hybrid culture kid." Our understanding of MK education should be updated accordingly.

Churches in Korea need to set aside an agreed upon portion of their mission budget to support educators of missionary children, because these lay missionaries, who are not directly involved in evangelism and church planting, find it hard to raise support for their ministry. God's people who accept the lordship of God and yearn for the progress of his kingdom need to pay more attention to MKs. Though these children are often richly gifted, they are sometimes neglected. God's mission is cross-cultural and also cross-generational.

Educational missions. In 2013 KRIM conducted research on the educational ministries of Korean missionaries. From September to December, qualitative field-based research was carried out in six countries, augmented by a questionnaire survey at the end of the year. Sixty mission executives filled out the questionnaire form. At the conclusion of 2013, Korean missionaries involved in educational missions made up 17.0 percent of the total Korean missionary force.[10] This figure included missionaries engaged in theological education. Together they had established 810 educational institutions, encompassing 104 elementary schools, 55 secondary schools, 44 universities and colleges, 389 seminaries, 183 after-school learning centers, and 35 vocational training centers.

The 810 educational institutions are located on every continent. Of the 423 schools (52 percent of the total) for which KRIM has an address, 62.4 percent are located in Asia, 18.0 percent in Africa, 13.0 percent in Latin America, 3.3 percent in Europe, 1.9 percent in the former USSR, and 1.4 percent in Oceania. See the accompanying table.

---

10. The survey of the educational missions of the Korean churches began at the end of December 2013 and was completed at the end of February 2014. Fieldwork involving observation and interviews was conducted in six countries—Mongolia, Bangladesh, Nepal, Indonesia, Cambodia, and Cameroon—from September 2013 through December 2013. The research team visited 14 educational institutions and interviewed 112 persons (71 students, 20 professors/teachers, and 21 administrators). The recorded interview sessions were transcribed, producing interview notes of 268 pages (A4, single space), which were analyzed qualitatively. The results of this research project were published in Korean as a booklet; see Steve Sang-Cheol Moon, *Hankuk Kyohoeeu Kyoyukseonkyoeu Hyeonhwangkwa Baljeonbangan* [The status of educational missions of the Korean church and suggestions for development] (Seoul: GMF Press, 2014).

School level	Asia	Africa	Latin America	Europe	Former USSR	Oceania	Location not available	Total
Elementary	31	18	8	1	1	0	45	104
Secondary	21	6	6	1	0	2	19	55
Universities and colleges	10	3	2	1	1	0	27	44
Seminaries	60	5	12	9	3	4	296	389
Vocational training centers	23	9	2	1	0	0	0	35
After-school centers	119	35	25	1	3	0	0	183
Total	264	76	55	14	8	6	387	810

Table 2.1. Korean mission schools by geographic region

To assess the attitude of Korean mission executives toward the educational ministries of Korean missionaries, we asked them to answer ten questions.

The first question asked for an overall evaluation of the effectiveness of the educational ministries of Korean missionaries. The executives' response was strongly positive (80.0 percent), with 58.2 percent positive and 21.8 percent very positive. Negative responses came to only 3.6 percent and 0.0 percent for very negative. A somewhat larger group (16.4 percent) recorded a neutral opinion.

The second question asked the executives to identify the most positive component of Korean missionaries' educational ministries. Fully 62.5 percent chose the benefit that educational missions provide to poor students who otherwise lack educational opportunity. Only a small number of respondents (5.4 percent) highlighted missionary provision of an elite education that local schools in their countries of service do not provide. The cause of specialized education was supported by 12.5 percent, the provision of Korean-style education by only 5.4 percent, and other aspects by 14.3 percent.

The third question sought to identify the most negative component of Korean missionaries' educational ministries. The most common response (46.4 percent) pointed to mission schools' inability to become self-supporting and their continuous need for support from Korean churches. The second most negative aspect identified (19.6 percent) was the lack of long-term stability, caused by sociopolitical instability in the field. Other opinions were a low level of effectiveness in comparison to the enormous financial needs (12.5 percent), duplication of local schools or competition with them (10.7 percent), and others (10.7 percent).

The fourth question elicited ways the educational ministries of Korean missionaries might be improved. About half of the respondents (50.9 percent) selected from a list of pre-supplied responses that missionaries in educational ministries should assess the educational needs of their respective fields and plan and run schools of optimal size. Two other common answers proposed cooperation with schools in the field and in Korea, avoiding duplication (22.6 percent), and running schools in ways that take trends in globalization and international exchange into account (13.2 percent). The idea of running the schools in a Korean way, however, reflecting the characteristics of the Korean educational system, received minimal support (1.9 percent). Other opinions (11.3 percent) included having a long-term perspective when operating schools, raising the level of awareness of educational ethics, improving educational administration, strengthening ties with the parents of students, and strengthening relationships with local communities and societies.

The fifth question addressed self-support for educational ministries. A majority of the survey respondents (56.0 percent) recommended being flexible in applying policies on self-support, in light of differences within each field's local context. One in five respondents (20.0 percent) endorsed the goal of achieving complete self-support within ten years. More than one in ten respondents (12.0 percent) expressed the opinion that due to their special character, educational missions will need external support on a long-term basis. Only a small proportion of respondents (4.0 percent) supported the idea that educational missions should depend on tuition and other internal income sources from the very beginning. Other suggested arrangements (8.0 percent) included the idea of receiving support until complete self-support becomes possible and the idea of raising support from other churches, organizations, and individuals in a third country.

The sixth question covered leadership succession within educational ministries. One important response (37.7 percent) was that missionaries need to recruit faculty members from among the local people from the start and, for the sake of a smooth changeover, to give thought to the process of leadership transition from missionaries to local leaders. Other respondents (28.3 percent) stated that missionaries need not only to plan leadership transfer from the start but also to finish it within ten years; an almost equal number (26.4 percent) advocated being flexible and not adhering to a fixed approach since local situations differ. The remainder (5.7 percent) encouraged planning for leadership succession from the start but carefully considering the progress of the ministry and changes in the ministry environment as decisions are made.

Question seven addressed the issue of property ownership and management. More than half of the respondents (53.7 percent) observed that a universal policy is hard to apply; approaches need to be flexible in light of varying local contexts. One out of three mission executives

(33.3 percent) stated that school ministries should not be entered into unless the property to be used is owned by a legal body. Only a small number of respondents supported either ownership by multiple individuals (1.9 percent) or ownership by a missionary or missionary team in situations where foreigners can possess property (1.9 percent). Others (9.3 percent) suggested consulting with local experts concerning the ownership and management of educational properties.

Question eight focused on the qualifications of educational missionaries. A large majority of respondents highlighted educational philosophy and conviction (67.3 percent). Passion about caring for students ranked second, but some distance behind (19.2 percent). Less emphasized were experience in school administration (7.7 percent), including fund-raising, or as a teacher (3.8 percent). A few (1.9 percent) stated that all of the above components should be combined within the qualifications of educational missionaries.

Question nine looked to future prospects for educational ministries. A large majority of respondents (69.2 percent) forecast that such ministries would have an enhanced role in the twenty-first century due to the influence of globalization and educational exchanges. One in five persons (19.2 percent), however, forecast a diminished place for educational ministries, judging that they would be confined to certain regions and areas and that the need for small-scale ministries would be limited. Also, a small number of mission executives (7.7 percent) believed that the need for educational missions would dwindle due to the development of indigenous educational institutions. Other responses (3.8 percent) highlighted the need to use English and to focus on the poor in educational ministries.

Question ten sought to identify niches appropriate for educational missions in the twenty-first century. Answers to this question were widely dispersed. Perceived need for diverse regular schools (32.7 percent) was balanced by equal emphasis on the need for vocational training centers (32.7 percent). Respondents also mentioned needs for specialization and differentiation in regular schools (15.4 percent), for after-school learning centers (11.5 percent), and for e-learning and vocational training in Islamic countries (7.7 percent).

Qualitative research on Korean missionaries' educational ministries involved visiting educational institutions in six countries and interviewing the schools' leaders or administrators, professors and teachers, and students, which was followed by transcription of the interviews and analysis of interview notes. How do the findings obtained through qualitative data analysis differ from those provided by statistical data analysis?

The data derived from the interviews were generally consonant with the results of the quantitative data analysis. In other words, the judgments expressed by the mission executives on the basis of their personal experience were not markedly different from the research team's conclusions reached through systematic data gathering and evaluation. Mission leaders in Korea understand the situation in the field well, and their judgment can be relied on as being objective.

Both the questionnaire and the qualitative field study produced positive evaluations of the overall effectiveness and efficiency of the educational ministries of Korean missionaries. The aim of appreciative inquiry is not only to evaluate strategically and realistically but also to encourage insightful strengthening of educational competencies.[11] Our appreciative inquiry presupposed that a school can be strong in some areas but weak in others. The field study's main purpose was to flesh out the strengths of particular organizations so that others could benefit through comparison and self-evaluation. The overriding concern was how to increase strengths and compensate for weaknesses creatively.[12]

Under the categories of attitude and know-how we find elements that could be shared with missionaries in other parts of the world and with generations to come. Desirable attitudes for good educators are love for students, a desire to uncover students' strengths and potential, patience, listening skills, a cooperative mind, creative thinking, and the ability to motivate. Know-how that could be shared includes understanding of

---

11. Scott Johnson and James D. Ludema, eds., *Partnering to Build and Measure Organizational Capacity: Lessons from NGOs around the World* (Grand Rapids: Christian Reformed World Relief Committee, 1997), 9.

12. Suresh Srivastva and Frank J. Barrett, "Appreciative Organizing: Implications for Executive Functioning," in *Appreciative Management and Leadership: The Power of Positive Thought and Action in Organization*, ed. Suresh Srivastva and David L. Cooperrider, 392–97 (Euclid, Ohio: Williams Custom Publishing, 1999).

the educational policies of the host country, identification of the niches for educational ministries, consideration of the conditions of the host location, the establishment of an effective information system, cooperation with NGOs, the conduct of periodic diagnosis and evaluation, and understanding of changes in the Korean educational system and environment.

That educational ministries not repeat past mistakes is important, but to make progress by drawing on accumulated knowledge and wisdom in educational missions is even more important. As conscious effort is invested for maturation and improvement, educational missions will be an important genre of the Korean missionary movement in the twenty-first century.

CONCLUSION

The minitrends apparent over the seven years from 2006 through 2013 show that the Korean missionary movement is stagnating. Although the number of missionaries is still growing, the decline in the rate of increase indicates a slowdown in quantitative growth.

The reports I prepared during this time period brought to the fore certain issues as I interacted with Korean mission leaders, Korean church leaders, international mission leaders, and others active in God's global mission. The reports focused on the issues of strategy, leadership, accountability, finance, MK education, and educational ministries. Analyses and discussions on these topics led me to highlight procedures and decisions that need to be made for the maturation of Korean missions. From a long-term perspective this time period may prove to be a period of transition from rapid growth to stagnation in numbers. It could also, however, be a *kairos* moment for advancing qualitative maturation and building strength for the long run. The foundations have been laid; observing trends carefully, we need to consolidate gains made and build well on those foundations so as to advance missions from Korea.

3

MISSIONS FROM KOREA 2013:
Microtrends and Finance

The Korean missionary movement continues to slow down; the survey of the Korean missionary force and mission agencies conducted by the Korea Research Institute for Mission in 2012 shows that though the aggregate number of foreign missionaries is larger, the annual rate of growth continues to decline. In 2012 there were a total of 19,798 Korean missionaries serving in countries outside South Korea.[1] One year earlier, in 2011, there were 19,373 foreign missionaries, yielding an increase of only 425, or 2.19 percent annual growth.[2] Fifty-five agencies reported membership growth in 2012, whereas thirty-five agencies experienced membership decrease, due to attrition or transfer to another agency. The total number of missionaries serving with denominational agencies increased by 6.0 percent, while the larger number of missionaries serving with interdenominational agencies decreased by 0.9 percent.

Since 2008, because of closures, mergers, and inactivity, the number of mission agencies has decreased from 190 to 167. In 2012, three agencies closed their ministries and two new agencies began, for a net

---

Originally published as "Missions from Korea 2013: Microtrends and Finance," *International Bulletin of Missionary Research* 37, no. 2 (April 2013): 96–97, this chapter is reprinted by permission.

1. Originally published as "Missions from Korea 2013: Microtrends and Finance," *International Bulletin of Missionary Research* 37, no. 2 (April 2013): 96–97, this chapter is reprinted by permission.
The total number of missionaries reported by Korean agencies for 2012 is 20,840. Of these, 1,042 are counted twice (i.e., they appeared on the list of more than one agency); the net total is 19,798.

2. The average annual growth rate since 2008 has been 2.36 percent.

decrease of one from the total for 2011. In 2012 these 167 agencies included 118 sending agencies and 49 supporting agencies; 152 of the mission agencies were interdenominational, and only 15 were denominational. Korean missionaries are active in 175 countries.

More than half of all Korean foreign missionaries are working in Asia (52.9 percent), and more than a quarter in countries that are majority Islamic (26.9 percent). A large majority of them are involved in traditional soul-winning ministries, including Bible translation, church planting, discipleship training, educational ministry, itinerant evangelism, and theological education (81.3 percent).

Changes in Korean missions since 2008 include:[3]

- The proportion of Korean missionaries working in Asia has grown, increasing from 47.3 percent in 2008 to 52.9 percent in 2012.
- Korean missionaries working in Eurasia or the former USSR decreased from 14.6 percent to 9.2 percent. Government restrictions or termination of visas caused much of this decline.
- A slight increase in the proportion of Korean missionaries working in Western Europe—from 3.9 percent to 5.0 percent—reflects recent calls for missionaries to engage in the challenge of re-evangelizing Europe.
- Missionaries pursuing soul-winning ministries decreased from 90.7 percent to 81.3 percent; conversely, missionaries pursuing holistic ministries increased from 9.3 percent to 18.7 percent. In part, this change reflects recent emphasis on the need for holistic approaches such as community development.
- Emphasis on missionary deployment to Islamic blocs has led to an increase from 23.2 percent to 26.9 percent.
- The proportion of Korean missionaries focusing solely on reaching non-Koreans with the Gospel has increased noticeably, from 82.6 percent to 89.2 percent.

---

3. So as to indicate trends in missionary personnel and finance between 2008 and 2012, the starting point figures in the following draw on a survey conducted in 2008.

- The proportion of Korean missionaries joining denominational agencies instead of interdenominational agencies has grown from 46.7 percent to 48.5 percent. This trend arises from churches' preference for seminary graduates with theological education rather than laypersons when choosing new missionaries to support.
- Accordingly, ordained clergy (including spouses) have increased from 64.0 percent to 70.4 percent.
- Also related is a sharp increase in full-time (vs. bivocational) missionaries from 75.8 percent to 92.5 percent.
- The proportion of missionaries working with Korean (vs. international) agencies increased significantly from 78.2 percent to 88.1 percent.
- Missionaries working with "regular missions" (vs. "frontier missions") grew from 59.0 percent to 65.0 percent.
- The majority gender for Korean missionaries changed from male (52.0 percent in 2008) to female (53.7 percent in 2012).
- Single missionaries increased from 10.3 percent to 13.8 percent.
- Composition of the missionary population by age groups has changed. Korean missionaries age fifty or older have grown from 24.4 percent in 2008 to 35.6 percent in 2012, pointing to the increased need for retirement plans and preparations.
- Continuing increase is noticeable in missionaries' educational level. Missionaries with an undergraduate or higher degree increased from 95.5 percent to 97.2 percent. Those with a master's degree as their highest degree jumped from 27.3 percent to 33.3 percent over the last four years.

These microtrends are intertwined with financial issues, to which several survey questions were directed for the first time. These questions revealed the following:[4]

The total amount of mission finance channeled through mission agencies is estimated to be Korean won (₩) 385,874,403,850, or an equivalent

---

4. KRIM researchers Jung Ju Lee and Mi Suk Chae contributed significantly to the collecting and analysis of the data presented in this article.

of US$363,005,083, in 2012.[5] The organizational budget per person was ₩18,809,194 (US$17,694) in 2011, and it grew to ₩19,490,575 (US$18,335) in the estimated budget of 2012. For 2009–12, aggregate income for all agencies grew 4.29 percent annually, which exceeded the annual rate of increase in personnel (2.36 percent) for the same period.

In 2012, support for mission finances came from local churches (41.6 percent), individual supporters (34.9 percent), organizations (9.8 percent), and others (13.7 percent). Categories of mission expenditures were missionaries' living costs (41.9 percent), field ministry funds (23.9 percent), home administration and other maintenance costs (13.2 percent), project costs at the organizational level (2.8 percent), and general fund/other (18.2 percent).[6]

The average expenditure per month for living costs for a four-person missionary family was ₩1,614,358 (US$1,518), ranging from a minimum of ₩400,000 to a maximum of ₩2,500,000.[7] The average educational cost for the same four-person missionary family was ₩591,082 (US$556), ranging from a low of ₩200,000 to a high of ₩1,000,000. The average ministry fund was ₩863,933 (US$812), with a spread extending from ₩300,000 to ₩2,000,000.

The current level of Korean mission finance, which is not adequate to support increases in the number of missionary personnel, impedes further growth of the Korean missionary force, both quantitatively and qualitatively. New missionaries as well as seasoned laborers are struggling under burdens caused by financial shortage. Creative and innovative ways need to be developed to fund strategic missionary services.

---

5. This amount does not include mission funds that were sent directly to foreign countries by local churches. Such funds are hard to trace. The exchange rate on December 31, 2012 (US$1 = ₩1,063), is used here.

6. In many mission agencies, expenditures for field projects are managed in the category of general fund. Funds for missionary member care are also included here.

7. The disparity in living standard among missionaries needs careful attention. What does it mean for missionaries to relate to one another and to serve incarnationally in light of such disparity? For a significant review of these and related issues, see Jonathan J. Bonk, *Missions and Money: Affluence as a Missionary Problem Revisited*, rev. and expanded ed. (Maryknoll, N.Y.: Orbis Books, 2006), 172–79, 182–88.

Missionaries						19,798
Mission agencies						167
sending/supporting						118/49
interdenominational/denominational						152/15
Receiving countries						175
Deployment (percentage)						
by continent/region						
Asia	52.9	Latin America	5.2	Oceania		1.9
North America	9.4	Western Europe	5.0	Other		2.7
Eurasia/former USSR	9.2	Middle East	4.5			
Africa	7.3	Eastern Europe	1.9			
by religious/cultural bloc						
Christian	27.5	Buddhist	14.3	Other		5.8
Islamic	26.9	Hindu	4.1			
Communist	18.7	Animist	2.7			
by ethnic/linguistic focus						
non-Korean	89.2					
ethnic Korean	8.1					
non-Korean and ethnic Korean	2.7					
by ministry type						
church planting	45.3	community development	4.2	Bible translation		1.4
discipleship training	16.1	social service	3.9	Other		9.2
educational ministry	10.4	itinerant evangelism	1.5			
theological education	6.6	medical service	1.5			
Personal data (percentage)						
male/female						46.3/53.7
married/single						86.2/13.8
clergy (including spouses)/lay						70.4/29.6
full-time/bivocational						92.5/7.5
serve with interdenominational/denominational agency						51.5/48.5
serve with Korean/international agency						88.1/11.9
serve in "regular"/"frontier" mission field						65.0/35.0
age distribution						20s (4.4), 30s (17.9), 40s (42.2), 50s (28.4), 60s and up (7.2)
missionary experience						<4 years (25.3), 4–8 (28.2), 8–12 (15.3), 12–16 (12.8), >16 (18.6)
highest degree						doctorate (4.2), master's (33.3), bachelor's (59.6), high school (2.8)
Missions finance (in US$, per year)						
total missions income						363,005,083
annual rate increase						4.29%
sources of income (percent)						local churches (41.6), individuals (34.9), organizations (9.8), other (13.7)
expenditures (percent)						missionaries' living costs (41.9), field ministry funds (23.9), home administration (13.2), organizational projects (2.8), general fund/other (18.2)
cost per missionary						17,694
living expenditure per month for four-person family						1,518
educational expense per month for four-person family						556
ministry fund per month for four-person family						812
missionaries with adequate support						47.8%
portion of aggregate support need met						62.3%
trends in individual support raising						decreases (42.9), no change (25.0), increase (28.6), other (3.6)

Table 3.1. Korean missionary totals as of December 2012

4

THE KOREAN MISSIONARY MOVEMENT IN A GLOBAL AGE (2000)

In former days the route traveled by the Korean missionary movement was a narrow alleyway, but now in the year 2000 it travels with great rapidity on a wide road. At the same time, the passageway has become more complex. More objects fill the way, more distractions pop into view, more traffic competes for attention, more signs and signals announce more regulations to be followed—in sum, much heavier demands are placed upon our attention. With the enlarged scale of the Korean missionary movement comes greater responsibility. A mindset inherited from the past is no longer adequate for addressing the new issues and challenges facing us today.

In 1990 the Korea Research Institute for Mission (KRIM) began to conduct research on the status of the Korean missionary movement, compiling data sets on mission agencies and on missionaries sent by Korean churches, research that had been pioneered by Marlin L. Nelson, who for forty years served in Korea as a missionary and professor of mission.[1] The questionnaire for KRIM's biennial surveys establishes statistics not only for current ministries but also for new issues such as investment in information technology, missionaries' ministry fund (that is, money allocated to them for ministry purposes), member care, and cooperation with other mission agencies. This analytical report for 2000 focuses on general trends in Korean missions in this ever-globalizing world.

Originally published in Korean in the electronic edition of *Korean Mission Handbook* (Seoul: GMF Press, 2000), this chapter is published here for the first time in English; translated, edited, and reprinted by permission.

1. For a timeline of Marlin Nelson's study of the Korean missionary movement, see chapter 1, endnote 1.

THE CONTINUAL GROWTH OF KOREAN MISSIONS

Some factors in the development of a missionary movement cannot be quantified. This report focuses on measurable indicators of the Korean missionary movement's growth, including numbers of missionaries, mission agencies, and countries of service. Changes and trends are noted, and issues related to qualitative growth are also discussed.

Increase in the Number of Korean Missionaries

At the end of 2000, missionaries sent by churches in Korea totaled 8,103 missionaries working in 162 countries through 136 mission agencies. In terms of Protestant foreign missions, Korea sends more missionaries than other country with the exception of the United States.[2]

Nelson's first tabulation of Korean missionaries, in 1979, reported the existence of 93 missionaries, counting only the husbands (for married missionaries) plus single missionaries.[3] By 1989, with couples (husbands and wives) being counted as two missionaries, the number had grown to 1,178, for a 1,266 percent increase between 1979 and 1989.

According to KRIM's first research on this movement, in 1990 the number of Korean missionaries was 1,645; that figure would grow to 8,103 in 2000. The growth rate in the 1990s was 492.6 percent, much lower than in the previous decade but still a remarkable increase. The total of 8,103 includes only missionaries who belong to mission agencies and not the so-called independent missionaries, who do not belong to any mission agency. The number also does not include short-termers, who are involved in field ministries for less than two years, or ministers who emigrate to minister to diaspora Koreans overseas. The figure of 8,103 is therefore conservative.

---

2. India comes before Korea in terms of number of cross-cultural missionaries. Most Indian missionaries work within the national boundaries of India, however, and therefore Korea has more Protestant missionaries in terms of number of foreign missions. Patrick Johnstone and Jason Mandryk, with Robyn Johnstone, make this point clear in *Operation World* (Cumbria: Paternoster Publishing, 2001), 388.

3. Marlin L. Nelson, *Directory of Korean Missionaries and Mission Societies* (Seoul: Asian Center for Theological Studies and Mission, 1979).

The economic crisis of 1997, caused by a shortage of foreign currency, raised concerns about a potentially negative impact on the development of Korean missions, but the missions continued to grow, even at an accelerated pace. The growth rates through the 1990s are as follows: 1990–92: 56.6 percent, 1992–94: 27.0 percent, 1994–96: 34.5 percent, 1996–98: 35.1 percent, and 1998–2000: 36.2 percent. This trend shows that growth of the Korean missionary movement was apparently unaffected by financial concerns within its support base.[4] The current annual growth rate of 17.7 percent indicates that approximately 1,000 new missionaries are being sent yearly from Korea, which positions the Korean church as an important harvest force.

The vast majority of Korean missionaries (87.3 percent; 7,072 persons) are married. The proportion of single missionaries has continued to drop, from 20.0 percent in 1994 to 16.0 percent in 1996 to 15.0 percent in 1998 and to 12.7 percent (1,031 persons) in 2000. The increasing ratio of married missionaries to single missionaries has to do with the development of denominational mission agencies with their preference for married missionaries who have finished theological training. Although the attrition rate among single missionaries is higher, perhaps a sign of their being less fixed in the course of their lives, the role and contribution of single missionaries need to be given greater recognition.[5] Single missionaries, since they do not need to wait until they are married and have finished their theological education, can enter the mission field much earlier in their lives. The general trend that finds missionary candidates leaving for the field in their mid-thirties or older is not desirable,

---

4. Although this statement is generally true, the Korean missionary movement faces difficulties that are a result of the economic recession, especially in the area of long-term investment for maturation. Responding to my report that Korean missions have continued to grow numerically despite economic difficulties, Paul McKaughan, executive director of the Evangelical Fellowship of Mission Agencies, confirmed in a personal conversation that the American missionary movement had not been seriously impeded by economic difficulties in its history.

5. KRIM's survey of missionary attrition, conducted in 1994, showed that while 20.0 percent of Korean missionaries were single, they constituted 45.9 percent of attrition cases. See Steve Sang Cheol Moon, "Missionary Attrition in Korea: Opinions of Mission Executives," in *Too Valuable to Lose*, ed. William D. Taylor (Pasadena, Calif.: William Carey Library, 1997), 135.

because they lose the opportunity for training in cultural sensitivity and ministerial creativity through trial and error at a young age.

The rapid increase in the number of missionaries highlights the need to develop missionary member care systems. If one team leader is needed for every 10 missionaries, 810 well-trained leaders are needed at present. Moreover, if one country coordinator or regional leader is needed for every 50 missionaries, 160 such experts are needed for the care of the missionaries. In practice, since missionaries are dispersed throughout numerous countries, more leaders are needed than these figures suggest. As the number of Korean missionaries continues to grow, weakness in the leadership pool will become all the more evident. Korean churches and mission agencies need to make a joint effort to overcome this problem if the movement is to continue to develop well.

Increase in the Number of Korean Mission Agencies

In two decades the number of Korean mission agencies has grown, from 21 in 1979 to 74 in 1990, 127 in 1998, and 136 in 2000.[6] There are now 98 sending agencies, 11 missionary training centers, 4 research institutes, 6 associations of mission agencies, and 17 supporting and cooperating organizations. Of the 136 agencies in 2000, 22 are denominational and 114 are interdenominational. Seven out of the nine newly added mission agencies are sending agencies. The number of mission agencies is not growing at the same rate as the number of missionaries, because missionaries prefer to join large, well-established mission agencies.[7]

In 1998 the largest missionary sending agency was the University Bible Fellowship (UBF); by 2000 the Global Missionary Society

---

6. Marlin L. Nelson's original research reported the number of Korean mission agencies to be 89 in 1986 and 92 in 1989, but KRIM's research team has reduced these figures to 65 and 66, respectively, after removing general Christian organizations unrelated to cross-cultural missions. These changes make the totals shown consistent with the categorization applied by KRIM since 1990.

7. So-called venture missions face particular challenges, just as venture business start-ups are not easy. New missionary candidates must be aware of both the benefits and the potential disadvantages of joining a newly born mission agency.

(GMS), with 1,021 missionaries, had surpassed the UBF, with 889 missionaries. These two are followed by the General Assembly of Presbyterian Church (Tonghap), with 616 missionaries, and the Methodist Church, with 592 missionaries. In terms of long-term career missionaries, Global Missionary Fellowship is Korea's largest interdenominational missionary sending agency, with 310 members working through its three sending arms. Other large missionary sending agencies include the Foreign Missions Board of the Baptist Convention (277 members), the Assemblies of God (269), Presbyterian Kaehyuk (Reformed) (231), Presbyterian Koshin (213), and the Holiness Church (197).

The list of the ten largest missionary sending agencies in 2000 shows a transition from interdenominational to denominational agencies, and also from student fellowships to specialized missionary sending agencies. The change from UBF to GMS as the largest missionary sending agency is typical of this transition. The rise of denominational mission agencies reflects the reality that in general the support base of such agencies is stronger than that of interdenominational sending agencies. A potential danger is amplified by this trend as denominational mission agencies may rigidly transplant a particular theological orientation into a cross-cultural setting.

The 1990s saw the rise of large mission agencies. In 1992 one mission agency had a membership of over 300 missionaries, then in 1994 the largest membership was over 400, in 1996 over 500, in 1998 over 700, and most recently, in 2000, over 1,000. As of 2000, four mission agencies report that they have over 500 missionaries, 24 agencies that they have over 100 missionaries, and 33 agencies that they have over 50 missionaries. The number of mission agencies with over 100 members was four in 1990, but grew to be 24 in 2000. This trend of growth in membership continued despite Korea's economic crisis in 1997. The number of mission agencies with over 500 members grew from two in 1998 to four in 2000, and the number of mission agencies with over 200 members grew from seven in 1998 to nine in 2000.

Becoming self-satisfied with numerical growth can hinder development in other areas, such as the area of expertise. The big mission agencies need to set a good example for excellence in member care, contingency planning, and infrastructure as well as in development of mission-related expertise. Large mission agencies need to cooperate for the sake of enhancing the performance of Korean missions in general through sharing knowledge and specialist personnel across organizational boundaries. They also need to make the results of their research available as resources in support of smaller organizations.

Increase in the Number of Receiving Countries

The number of countries receiving Korean missionaries grew from 26 in 1979 to 87 in 1990, 145 in 1998, and 162 in 2000. In terms of the number of countries receiving its missionaries, Korea appears in second place, with only the United States ranking higher.[8] Ironically, today the Korean people are one of the most scattered people groups in the world, whereas for over a thousand years they lived only within the Korean peninsula. One of the reasons they are so dispersed is that so many Koreans seek to preach the Gospel. The Korean missionary movement is evidence of God's providential work, in which the foolish of the world shame the wise and the weak things of the world shame the strong (1 Cor. 1:27).

In 2000, Korean missionaries are working in Asia (45.3 percent), Eurasia (former USSR, 10.3 percent), Europe (8.9 percent), Africa (6.9 percent), Latin America (7.0 percent), the Middle East (5.4 percent), Oceania (3.3 percent), North America (2.8 percent), and other regions (9.9 percent). The proportion working in Asia grew from 41.6 percent in 1998 to 45.3 percent in 2000, and over the same period the proportion working in the Middle East grew from 4.5 percent to 5.4 percent. The proportions working in Latin America, Eurasia, Europe, Africa, and other regions decreased over those two years. Cultural proximity may account for the increase in the proportion working in Asia, with another contributing factor being that Asia is the least evangelized continent. The increase in the Middle East should be attributed to the advance of the frontier missions movement in Korea in the 1990s.

---

8. According to the *Mission Handbook 1998–2000*, the United States has missionaries in 197 countries; see John A. Siewert, ed., *Mission Handbook 1998–2000: U.S. and Canadian Christian Ministries Overseas*, 17th ed. (Monrovia, Calif.: MARC, 1997), 88–93.

The ten countries that receive the largest number of Korean missionaries are China (781), the Philippines (527), Japan (463), Russia (359), Germany (288), Thailand (233), Indonesia (216), the United States (183), India (160), and Uzbekistan (138).[9] In 1979, when research on Korean missions was first conducted, Japan was the largest mission field for Korean missionaries.[10] Now in 2000, however, China has become the largest receiving country for Korean missionaries, which is all the more remarkable in light of the many restrictions that country places in the way of mission work. This change in deployment expresses the changing emphases in the Korean missionary movement.

As the number of receiving countries continues to grow, so too does the need to study the situation in each country and to plan appropriate strategies for reaching the people with the Gospel. Awareness of this need is higher among younger missionaries than among those who have been serving longer in the mission field. How many among the over 8,000 Korean missionaries can be considered to be expert on a region or culture? Experienced missionaries need to expend more effort in advising and leading younger missionaries in acquiring such knowledge. Korean missionaries are involved in traditional forms of ministry, but such traditional ministries need to be conducted in light of new insights and with new approaches. Overcoming a tendency toward activism in mission, which does not pay due attention to the importance of reflection and strategizing, is an issue to be addressed through research.

It is encouraging to know that even as church growth within Korea stagnates and even during an economic recession, 8,103 Korean missionaries are working with 136 mission agencies in 162 countries. A greater number of missionaries means, however, greater need for support. Rapid growth has not allowed time to address growing pains. Missionaries need systematic care; mission agencies need more support for development; and mission fields need strategic investment. For the

---

9. These are minimum figures for the number of working missionaries in each country; each number has been verified against the names of missionaries. Additional missionaries in creative access countries at times wish to remain anonymous for reasons of security. Many more Korean missionaries work in China than reported here.

10. Nelson, *Directory of Korean Missionaries and Mission Societies*, 44.

sake of further growth and maturation, the missionary movement in Korea needs to address such issues, which accompany growth.

WHAT MISSION AGENCIES NEED TO DO

In the early stages of its development, the emerging Korean missionary movement could claim the inexperience of youth, and progress through trial and error seemed reasonable. Now as a leading force in global missions, Korean missions need formal criteria and a new mindset. The nature of missions is innately both local and global, and therefore both localization and globalization must be acknowledged.[11] The standards and criteria of experienced missionary sending countries need to be applied to Korean missions' practice of member care, sending structures, and field strategy.

Member Care: From Noninterference to Systematic Care

Korean mission agencies' pursuit of growth in membership has led more attention to be given to recruiting and mobilization than to member care. Field missionaries also have preferred to work by themselves and to make decisions independently, without close supervision. Weak member care, however, bars the way to advanced mission practice.

Protestant missions value personal autonomy over systematic supervision more highly than do Roman Catholic missions. One wonders whether this tendency to overvalue personal autonomy is also true for other streams of Majority World missions. The weak accountability structures in Korean missions have grown out of an individualistic orientation among the Korean churches. One systemic cause of this

---

11. See Sherron Kay George, "Local-Global Mission: The Cutting Edge," *Missiology: An International Review* 28, no. 2 (2000): 195. Dana Robert has emphasized that the need for a balance between the local and the global will characterize Christian missions in the twenty-first century; see Dana L. Robert, "Shifting Southward: Global Christianity since 1945," *International Bulletin of Missionary Research* 24, no. 2 (2000): 57. Roland Robertson has termed the combinational process of localization and globalization as "glocalization," as cited in Robert Schreiter, *The New Catholicity: Theology between the Global and the Local* (Maryknoll, N.Y.: Orbis Books, 1999), 12.

phenomenon can be identified in the number of missionaries who were sent to the field before relevant systems for placement and supervision were established. Missionaries need to be supervised and cared for systematically if they are to serve well in a foreign land.

Rather than prioritize the regulation of field ministries, however, mission administrators should seek to support and assist missionaries in doing their work well. More important than systematic management is recognition of the guidance of the Holy Spirit, who empowers and grants gifts to missionaries. If noninterference is one extreme, the other is a controlling mindset. A balance must be maintained, with both missionaries and mission administrators exercising stewardship in their use of time, resources, and planning. Observing the principles governing the conduct of missions in general and being attentive to regulations developed by one's mission agency or team are needful steps toward best practice in mission.

To care for missionaries well, systems are needed, and systems need experts. Health care specialists, counselors, and educationalists are required. If such specialists cannot make a full-time commitment, they might form a network that provides member care for missionaries on a voluntary basis. A greater number of full-time qualified mission administrators should be recruited to work with the over 8,000 missionaries. Furthermore, churches need to support the ministries of these specialists on a long-term basis.

Sending Structures: From Imitation to Innovation

As Koreans gain experience in the mission field, the organization of mission personnel according to a reasoned plan becomes increasingly important. In the 1994 survey, 68.0 percent of Korean missionaries had field experience of less than four years, but their proportion decreased to 39.0 percent in 2000. During the same period, the number of missionaries with over twelve years of experience grew from 3.0 percent to 8.0 percent. Experienced missionaries need to spend time taking care of novice missionaries.

Missionary sending structures in Korea have been modeled after Western structures largely developed in the United Kingdom and the United States. Should the same organizational rules and regulations be rigidly applied regardless of context? Or should they be adapted to a new organizational environment? Both the commonalities and the disparities of the established model of Western missions and the emerging model of Majority World missions need to be considered wisely. Might Korean missions, positioned between these two paradigms, suggest a third model?

Indigenous Korean mission agencies tend to be weak in structure because they are dependent on entrepreneurial leaders, who in many cases remain in place. In such situations, leadership transition becomes a major issue for the whole organization. Indigenous mission agencies need to overcome their person-centered orientation so as to pursue system-centered management.[12] We can expect a shift toward a more horizontal and flexible organizational practice to accompany the influx of younger generations of missionaries.

For their part, international mission agencies need to adapt to the new organizational soil of Korea. A uniform structure that fails to reflect the diversity of cultural contexts is no longer competitive in this ever-diversifying world. Big organizations tend to be slow to respond to calls for change, so they need to become more streamlined by delegating decision making to lower units. Instead of working as a branch of a huge international conglomerate, international mission agencies need to consider implementing a horizontal partnership model. Decision making needs to reflect the cultural characteristics of each sending country.

In order to function relevantly in this global age, both indigenous and international mission agencies need to be innovative in their sending structures.[13] Relevance demands both high effectiveness and high efficiency. International mission agencies with a Western background face the problem of high costs, whereas indigenous Korean mission agencies face the problem of low investment. To function efficiently at

---

12. Recently, international mission agencies have been going through a transition in leadership, and Korean mission agencies are following the same pattern. Efforts toward "organized improvement" should go hand in hand with leadership transition; see Peter F. Drucker, *Management Challenges for the Twenty-First Century* (New York: HarperBusiness, 1999), 80.

13. Drucker (*Management Challenges*, 119) emphasizes that in the midst of a variety of competences, all organizations need one common core competence—innovation. This observation is also true for missions.

low cost requires swift and adept action by autonomous small units.[14] Small mission agencies need to seek partnerships and strategic alliances to achieve common goals. Mission structures need to allow units to be proactive, with new technological alternatives taken into consideration in planning structural innovations or changes in their programs.

Our survey indicates that Korean mission agencies are not actively investing in information technology (IT) for ministry. Only twenty mission agencies have at least one member of staff for IT, with only 28 IT staff members in total. Only eleven mission agencies budget for IT-related work, which means that although many mission agencies are concerned about the need for IT support, few have a specific IT plan in place to support ministry.[15] The main reason for this deficiency is insufficient budget.

Korean mission agencies in general cut their overall budget in 2000. The average monthly support for a missionary family with two children ranged from US$2,340, the highest level, down to US$780. For single missionaries, monthly support ranged from US$1,404, the highest level, down to US$390. The direct expense of support for missionaries seems to compose the bulk of mission agencies' budgets. Most domestic or home-office expenses are for personnel, rent, and management. This reality renders it difficult for Korean mission agencies to innovate creatively.[16]

---

14. Ric Duques and Paul Gaske advise that big companies should act like small companies in order to raise the urgency of innovation, to strive for lean and value-laden group functions, and to create a corporate culture that generates the type of vitality that can produce continuous success and development; see Ric Duques and Paul Gaske, "The 'Big' Organization of the Future," in *The Organization of the Future*, ed. Frances Hesselbein, Marshall Goldsmith, and Richard Beckhard (San Francisco: Jossey-Bass, 1997), 33–42.

15. The mission agency Every Nation Mission made the largest financial commitment to IT, with approximately US$70,000 budgeted for IT in 2000.

16. In the case of HOPE, a sending arm of Global Missionary Fellowship, the direct budget for missionaries takes 87.1 percent of the total budget, leaving the remaining 12.9 percent for domestic use in the home office. More than a third of the domestic budget (36.5 percent) is used for employment; other costs include maintenance and public relations. This pattern in the distribution of funds, in which HOPE is not exceptional, hinders long-term investment for Korean missions.

Nevertheless, Korean mission agencies need to be proactive in pursuing structural and technological innovation regardless of weak financial support. With more IT specialists working in missions, it will be possible to have more specialized member service and greater church-missions cooperation, interagency cooperation and partnership, and field-home communication and coordination. The churches in Korea need to recognize this need and invest in it.

Field Strategy: From Competition to Cooperation

In 2000, Korean missionaries are deployed in 162 countries, which means that many missionaries are working on their own and are not on a team in a particular country. Most Korean mission agencies do not have a specific regional focus, but send their members to any country around the world. For this reason, the agencies need to create partnerships with other mission agencies, local churches in the field, and local churches in the home country.

Competition decreases the possibility of partnership with other organizations, and a competitive mindset poses a threat to synergistic partnership in missions. We need to make a conscious effort to overcome a competitive mindset that is rooted in the worldview of peasant societies and has been reinforced in Korean society through education.[17] As mission agencies try to pursue vision-centered alliances across organizational boundaries, more creative ways for synergistic partnership will arise.[18]

Unfortunately, cooperation between two Korean mission agencies can be more difficult to achieve than is cooperation between a Korean

---

17. George Foster's concept of limited good suggests that people in peasant societies compete over goods such as land because these items are limited. If one person gets more, another gets less. See George M. Foster, "Peasant Society and the Image of Limited Good," *American Anthropologist* 67, no. 2 (1965): 296–97; and Paul G. Hiebert, *Cultural Anthropology* (Grand Rapids: Baker Books, 1976), 265.

18. Drucker notes that the workforce increasingly participates in a network society rather than an employee society; see Drucker, "Introduction: Toward the New Organization," in Hesselbein, Goldsmith, and Beckhard, *The Organization of the Future*, 2. Companies and not-for-profit organizations need to overcome an inward-looking consciousness. In place of merely belonging to an organization or agency, they should pursue the benefits to be found through outward-looking networking.

mission agency and an international mission agency, because mission leaders tend to be concerned more about the development of their own organization than about working together synergistically. As a means of surviving and thriving, many organizations pursue independence over interdependence. Duplication of investment as a result of competition leads to mistrust and a defensive mentality. Mission agencies and missionaries need to check closely to see whether their new ministry plans threaten to overlap with the programs of others.

Both associations of missionaries in the field and associations of mission agencies in Korea have important roles to play in promoting cooperation and partnership in missions. Building trust among members or member organizations is more important than extending organizational scope or capacity. Fair representation must be given to the various mission entities. Mission associations should not act like mission agencies. They should be as inclusive as possible.

When megachurches in Korea try to do field ministries directly, bypassing mission agencies, problems associated with limited specialization arise. Viewed realistically, remote control poses a threat to the contextualization of field ministries. In place of mission leaders, church leaders could become the voices determining what is important in the field. Direct intervention by megachurches in field ministries raises the specter of a new mode of imperialism in missions.

That Korean mission agencies and missionaries will work with mission agencies and missionaries from different national backgrounds is inevitable, but knowing one's partners and partnering organizations well before working with them is important. On the one hand, in order to exercise leadership in the mission field and in the international arena, Korean mission agencies need to cultivate experts and specialists in different fields. Korean churches need to consider the leadership potential of missionaries when they invest and not help poor missionaries just out of pity. On the other hand, Korean missionaries who belong to international mission agencies need to remember their cultural identity as they grow as leaders in a multicultural setting. They need to seek to represent the realities of Korean churches, mission agencies, and missionaries well.

In building trust between organizations, the role of a partnership facilitator is important. Specialized organizations and leaders who work to facilitate partnership among missionary teams should be given recognition. At present the number of people and organizations in Korean missions circles that work toward this goal is not large. Cooperation and partnership should be functional, not just an abstract cause. In many cases, in attempting to build cooperation and partnership, missionaries need to begin small. To facilitate cooperation and partnership, the neutrality of the varied stakeholders needs to be secured, and common purposes and goals must be elevated above individual agendas.

In their essence, cooperation and partnership require pure motivation for a common cause. Competition makes people feel uneasy toward each other. Cooperation leads people to trust and respect each other. Pure motivation instead of human ambition will bless and enrich kingdom ministry. We need to remember to place the cause of God's global mission above all.

International cooperation is a necessary condition for a successful ministry both overseas and at home. Local churches in Korea need to consider the changing realities of the pastoral environment. It may be that as time passes, the intercultural dimension of church ministries will be increasingly emphasized. When churches support mission leaders who are involved in fostering cooperation and partnership across cultures, they invest in the future of the Korean church. Churches are being globalized as their missions are being globalized.[19]

WHAT LOCAL CHURCHES NEED TO DO

In advancing the Korean missionary movement, the churches' role is crucial. Although mission agencies are on the front line, the initiative and dynamics of missions belong to local churches. The level of

---

19. For example, studying English in English-speaking countries is becoming a trend among Koreans. By employing their missional experiences and networks, churches and mission agencies could become more effective than secular companies and organizations in running such programs. Churches and mission agencies need to see the opportunities for evangelism through English education, although at the same time they must guard against the dangers of secular commercialism.

commitment of the Korean churches determines the degree of maturity of Korean missions. Missions is about the lifestyle of Christians and is an expression of faith shared within a community. Korean churches need to embrace globalism, leaving behind parochial individualism.[20]

Support for Member Care Specialists

Missionaries are not spiritual giants; they need holistic support. The apostle Paul recognized the companionship of his colleagues in missions in Romans 16. He deliberately spent times of rest and renewal with Timothy and Titus (2 Tim. 4:9, 21; Titus 3:12). In light of this biblical principle, Korean churches need to make the effort to care for missionaries well.

Although missionaries can care for missionaries, specialists trained in counseling and other fields can also be of significant help. Korea has many Christian counselors and psychiatrists. Churches could encourage them to set aside some portion of their time for missionaries. Churches also need to help with the travel expenses of specialists who offer short-term counseling to missionaries or missionary teams overseas. If specialists wish to commit themselves to full-time missionary member care, churches should support them as specialized missionaries. Churches must recognize the fruits of this kind of ministry, even if those fruits are not highly visible.

Support for Long-Term Development of Mission Agencies

Many churches give toward the support of mission agencies directly, as well as giving in support of specific missionaries. Korean mission agencies still have a significant need, however, for long-term development in many areas. They require headquarters, guesthouses, dormitories, other facilities, and equipment. Only a small number of pastors or churches are concerned about these needs. Churches have been more interested in supporting construction projects in the mission field, but the effectiveness and strategic relevance of such projects can at times

---

20. Sherron Kay George ("Local-Global Mission," 190) succinctly points out that the global church is a key player in all mission endeavors and that the local congregation is a primary agent of the mission of God.

be questioned. The development of the home infrastructure of Korean mission agencies now lags behind their growing membership and lengthening history.

The advancement of missions presupposes unconditional giving. Just as unconditional love is moving and influential, unconditional giving is powerful in this condition-bound world. When Korean churches give unconditionally in support of the vision and purpose of a project involving a community of missionaries, Korean missions come closer to the biblical ideal of missions. The Korean missionary movement keeps growing in terms of number of missionaries, but little space has been given to long-term investment for mission agencies. For example, does the Korean missions circle need to develop a good digital library for missionaries? Korean churches, especially megachurches, must meet these neglected but important needs.

Support for Field Research and Networking

Due to their traditional, monocultural background, Koreans largely experience other cultures only in a foreign land. Understanding both the breadth and depth of other cultures is an important prerequisite for successful cross-cultural ministry. Such understanding is also necessary for the exercise of leadership in a multicultural setting. Korean churches need to become more aware of and more ready to support this increasing need.

The business sector recognizes that it is hard to achieve long-term goals without investing in research and development. Without such investment in missions now, we cannot expect fruit in the next generation. One of the criteria of a missional church should be whether research on the cultures and worldviews of other regions is being undertaken.

Korean churches need to support their missionaries in developing their expertise through continuing education and leadership development programs. Most missionaries cannot afford the costs of either degree or nondegree programs, and therefore churches should selectively support potential leaders so that they can receive appropriate leadership training. With the support of churches, missionaries need to grow in expertise related to their region through field-based research.

It is important to remember that networks are a kind of resource. This significant invisible resource is directly related to the maturation of missions. By subsidizing registration fees for seminars and consultations, churches can help missionaries extend their networks to include local leaders, other missionaries of different nationalities, and other specialists in various fields.

With local churches that are proactive in support of member-care specialists, long-term development of mission agencies, and field research and networking, Korean missions can be in the vanguard of Majority World missions.

CONCLUSION

The Korean missionary movement is now at a crossroads. New expectations and a different dynamic are intersecting—one way runs toward rapid numerical growth, another way beckons to qualitative maturation. We need to decide upon the merits of each path. We can find wisdom both in taking advantage of being Korean and in learning from the accumulated global experience of missions.

Korean mission agencies need to move forward, from noninterference to systematic care for their missionary members, from imitation to innovation in sending structures, from competition to cooperation in field strategy. In order to set an example of forward-looking missions in the Majority World, Korean churches are called to support member care specialists, long-term development of mission agencies, and field research and networking of missionaries.

By addressing these developmental issues well, the Korean missionary movement will signal that it is overcoming the inevitable weaknesses and limitations of an emerging missionary movement. To complement or offset one's vulnerability though learning and conscious effort is a Christian attitude. It also displays a global mindset. The Korean church is becoming global through its global missions.

5

THE RECENT KOREAN MISSIONARY MOVEMENT:
A Record of Growth, and More Growth Needed

Since 1990 the Korea Research Institute for Missions (KRIM) has conducted biennial research projects on the missionary movement in Korea. The most recent survey, done at the end of the year 2000, studied the usual questions regarding the number of missionaries and mission agencies, and the number and type of mission fields. The 2000 survey also focused on the issues of information-technology investment, member care, and cooperation among mission agencies. This article highlights some important trends of the Korean missionary movement and issues needing attention for its further growth.[1]

KOREAN MISSIONARIES

According to KRIM statistics, 8,103 Korean missionaries were at work outside of Korea at the end of 2000. This total makes Korea the second largest missionary sending country in the world, ranking only after the United States in its number of overseas missionaries.[2] This number

---

Originally published as "The Recent Korean Missionary Movement: A Record of Growth, and More Growth Needed," *International Bulletin of Missionary Research* 32, no. 2 (January 2003): 11–17, this chapter is reprinted by permission.

1. This article is based on a paper the author presented at the Global Congress on Church Ministry and Mission, Pattaya, Thailand, in October 2001.

2. If we consider the broader category of cross-cultural missionaries, India ranks ahead of Korea, for in 1997 it had 15,000 missionaries working cross-culturally, many of them in ministries within their own country. Patrick Johnstone cites the rank of Korean overseas missions in *Operation World*, 6th ed. (Carlisle, Cumbria: Paternoster Lifestyle, 2001), 388.

is conservative, for it includes only missionaries belonging to mission agencies, not independent missionaries sent directly by a local church. Nor does it include workers who committed themselves to missionary service for less than two years, or those who have given up Korean citizenship for the sake of their work.[3]

Marlin L. Nelson's first research on the missionary movement in Korea, in 1979, reported the existence of 93 overseas missionaries. His last report, in 1989, identified 1,178 Korean missionaries, more than a twelvefold increase in that decade. For the next generation of KRIM research, surveys showed a growth from 1,645 (1990) to 8,103 (2000), almost a fivefold increase. The growth rate thus slowed during the 1990s, but still it represents one of the fastest growing national missionary movements in the world.

At the time of the 1997 Korean economic crisis over the shortage of foreign currency, concern was expressed about the possible negative impact on the missionary movement. Our recent research shows, however, that economic problems have not slowed growth.[4] In fact, every two-year period throughout the decade showed a strong increase. See table 5.1.

---

3. If we included independent missionaries, the number would be more than 9,000. We counted a missionary husband and wife as two units but did not include children unless they themselves had been admitted as adult missionaries. The pastors of Korean churches in the United States and Canada, as well as salaried staff members of mission agencies, were not included in the total of 8,103 missionaries. However, those working full-time in home offices as full members of the missions and who are supported directly by churches and individuals were considered as missionaries working in the headquarters. Missionaries who belonged to more than one agency were counted only once. In general, our number is a conservative one. Johnstone's numbers of 10,646 foreign missionaries and 12,279 cross-cultural missionaries (*Operation World*, 749) include pastors of Korean churches overseas and double-count members who belong to two mission agencies.

4. My observation is that Korean churches make the support of individual missionaries a high priority, but they are less willing to invest in missions on a long-range basis. The recent economic constraints seem to have had an adverse effect on the attitudes of churches. For comparison, consider the story of American churches, which continued to support the cause of world missions despite the woes of the Great Depression in the 1930s (Ruth Tucker, *From Jerusalem to Irian Jaya: A Biographical History of Christian Missions* [Grand Rapids: Zondervan, 1983], 323–24).

Year	Missionaries	Two-Year Growth %
1990	1,645	—
1992	2,576	56.6
1994	3,272	27.0
1996	4,402	34.5
1998	5,948	35.1
2000	8,103	36.2
2002	10,745	32.6 (est.)

Table 5.1. Percent growth in number of missionaries, 1990–2002

The approximately 1,000 new missionaries now being sent out each year from Korea have more than compensated for the missionaries leaving the field because of retirement or attrition.

Married missionaries outnumbered singles in the missionary force by a ratio of almost 7 to 1. The percentage of single missionaries fell from 20.2 percent in 1994 to 12.7 percent in 2000. The decreasing percentage of single missionaries can be traced to the gradual development of denominational mission agencies, whose members are largely seminary graduates and married, and also to the preference of large interdenominational agencies for married members over singles.

Married missionaries have a lower attrition rate than singles, which suggests that the recent increase in the ratio of married workers is to be welcomed.[5] In some fields, however, single missionaries can work more effectively. Also, given the typical cultural experience of Koreans, whose society is one of the most homogeneous in the world, it would seem wise to encourage young, single missionaries to gain intercultural exposure and missionary experience as soon in their lives as possible. Many Korean missionaries spend their twenties and early thirties on their own university education, military service, theological education,

---

5. In 1994 almost half (46 percent) of all attrition cases involved single missionaries. See Steve S. C. Moon, "Missionary Attrition in Korea: Opinions of Agency Executives," in *Too Valuable to Lose*, ed. William Taylor (Pasadena, Calif.: William Carey Library, 1997), 135.

and prefield missionary training. This unusually long period of preparation in the home country is disadvantageous in terms of intercultural adjustment, learning, and creativity, because these qualities are better acquired when one is younger.

The level of ministry experience among Korean overseas missionaries has risen in recent years. In 1994 less than one-third of the 3,272 missionaries serving overseas had as much as four years' field experience. By 2000 this proportion had risen to 61 percent. See table 5.2.

Years of Experience	Percentage 1994	Percentage 2000
< 4	68	39
4–8	24	33
9–12	5	20
> 12	3	8

Table 5.2. Missionary years of experience, 1994 and 2000, by percentage

In 2000 most of the 8,103 missionaries were focusing on church planting (37 percent) or discipleship training (27 percent). The remainder were divided among educational ministries (10 percent), theological education (7 percent), itinerant evangelism (6 percent), Bible translation or medical work (5 percent each), and social work (3 percent).

KOREAN MISSION AGENCIES

The number of mission agencies in Korea has grown steadily from 21 in 1979 to 74 in 1990, 127 in 1998, and 136 in 2000.[6] Of the 136 organizations, 98 are sending agencies, 17 are support organizations that do not themselves send missionaries, 11 are training centers, 6 are mission associations that facilitate cooperation and partnership among mission agencies, and 4 are research institutes. Altogether, 114 of the agencies are interdenominational, 22 are denominational.

---

6. Marlin Nelson's original research reported 89 mission agencies in 1986, and 92 in 1989. KRIM researchers, however, narrowed the definition of "mission agency" to those clearly dedicated to foreign missions, which reduced these figures to 65 and 66 respectively.

Although the total number of missionaries continues to rise dramatically, the growth in the number of mission agencies has slowed. These facts suggest that new missionaries prefer working with already existing, stable agencies. In all, 4,615 (57 percent) of the Korean foreign missionaries serving in 2000 belonged to one of the following ten agencies.

Global Missionary Society	1,021
University Bible Fellowship	889
Tonghap Presbyterian Mission Board	616
Methodist Mission Board	592
Global Missionary Fellowship	310
Baptist Mission Board	277
Assemblies of God Mission Board	269
Kaehyuk Presbyterian Mission Board	231
Koshin Presbyterian Mission Board	213
Holiness Church Mission Board	197

The 1990s have witnessed a rise in denominational agencies and a relative decline in campus ministries and interdenominational groups. Of the ten largest agencies in 2000, only the University Bible Fellowship is a campus ministry, and only the Global Missionary Fellowship is an interdenominational agency. Denominational missions often have an advantage in raising support, and they are typically better able to keep mission policies consistent and based on theological principles. Their drawback is the danger of inappropriately imposing denominational patterns in a mission field.

The size of mission agencies has grown over the years. In 1990 only four agencies had over 100 members; by 2000 there were twenty-four such organizations. The recent economic crisis seems not to have affected this trend. In 1998 two agencies had more than 500 members; two years later four agencies had grown to that size.

KOREAN MISSION FIELDS

In 1979 Korean missionaries were serving in 26 countries around the world. This number more than tripled by 1990 (87 countries), and then almost doubled again by 2000 (162 countries). In 2000 only the United

States (197 countries) sent missionaries to more countries.[7] For a mono-ethnic and monocultural people, it has been unexpected indeed to see the numbers of Koreans scattered around the world in so many places for the sake of preaching the Gospel. Given the numerous foreign invasions and occupations the Korean people have endured in their history, we can view Koreans' heavy involvement in foreign missions as one of the biggest surprises in the history of missionary movements. Certainly we must credit divine intervention and wisdom, which chooses what is foolish and weak in the world to put to shame the wise and the mighty (1 Cor. 1:27–28).

Not surprisingly, the largest number of Korean missionaries serve in Asia. Worldwide, the top ten host countries for the missionaries serving in 2000 were the following:[8]

China	781
Philippines	527
Japan	463
Russia	359
Germany	288
Thailand	233
Indonesia	216
United States	183
India	160
Uzbekistan	138

Overall, Asia is the place of service for the largest percentage of Korean workers (45.3 percent), followed by countries of the former Soviet Union (10.3 percent), Europe (8.9 percent), Latin America (7.0 percent), Africa (6.9 percent), the Middle East (5.4 percent), South Pacific and Oceania (3.3 percent), and North America (2.8 percent). The remaining 10.1 percent includes home staff members, itinerant workers, and people in training programs. It is natural and desirable for Korean missionaries to work in other Asian countries for cultural and geographic reasons,

---

7. John A. Siewert, ed., *Mission Handbook, 1998–2000: U.S. and Canadian Christian Ministries Overseas*, 17th ed. (Monrovia, Calif.: MARC, 1997), 88–93.

8. The number of missionaries in each country is to be understood as a minimum. In many "creative access" countries, missionaries use pseudonyms. While KRIM researchers did their best to identify all legal names and pseudonyms, the numbers here for such countries as China are no doubt actually higher than shown.

but their presence in the Middle East and other places distant from Korea reveals a certain pioneering spirit.

In terms of religious or cultural blocs served, two-thirds of all Korean foreign missionaries serve in areas that are culturally Christian (37 percent) or Muslim (29 percent). The remaining third is divided among peoples that are Buddhist (13 percent), Communist (11 percent), animistic (3 percent), Hindu (3 percent), or other (4 percent).

QUANTITY, BUT ALSO QUALITY

The fact that 8,103 Korean missionaries work with 136 mission agencies in 162 countries is certainly encouraging. Though church growth in the homeland is currently relatively modest, and despite national economic struggles, the missionary commitment and zeal of the Korean church remain high. In the overall scheme of world mission, the Korean missionary movement certainly seems to be playing a larger role than would have been anticipated in God's plans for world evangelization in the twenty-first century.

The rapid growth in the number of missionaries, however, has led to severe growing pains. There is clearly a need for more attention to the care of missionaries and to strategic development on the part of mission agencies and churches. The current socioeconomic stresses within Korean churches will likely limit bold investment in the long-range development of strategic expertise on the part of mission agencies. And we need further research on how mission workers from a monocultural background can become more effective in their work in the variety of global settings in which they serve. Thus, along with appreciation for the numerical growth of the Korean missionary movement, we need to address thoughtfully the issues that will promote continued growth and development.

Mistakes were made in the early, developmental stage of Korean missions, which were generally understood and excused by other missionary-sending countries and by the receiving countries. Now, however, as the second largest supporter of international missions, the Korean church must upgrade the criteria it uses for evaluating its mission personnel and programs. We certainly need more global criteria for judging the maturation of the missionary movement, for a wide variety of missions nowadays are simultaneously local and global.⁹ A review of the criteria used by the more experienced missionary-sending countries will shed light on what can be done to improve missionary practice. Here we consider the key issues of member care for missionaries, the management of the missionary home office, and ministry strategy in the field.

FROM NONINTERFERENCE TO SYSTEMATIC CARE

Overall, Korean mission agencies have pursued size. They have emphasized recruiting new missionaries and mobilizing churches for missionary support, yet to a great extent they have neglected member-care service. For their part, missionaries on the field have typically preferred to work under their own guidance and sense of direction rather than welcoming the supervision and management of their sponsoring organization. As a result of these two tendencies, Korean missionaries have often worked virtually alone, engaging in minimal interaction with others. A weak member-care system has prevented Koreans from doing mission faithfully and skillfully, even in terms of their specific mission organizations or of the national missionary movement as a whole, not to mention by global standards.

Autonomy, rather than submission to organizational rules and policies, characterizes Protestant missions generally (especially in contrast to Roman Catholic missions), but this characteristic is even more pronounced in the missionary movements of the Two-Thirds World. A critical review of the Korean missionary movement reveals that its relatively weak accountability structure and its individualistic mission style, which to some degree are culturally determined, have been aggravated by a generally weak sending structure, which has commissioned

---

9. Sherron Kay George, "Local-Global Mission: The Cutting Edge," *Missiology: An International Review* 28, no. 2 (2000): 195. Discussing the balance and harmony between the local and the global in the ministry of the church, Dana Robert posits that such a balance and harmony will characterize Christianity in the twenty-first century ("Shifting Southward: Global Christianity Since 1945," *International Bulletin of Missionary Research* 24, no. 2 [2000]: 57). Roland Robertson uses the term "glocalization" in talking about the combination of localization and globalization (cited in Robert Schreiter, *The New Catholicity: Theology between the Global and the Local* [Maryknoll, N.Y.: Orbis Books, 1999], 12).

missionaries before the sending bases were well formed, and by a weak member-care system, which has not been adequate for the numbers of missionaries actually sent out.

The general policy of noninterference and letting alone is undesirable, for missionaries need to work responsibly as members of an organization or team, being accountable to their supporting churches. Korean missionaries seem to be given, and to take, more individual latitude than missionaries from any other countries. They would be well advised, however, to regard systems for supervision and care as minimal protective devices and to cooperate with them both for their personal well-being and for the sake of organizational solidarity.

On their part, mission administrators and supervisors need to remember that their role is not to control but to serve and to care for missionaries. Here the work of the Holy Spirit should be well considered because the Spirit pours out gifts on, and works through, individual persons in different ways, including those in support roles. Member-care personnel need to keep a balance between the extremes of noninterference and control. In this balance, both mission administrators and missionaries should be transparent in their use of time and finances, planning their respective ministries as good stewards for God. When all persons involved in the missionary effort fulfill their roles faithfully, observing biblical principles and organizational policies, missions will be more relevant and powerful.

Effective member care requires appropriate systems and experts who can maintain the systems. Health-care personnel, counselors, and educational specialists are most urgently needed, whether professionals who work full-time for missions or a network of experts who devote a percentage of their time to missions. Skilled administrators are needed both in the mission fields and in the home offices.

KRIM's survey for the year 2000 identified 47 member-care personnel in 12 agencies, a number that is far from adequate in light of the actual needs of the 8,103 missionaries. Enlisting enough well-qualified people for member care will require a new degree of cooperation and support from churches.

SENDING STRUCTURES: FROM IMITATION TO INNOVATION

Missionary-sending structures in Korea have generally been modeled after Western agencies developed in Britain, the United States, and Canada, agencies whose structures reflect more than two centuries of refinement and change. Now, however, as the center of gravity in missions shifts to the non-Western world, there is an urgent need to review the appropriateness of using Western sending structures in the Two-Thirds World. In this transitory period non-Westerners need to be both appreciative and critical of the old as we develop models to face the new issues and challenges before us.

Indigenous mission agencies tend to be weak in establishing sending structures. In many cases an agency's entire operation revolves around a charismatic leader, with little commitment to developing a structure that will allow the organization to survive after the passing of the leader. Leadership transition will be a crucial factor determining the progress of Korean mission agencies in the next several years.[10] Developing sending structures based on contextualized ministry rather than on a single strong personality is a clear need, especially when we consider the involvement in missions of the younger generations. In our ever-globalizing world, this group calls for structures that are more horizontal than vertical.[11]

In order to function both effectively and efficiently, mission agencies—especially the larger ones—need to act small, delegating more decision-making responsibility to lower units.[12] Small mission

---

10. In some cases Korean missions have indeed experienced stable leadership transition. The important issue is to pursue "organized improvement," not simply to survive the leadership transition itself (Peter F. Drucker, *Management Challenges for the Twenty-First Century* [New York: HarperBusiness, 1999], 80).

11. George also posits that we are moving from a model of centralization and top-down hierarchies to one of global and grassroots networking ("Local-Global Mission," 191).

12. Ric Duques and Paul Gaske argue that big companies should "act like small companies," "create the urgency for innovation," "create the lean, value-added corporate function," and "create an energizing culture" ("The 'Big' Organization of the Future," in *The Organization of the Future*, ed. Frances Hesselbein, Marshall Goldsmith, and Richard Beckhard [San Francisco: Jossey-Bass, 1997], 33–42).

agencies need to pursue organizational innovation through partnership and networking in order to give stability to their organizational practice.

Branches of international mission agencies need to pursue more innovative structural alignments that will allow them to work effectively across cultural boundaries. Management theorists have long suggested that uniform structures are no longer competitive in today's global age. Megastructures, unless they act small, are ineffective in noticing and reacting to changes in their environment. A better option for international agencies seems to be to structure them as a federation of autonomous entities that give significant freedom to the operation of national councils.[13] Such a decentralized model gives more sense of ownership to the supporting churches and national leaders in each sending country. Within such a structural model, Korean missionaries might feel less like a minority in a conglomerate international structure and more like part of a responsible leadership group. Embracing such a model will involve the radical restructuring of sending agencies; merely tinkering with the present model will produce no significant change.

Finally, all mission agencies, both large and small, need to explore the innovative possibilities of information technology (IT) and redefine their organizational functions accordingly. The recently conducted survey by KRIM shows that Korean mission agencies are generally passive in their investment in IT. Of the 136 mission agencies, only 20 designate anyone as responsible for IT, and only 12 specifically mention IT in their budget. In all the agencies together, only 28 people are considered IT personnel. While many mission agencies are generally interested in IT and its related areas, few have developed concrete plans for creatively using IT in future ministry.[14]

One of the main reasons behind the passive attitude toward IT among Korean mission agencies is lack of finances. Indeed, from 1999

---

13. Peter Drucker argues that every structural unit must have one core competency, although areas of core competency could differ among the various structural units. To Drucker, the correlation of core competencies is key to structural innovation (*Management Challenges*, 119). I think the same is true for mission structures.

14. One exception was the Segyero Mission, which reported an IT line item in its 2001 budget of US$63,000.

to 2000 a majority of Korean mission agencies cut their budget. The recent survey indicates that the monthly allotments for missionaries are indeed extremely modest: for a family with two children, the range is from US$780 to US$2,340; for single missionaries the range is from US$390 to US$1,404. For most Korean mission agencies 90 percent of the total mission budget goes directly to missionary support, leaving little for the home office. Most of the remaining 10 percent goes to salaries and maintenance fees for the home office, which hinders any new development of innovative technologies.

Korean mission agencies need to be proactive in attempting structural and technological innovation, notwithstanding their financial problems. With more IT experts, for example, more effective and efficient member service will be possible from the home office through better means of communication among supporting churches and missions, the home office, and missionaries on the field. Local churches have a significant role to play in making these advances possible.

FIELD STRATEGY: FROM COMPETITION TO COOPERATION

The fact that Korean missionaries work in 162 countries points to the need for field-based cooperation among mission agencies and missionaries. Since most Korean mission agencies do not operate solely within a single region, the need for cooperation is great. Partnership and cooperation are needed, not only among mission agencies, but also between mission agencies and churches in the mission fields, and between mission agencies and supporting churches in the home country.

Korean missionaries and their agencies need to work synergistically across organizational boundaries to achieve a common vision. In Korea competition rooted in the consciousness and mentality common to peasant societies has been strengthened by the national educational philosophy and system.[15] Only by consciously embracing a truly kingdom

---

15. George Foster's concept of "the image of the limited good" illustrates how members of peasant societies compete with one another over things desired, such as land, which is limited. People who live in this type of society tend to think they can improve their socioeconomic status only at the expense of other members and outsiders of the society (Foster, "Peasant Society and the Image of Limited Good,"

vision will we be able to understand and practice "boundarylessness";[16] only when mission agencies are able to think across organizational boundaries can they enjoy synergy through functional partnership.[17] Cooperation between mission agencies is difficult when mission executives are more concerned about the organizational development of their own agency than about the ultimate cause of the evangelization of the world. Duplicate investment by mission agencies, often a result of competition, sows the seeds of mistrust and a defensive mentality and thus jeopardizes partnership opportunities.

The role of associations of mission agencies is crucial in facilitating a spirit of partnership. Associations, both national and international, should provide sound platforms for cooperation and partnership based on recognized missiological principles. In negative cases, mission associations act like a separate mission organization, undermining partnership. Voluntary cooperation based on mutual trust is possible only when mission associations maintain an open, servant attitude.

It is becoming increasingly common for large churches to send out missionaries directly, bypassing mission agencies altogether. When local churches function also like mission agencies, however, contextualization of the Gospel is less likely to happen in the field because of the tendency of the sending church to exercise tight control over the mission work. Local church leaders, who often lack expertise in intercultural ministry, may exercise undue influence in determining field strategy. In worst cases, the direct involvement of local churches in field ministry might produce a new kind of imperialistic paradigm of missions.

American Anthropologist 67 [1965], 296–97; Paul G. Hiebert, *Cultural Anthropology* [Grand Rapids: Baker, 1976], 265).

16. Ron Ashkenas, "The Organization's New Clothes," in Hesselbein, Goldsmith, and Beckhard, *The Organization of the Future*, 104.

17. Drucker asserts that the coming age is "a network society rather than an employee society," which suggests that companies and nonprofit organizations should cultivate functional networks involving other groups rather than working only with their own people within the boundaries of their own organization ("Introduction: Toward the New Organization," in Hesselbein, Goldsmith, and Beckhard, *The Organization of the Future*, 2).

Korean mission agencies and missionaries cannot avoid working with mission agencies and missionaries from other countries. Indeed, in this global age, we need to learn from one another in doing missions. Such learning across cultural and linguistic boundaries will help prevent mistakes otherwise easy to make. Korean mission agencies, however, now generally lack leaders prepared to work with representatives of mission agencies from other countries. Existing international agencies have more opportunities for raising up international leaders from among their member missionaries, but much time and encouragement are needed to cultivate well-prepared leaders. Church leaders in receiving countries should also take more initiative to foster partnership with Korean missionaries and agencies. Once adjusted to the concept of working in partnership and feeling comfortable with other stakeholders, Korean missionaries will become even more effective in serving the cause of kingdom partnership.

QUALITATIVE ISSUES FOR LOCAL CHURCHES

Local churches play a crucial role in advancing the missionary movement. Mission agencies are on the front line of world evangelization, but local churches are the driving forces of missionary movements. The rapid growth of the missionary movement in Korea is rightly attributed to the zealous commitment and faithful support of Korean churches to the cause of reaching the unreached with the Gospel. It is time, though, for Korean churches to think less about the quantitative side of their missions growth and to reflect more on issues of qualitative growth. In general, the Korean church should now pursue a globalization of its missionary movement, overcoming parochialism for the sake of world evangelization in this global age.[18] Specific issues now facing local churches involve the support of missionary care, the development of infrastructures in support of missionaries, and the encouragement of mission innovation.

---

18. George emphasizes that "the global church is a key player in all mission endeavors today," whereas "every local congregation is a primary agent in God's mission" ("Local-Global Mission," 190).

Experts in missionary support say that member-care personnel in mission agencies alone cannot meet the needs for missionary care. Workers on the field need assistance and support from the rich pool of people resources in the local churches. There are medical doctors, counselors, and many others with valuable skills and experience who could make major contributions to the care of missionaries. Local churches should allow mission agencies to tap into their rich personnel resources.

An example of broader personal involvement of local churches comes from Tae-Kwon Kim of Namseoul Pyongchon Presbyterian Church, who has made it a policy of his church to assign a single missionary or missionary family to each of his church's cell groups, which then regularly prays for and contacts its missionaries. Cell group leaders are aware of their missionaries' schedules and are the first to contact them when they return for a home visit.

A different source of support is the E-Land Group, founded in 1980 by Song-Su Park with the goal of using business as a vehicle for ministry and witness. The group has recently been developing ways to help mission agencies provide medical checkups for their missionaries. En-sup Sohn, director of the E-Land Group's Hanse Clinic, has a vision of forming a network of medical doctors, nurses, and counselors who would be dedicated to missionary care.

Korean churches have generously given funds for constructing churches, schools, and hospitals in the mission fields. Now they need to give equally generously in developing the infrastructure in Korea in partnership with the mission agencies. Missionaries need housing while on home assignment, guest houses for short visits, sometimes youth hostels for their children, mission libraries for their continuing education, educational facilities for self-study, office space for administrative work, pensions for their lives after retirement, and many other provisions and facilities. Many churches in Korea run mission homes for missionaries on home assignment. Now a much broader vision of missionary support is needed, not only in the home country but also in the mission fields.

The newest technologies and skills must be used innovatively for ministry. Today one cannot talk about the future of missions without considering the Internet and the information revolution.

Korean churches need to take advantage of the advanced IT industry in Korea. Korean Christians, living in an environment where the information superhighway is more easily accessible than in any other country, must learn how to use the nationwide infrastructure and information technologies for missionary purposes. Perhaps one church could support not only its own Web page but another for missionary purposes in another language, in partnership with Korean missionaries or other Asian missionaries. Various sites could be run for direct evangelism, counseling, children's education, or friendship building in different local languages.

Computer animation is one possible area of innovative ministry in the future, aimed at both children and adults. Bible stories and other stories of faith could be dubbed in different languages to be distributed in CDs, videotapes, or on Web sites. Perhaps Korean churches could overcome their monolingual background by partnering with Indian, Singaporean, and other Asian churches for production and distribution of these projects, thus helping develop genuinely cross-cultural ministries.

LOOKING TO THE FUTURE

The global mission of God finds various expressions in different ages and cultural settings. The phenomenal growth of the Korean missionary movement has been an unexpected expression of God's providential work, which works through the foolish and the weak. The movement has its own strengths and weaknesses as it continues to evolve. Along with rapid quantitative growth, there is need to upgrade the national missionary movement to become a fully global movement that encourages other local missionary movements throughout the world. Such a task requires a thorough evaluation of the effectiveness of Korean missionary practices, using global criteria and standards.

A global mind-set requires learning across cultural and national boundaries. Korean missionaries need understanding and encouragement from Christian brothers and sisters of other countries, as they must give the same to the rest of the Christian world. Missionaries from Korea are eager to be part of the unified adventure of future missions, taking their part in God's multinational, multicultural, and multilingual teams.

6

THE PROTESTANT MISSIONARY MOVEMENT IN KOREA:
Current Growth and Development

The Protestant missionary movement in Korea has recently gone through a period of growing pains and now stands at a crossroad. Careful analysis is needed to determine the direction it should now take. This report is based on the most recent survey, conducted by the Korea Research Institute for Missions (KRIM) between January and August 2007. The survey notes both the increasing elements of globalization of the Korean missionary movement and the developmental issues that must be addressed for qualitative growth.

THE GLOBALIZING MISSION MOVEMENT

The number of Korean Protestant missionaries who were at work in other countries as of the end of 2006 is shown in table 6.1, as well as the number of Korean mission agencies and the number of countries in which they were serving. Marlin L. Nelson's first research on the Korean missionary movement, in 1979, reported the existence of 93 missionaries. His last report, in 1989, identified 1,178 Korean missionaries. For the next generation of KRIM research, surveys showed a growth from 1,645 (1990) to 8,103 (2000), and then to 14,905 (2006).[1] That is, during

---

Originally published as "The Protestant Missionary Movement in Korea: Current Growth and Development," *International Bulletin of Missionary Research* 32, no. 2 (April 2008): 59–64, this chapter is reprinted by permission.

1. Our operational definition of "missionary" does not include independent missionaries who do not belong to any agency or pastors of diaspora churches who do not belong to mission agencies. People who work with migrant workers in Korea are also not included. Korean missionaries sent by diaspora churches are

the twenty-seven years from 1979 to 2006, the number of missionaries grew 160-fold! Throughout the 1990s the annual growth rate was 25 percent, which fell to 7.6 percent in the 2000s.[2]

Year	Missionaries	Mission agencies	Countries of service
1979	93	21	26
1982	323	47	37
1986	511	65	47
1989	1,178	66	72
1990	1,645	74	87
1992	2,576	90	105
1994	3,272	113	119
1996	4,402	113	138
1998	5,948	127	145
2000	8,103	136	162
2002	10,422	163	164
2004	12,874	165	160
2006	14,905	174	168

Table 6.1. Korean missionary movement, 1979–2006: missionaries, mission agencies, and countries of service

The change in growth rates indicates that the missionary movement entered a stabilizing period in the 2000s, which allows us to project growth to a maximum of 35,000 career missionaries in the next twenty-five years. One factor explaining this rather conservative projection is the stagnated growth of Korean Protestantism. Nevertheless, with an annual growth rate of 7.6 percent, we can expect Korean churches

---

not included in this number, although we know that there are some. The number 14,905 is thus conservative. For comparison, the number of Roman Catholic missionaries from Korea at the end of 2006 was 634 according to the Catholic Bishops' Conference of Korea.

2. For the two-year period 1990–92 the growth rate was 56.6 percent, which decreased in subsequent two-year periods to 27.0 (1992–94), 34.5 (1994–96), 35.1 (1996–98), 36.2 (1998–2000), 28.6 (2000–2002), 23.5 (2002–04), and 15.8 (2004–06).

each year to send out over 1,000 new foreign missionaries, which still represents one of the fastest growing national missionary movements in the world.³

The number of Korean mission agencies grew steadily from 21 in 1979 to 74 in 1990, then to 136 in 2000 and 174 in 2006. In recent years the number of mission agencies has not grown as rapidly as it did in the 1990s, which indicates that the sending structures are being established and stabilized. From another angle, we could say that new missionaries prefer working with already existing, stable agencies, a preference that matches the growth in size of mission agencies over the years. In 2006 there were two sending agencies with over 1,000 members, six with 500–999 members, twenty-eight with 100–499, fifteen with 50–99, eighty-nine with less than 50 members, and 34 supporting agencies such as missionary training centers. In 2006 the ten largest mission agencies were as follows:

Agency	Members
Global Missionary Society (Hapdong)	1,835
University Bible Fellowship	1,463
Presbyterian Mission Board (Tonghap)	927
Methodist Mission Board	750
Assemblies of God Mission Board	664

---

3. According to the most recent *Mission Handbook*, there are 44,384 fully supported overseas missionaries from the United States (Linda J. Weber and Dotsey Welliver, eds., *Mission Handbook: U.S. and Canadian Protestant Ministries Overseas, 2007–2009* [Wheaton, Ill.: Evangelism and Missions Information Service, 2007], 13). According to *Operation World*, there are 41,064 Indian missionaries, most of whom work cross-culturally within India. These countries are followed by the United Kingdom (8,164 missionaries, including 5,666 overseas), Canada (7,001, including 4,337 overseas), and Brazil (5,801, including 1,912 overseas) (Patrick Johnstone, Robyn Johnstone, and Jason Mandryk, *Operation World: When We Pray God Works* [Carlisle, Eng.: Paternoster Lifestyle, 2001], 895–901). In the 2005 survey, the attrition rate for Korean missionaries was 3.4 percent (i.e., 34 missionaries out of every 1,000 return home sooner than expected). In 2004 the number of missionary early returnees was 443. For the time period 1995–2004, a total of 2,785 cases of attrition were reported. Important reasons for attrition, listed here in the order of frequency, were change of job, conflict with the home office, health problems, retirement, death, conflict with colleagues, and marriage with nonmissionaries.

Campus Mission International	561
Global Missionary Fellowship	560
Baptist Mission Board	550
Holiness Mission Board	420
Youth With A Mission	386

The development of sending structures for overseas missions in Korea is a facet of globalizing church structures that has been propelled by the globalization of Korean society in general. This development has been marked in particular by opportunities for unrestricted travel and overseas residence.[4]

In 1979 Korean missionaries were serving in twenty-six countries around the world. This number more than tripled by 1990, and then nearly doubled again by 2006 (see table 6.1). Such growth reflects the pioneering spirit of Korean missionaries. For a monoethnic and monocultural people, it has been unexpected indeed to see the numbers of Koreans scattered around the world in so many places for the sake of preaching the Gospel.

Not surprisingly, the largest number of Korean missionaries serve in Asia (47.3 percent). The rest are active in the Eurasian countries of the former USSR (14.6 percent), followed by North America (9.3), Africa (7.7), Latin America (5.8), the Middle East (4.5), Western Europe (3.9), the South Pacific (2.9), and eastern Europe (2.0), with the remainder in itineration and headquarters (2.0 percent). The comparatively large deployment of Korean missionaries in Asia is positive because Asia is the most populous, but also the least evangelized, continent. Worldwide, the major countries of service for Korean missionaries are China, United States, Japan, Philippines, Russia, Germany, Thailand, Indonesia, India, and Canada. Recently, many missionaries have been sent

---

4. Andrew F. Walls argues that democratic political systems that encourage voluntary organizations, unrestricted travel and flow of finance overseas in capitalist economic systems, and tax exemption for nonprofit organizations are important factors contributing to the growth of the American missionary movement (*The Missionary Movement in Christian History: Studies in the Transmission of Faith* [Maryknoll, N.Y.: Orbis Books, 2000], 221–40). Similarly, the globalization of society has affected the globalization of the church in Korea. The question is how the church should use its own global experience to contribute to the globalization of society.

to Japan, Russia, Thailand, and India. The missionaries in the United States, Germany, and Canada are mostly involved in campus ministries.

In terms of the religious or cultural areas served, over half of Korean Protestant missionaries are active in the Christian (29.1 percent) or Islamic (24.1 percent) blocs. The remaining half are divided among peoples that are Communist (18.7 percent), Buddhist (14.2), animist (4.1), Hindu (3.8), or other (5.9). It is noteworthy that, at present, more and more Korean missionaries are going to the Islamic world.

What reasons can we give for such a phenomenal growth of the Korean missionary movement over the last three decades? First, the explosive growth of churches in Korea in the 1960s and 1970s affected Korean mission growth beginning in the 1980s. The missionary movement was the child of church revival.[5] Second, the globalization of Korean society affects the missionary movement. Government policies that include unrestricted travel and overseas residence have facilitated the missionary movement. Third, a surplus of seminary graduates is another factor explaining the increase of expatriate Christian workers. Many young Christians who commit themselves wholeheartedly to the cause of Christ's kingdom decide to enter seminary, and then, since there are not enough ministry positions in Korea for all graduates from seminary, many look overseas for their future service. There are negative sides of this phenomenon, but one positive is that it is desirable that more qualified people go to the mission fields.

WHO ARE THE KOREAN MISSIONARIES?

Korean missionaries reflect the characteristics of Korean society and the Korean church. These characteristics, which highlight both the advantages and the disadvantages of being Korean, work either positively or negatively with respect to current global trends.

Slightly more than half of all Korean missionaries are female (50.3 percent). Married missionaries outnumber singles in the missionary force by a ratio of almost 8 to 1 (88.7 vs. 11.3 percent). The percentage of single missionaries fell from 20.2 percent in 1994 to 12.7 percent in

---

5. See ibid., 160.

2000, and still further to 11.3 percent in 2006. The decreasing percentage of single missionaries can be traced to the gradual development of denominational mission agencies, whose members are largely seminary graduates and married, and also to the preference of large interdenominational agencies for married members over singles.

In age, 71.8 percent of Korean missionaries are in their thirties and forties.

Age	Percent
20s	7.4
30s	32.0
40s	39.8
50s	17.0
60 or older	3.8

The age distribution is related to the extent of ministry experience.

Years of experience	Percent
< 4	29.0
4–8	25.2
8–12	22.3
12–16	15.2
> 16	8.3

The percentage of Korean missionaries with less than four years' experience is lower than in previous surveys (39 percent in 2000 vs. 68 percent in 1994), whereas the ratio of missionaries with over eight years' experience has increased (46 percent in 2006 vs. 28 percent in 2000 and only 8 percent in 1994). There have been concerns about the lack of veteran missionaries who could provide oversight for young and inexperienced missionaries, but the problem is being reduced. More systematic efforts are needed, however, to care for and support younger missionaries.

As for the level of education of missionaries, 4.3 percent of Korean missionaries have completed only high school, 65.7 percent have undergraduate degrees, 25.7 percent have master's degrees, and 4.4 percent have completed a doctorate. We find that increasing numbers of missionary personnel are educated at the doctoral level, many of them pursuing higher degrees in mission-related topics such as ethnology or area studies. The educational standard of Korean missionaries suggests that they are equipped to carry out highly specialized ministries globally, though certain formative informal and nonformal training is essential in addition to purely academic studies.

Over one-third of Korean missionaries are ordained pastors (36.6 percent), with pastors' wives and laypersons accounting for the other 63.4 percent. Since a majority of Korean missionaries have had education in theology, we count on them to be effective in discipleship training, church planting, theological education, and especially leadership development.

In the 1970s and 1980s the majority of Korean missionaries were involved in diaspora ministry; currently, however, only a small minority (9.6 percent) are involved in ministry to the Korean diaspora or in home ministries at the headquarters.[6] This percentage has increased a little recently because mission agencies now have more home officers, and some mission agencies have accepted new members who are currently involved in diaspora ministry but are targeting other population groups cross-culturally at the same time. Most Korean mission agencies do not consider diaspora workers as missionaries. If we include all of them in the number of missionaries, the total would be much higher.[7] Diaspora ministry is characteristic of a missionary movement with a monocultural background.

In terms of ministry focus, Korean Protestant missionaries in 2006 were divided as follows:

Ministry focus	Percent
Church planting	39.1
Discipleship training	21.5
Educational ministries	9.2

---

6. Here pastors of diaspora churches are included in the total number of missionaries if they belong to mission agencies with missionary vision, although not all of them are currently involved in cross-cultural ministry. The number of pastors involved in diaspora ministry is not large, however, because we do not include diaspora workers who are not related to a mission agency; and when diaspora workers form the majority of a mission agency, we do not count them as missionaries for the purposes of this survey.

7. Diaspora churches are important as bases of member care for cross-cultural missionaries and increasingly are becoming involved in cross-cultural missions.

Theological education	5.0
Itinerant evangelism	4.4
Social welfare	4.3
Community development	4.0
Medical missions	3.5
Business and IT-related	3.4
Bible translation	2.9
Other	2.7

Considering items 1, 2, 4, 5, and 10 above, we see that 72.9 percent of the missionaries in 2006 were directly involved in evangelistic and spiritual works, which reflects the conservative theological orientation of the Korean church. Korean missionaries, however, need to grow in practicing a more holistic concept of missions, as we see it expressed in other parts of the body of Christ around the world.

STRATEGIC AGENDA OF KOREAN MISSIONS

Korean missions must grow according to current global standards and needs, but they must not forget the need to adapt to local cultural situations. For meaningful further growth of the Korean missionary movement, efforts must be directed in both directions—global and local.

"Glocalizing" the missionary movement. To properly glocalize the Korean missionary movement, we must evaluate it with global standards and must also pursue development creatively in local environments. In both areas we need insight for growth and maturation from the global mission community.

Working with international agencies provides a good opportunity to learn what it means to work multiculturally. According to the 2007 survey, 18.6 percent of Korean missionaries are working with international agencies, versus 81.4 percent with Korean agencies. The percentage of missionaries working with international agencies was higher in the 1980s than it is now. In the 1990s the figure dropped significantly but now is increasing again. This growing percentage reflects the new generation's preference for international agencies over Korean agencies, which, considering the need for globalization, is a desirable trend.

International agencies need to complement their corporate structure and culture with significant input from local situations. In this global age it is no longer adequate to maintain uniform standards and regulations across an institution. Agencies need to learn and adopt local cultural traits and to maintain a spirit and philosophy of multiculturalism embracing both the global and the local. More and more international agencies are making efforts to localize their principles and policies in different parts of the world, although many still refuse to decentralize their functions. It is encouraging that a few have included Korean missionaries on their leadership team, but much more must be done by international mission agencies in sharing mission leadership with the Majority World church. Furthermore, glocalization efforts need to be more fully reflected in the corporate cultures of the agencies.

Where Korean agencies are weaker in the global aspect than in the local aspect, they need to cooperate closely with churches, missions, and missionaries from other countries. By doing so, their members can develop global expertise, as well as practice local diversity. Local agencies may feel uncomfortable about crossing organizational boundaries, but they nonetheless need to make conscious efforts to cooperate.[8]

As globalization deepens and widens, the need increases for tentmaking, which can often deal with global realities more sensitively and more creatively than traditional full-time missionaries can. Tentmaking ministries, through their greater economic opportunities, enable creative approaches to local cultural situations. Korean missions need to be creative in developing a wider range of tentmaking efforts, for currently only one-third of all Korean missionaries (33.5 percent) can be categorized as tentmakers, including those who are involved part-time in business. More experimental and creative minds and efforts are needed to suggest effective models of tentmaking. Concrete working models are needed, not merely further conceptual study. For example, a proper development of tentmaking requires marketing consultants for microbusiness.

---

8. The concept of boundarylessness is useful for promoting an active exchange and cooperation among mission agencies. The concept does not deny the existence of organizational boundaries but encourages and facilitates free movement and exchange across the boundaries (see Ron Ashkenas, "The Organization's New Clothes," in *The Organization of the Future*, ed. Frances Hesselbein, Marshall Goldsmith, and Richard Beckhard [San Francisco: Jossey-Bass, 1997], 104).

Frontier missions, which are more difficult and dangerous and which require more effort and careful attention than work in established missions, aim to experience the full cycle of missionary work. In 2006 a sizable minority (29.6 percent) of Korean missionaries were involved in frontier missions, a percentage that has been increasing over the years. In the summer of 2007 the Taliban in Afghanistan kidnapped twenty-three Korean missionaries, eventually killing two of them and releasing the others after several weeks. This incident shows how necessary it is to base frontier missions on a realistic assessment of risks and on adequate preparation. Passion and zeal are not enough. We need information, strategy, and wisdom in order to do frontier missions well, just as we need a balance between frontier and established missions. It is not a matter of either/or but of both/and. Proponents of frontier missions in Korea, however, typically emphasize only unreached peoples, neglecting areas that show receptivity to the Christian Gospel. We need to follow, rather than precede, the Holy Spirit in strategizing global missions, whether on a small or a large scale. Frontier missions requires long-time perspectives, but Korean missions and churches tend to be more short-term oriented, ready to plunge in, often without considering the local sociocultural situation. Korean missionaries need to learn to wait patiently for God's timing.

Strategizing for the Korean missionary movement. In the survey, Korean mission executives identified what they felt were the greatest single strength and the greatest weakness of Korean missions.[9]

Greatest strength	Percent
Personnel resources	75.0
Technological expertise	11.5
Know-how for missions	8.7
Financial supply	4.8

Greatest weakness	Percent
Weak supporting systems	45.1
Lack of know-how	25.2
Lack of experts	24.3
Poor application of technology	5.4

---

9. These and the following statistics are based on replies by 110 (or, in some cases, fewer) of the 174 mission executives surveyed.

It is curious to see mission know-how identified as both a strength and a weakness, a discrepancy that fuller definition of "know-how" might resolve. As for the top item identified as a weakness for Korean missions, it is clear that without proper supporting systems, the missionary movement cannot continue its growth. Agencies must therefore commit themselves to establishing better support systems both within Korea and abroad. Local churches need to invest in the establishment and strengthening of support systems rather than solely emphasizing the need to send missionaries to the "front lines."

Mission executives suggested several ways to improve support systems.

Ways to improve support systems	Percent
Introduce good models of ministry	46.3
Raise awareness of missions among churches	38.9
Control the number of missionaries	11.1
Raise individual and corporate support	3.7

Good examples and models of ministry can overcome mission fatigue among the stakeholders of missions. Short-term evaluation may lead to premature judgment, so long-term perspective is needed to monitor the fruitfulness of present ministries.

In response to an open question about the most urgent developmental issue facing Korean missions, mission executives pointed to the following areas:

Most urgent area of development	Percent
Missionary care	25.0
Leadership	21.4
Research and development	18.8
Missionary training	16.1
Missionary children's education	9.8
Support systems	8.9

Of the various ways to exercise care of missionaries, professional care by experts is emphasized (by 44.9 percent of respondents) more than mutual care among field missionaries, care by home staff members, or care by local church people in Korea. Missionaries often carry deep-seated personal problems and need professional care by counselors, psychiatrists, educators, and administrators. Such experts need to work closely with mission leaders and missiologists to give systematic care for the missionaries.

When it comes to children's education, Korean mission executives identified (47.3 percent) establishing the child's sense of identity as the most important factor; internal issues must be resolved before addressing other concerns. The identity issue seems to be a complex one indeed for a "missionary kid" who grows up in a complex cultural and educational milieu. Mission agencies and local churches therefore need to invest in developing educational programs to help establish and strengthen MKs' sense of identity.

Mission executives were asked to identify the area of research they viewed as most significant. The results highlighted the need for developing mission strategy.

Areas needing research	Percent
Mission strategy	45.7
Field research	26.7
Personnel research	23.8
Historical research	3.8

That is, pragmatic concerns were considered more urgent than theoretical and conceptual research such as in the theology of mission and mission history. Still, we cannot disregard theoretical and academic research, which in the long term will ultimately help mature the missionary movement. Mission executives, however, often seem to have little time to reflect on long-term goals.

On the question of which media are viewed as most significant for missionary work, mission executives identified the Internet (55.0 percent) and satellite broadcasting (27.5 percent). Both media are currently being used for missions by the Korean church, but more efforts are needed to make the best use of them for missions in this ever-globalizing world.

Mission executives identified several areas to be strengthened in missionary training.

Improvements needed in training	Percent
Character building	43.5
Community-life training	32.4
Area research	20.4
Missiological knowledge	3.7

Overall, personal and relational training is viewed as more needed than theoretical or methodological training. There are many Korean missionary training programs, but most of them focus on cognitive education for missiological knowledge. Mission executives, in contrast, consider personal stability and spiritual maturity to be more important than knowledge, experience, or managerial capability as important qualities of mission leadership.

The executives had different estimates of how much Korean missions would grow in the next twenty-five years.

Estimate for number of missionaries in 2030	Percent of executives
15,000–20,000	10.1
20,001–30,000	24.7
30,001–50,000	18.0
50,001–80,000	24.7
80,001–100,000	11.3
over 100,000	11.2

Although most mission executives do not expect to see 100,000 missionaries on the field in 2030, they nevertheless believe that the Korean church is able to send many more missionaries than the 14,905 on the field in 2006.

Which country will be the leading missionary sending country in the twenty-first century? The majority of respondents highlighted Korea.

Leading mission country	Percent
Korea	51.9
China	36.8
United States	7.5
India	2.8
United Kingdom	0.9

Collectively, the respondents assumed that the leading missionary countries will change dramatically from Western to Majority World countries. The U.S. church is underestimated perhaps because of lack of awareness of the size of the American missionary force and of the leading role the U.S. mission movement plays in foreign missions especially in terms of strategy development.

The mission executives were asked which Korean mission agency they thought was the best. The highest vote-getters were Global Missionary Fellowship (GMF, 10 out of 55 respondents), Global Bible Translators (GBT, the Bible translation arm of GMF and affiliated with Wycliffe Bible Translators, 10), and Global Mission Society (GMS, Presbyterian/Hapdong, 8). If we include all eight divisions of GMF, it was selected by approximately half of the mission executives responding. GMS effectively overcomes the recent stereotype that denominational agencies lack missiological expertise.

Respondents identified the Overseas Missionary Fellowship (OMF, 9 out of 51 responding), WEC International (8), and Wycliffe (WBT, 7) as the most excellent and respected international mission agencies, each of which has long been active in Korea. OMF has been in Korea for the longest time, both in receiving and in sending missionaries. WEC's recent progress is remarkable and can be attributed to the younger generation's preference for overseas training opportunities and its global network. WBT as a successful model of glocalization is known through GBT in Korea; although it is in third place here, its ministry in Korea is widely appreciated through its association with GBT. These international agencies are generally well accepted among the Korean churches because of their long history in Asia and Korea.

SUMMARY AND CONCLUSIONS

The Korean church is now not only a leading force in the Majority World mission movement but also an important part of the wider global mission movement. Korean missionaries are comparatively young but are rapidly accumulating cross-cultural ministry experience. In order to glocalize the global missionary movement, international agencies need to function like indigenous agencies, and indigenous agencies need to function like international agencies. In the changing climate of missions, the Korean church needs to cooperate with missionary forces from other countries, including the churches in the United States and China.

In conclusion, glocalization must be realized concretely in many mission fields in order for the missionary movement as a whole to advance. Qualitative growth according to global standards that allow space for local creativity is needed, and we need balance between them. Expertise in diverse areas must be developed to contribute to the global missionary movement more meaningfully and strategically. The process of this growth may include personal or institutional suffering. We must remember, though, that any such sufferings are not worth comparing with the glory that will ultimately be revealed in us (Rom. 8:18).

7

THE KOREAN MISSIONARY MOVEMENT AND LEADERSHIP ISSUES (2008)

This report provides an update on the progress of the Korean missionary movement followed by an in-depth analysis of leadership needs. The update and analysis are based on the biannual survey of the status of the Korean missionary movement conducted by the Korea Research Institute for Mission (KRIM) at the end of 2008.

UPDATED OVERVIEW OF KOREAN MISSIONS

According to KRIM's survey, at the end of 2008 the number of Korean missionaries reached 18,035. The annual growth rate in 2006–2008 was 10.0 percent. This rate is higher than in the period 2004–2006 (7.6 percent) but lower than the annual average for 2000–2008 (12.3 percent). It is much lower than the annual growth rate of 39.3 percent seen in the period 1990–99.

With 18,035 missionaries Korea is the third-largest missionary sending country within Protestantism, following the United States (44,384) and India (41,064), in terms of cross-cultural missions. If we calculate the number in terms of foreign missionaries, Korea comes in second, right after the United States.[1] The number of missionaries

---

This chapter appears in print for the first time in this book.

1. According to the *Mission Handbook* there are currently 44,384 fully supported overseas missionaries from the United States; see Linda J. Weber and Dotsey Welliver, eds., *Mission Handbook: U.S. and Canadian Protestant Ministries Overseas, 2007–2009* (Wheaton, Ill.: Evangelism and Missions Information Service, 2007), 13. Most of the 41,064 Indian missionaries work cross-culturally within India. The United States and India are followed in number by the United

continues to grow, but there are concerns about the managerial capacity of Korean mission agencies, concerns that are related to the lack of relevant support and member-care systems in churches.[2] Numerical growth alone does not guarantee the stability and maturity of a missionary movement.

The number of Korean mission agencies reached 190 in 2008. This number comprises 150 sending agencies (133 interdenominational and 17 denominational agencies), 14 support/mobilization agencies, 12 mission associations, 8 training centers, and 6 research centers. In 2008, there was one agency with over 2,000 members, three agencies with over 1,000, nine with over 500, and thirty-six with over 100. Mission agencies keep growing in size, but it is legitimate for us to raise questions about their functionality. Rather than competing over numbers, mission agencies need to develop expertise and managerial capacity to provide good service to their members and supporters. Mission agencies need to seek cooperation rather than being drawn into competition.

Korean missionaries in 2008 serve in 177 countries. Not surprisingly, the largest number of Korean missionaries serve in Asia (47.3 percent). The rest are active in the Eurasian countries of the former USSR (14.6 percent), followed by North America (9.3), Africa (7.7), Latin America (5.8), the Middle East (4.5), Western Europe (3.9), the South Pacific (2.9), and Eastern Europe (2.0), or are involved with itineration or work at headquarters (2.0 percent). Asia is the most populated but least evangelized continent, which explains the comparatively large deployment of Korean missionaries in Asia. The main hosting countries of Korean missionaries are China, the United States, Japan, the Philippines, Russia, Germany, Thailand, Indonesia, India, and Canada in descending order of the number of Korean missionaries present in each

---

Kingdom (8,164 missionaries, including 5,666 overseas), Canada (7,001, including 4,337 overseas), and Brazil (5,801, including 1,912 overseas). See Patrick Johnstone, Robyn Johnstone, and Jason Mandryk, *Operation World: When We Pray God Works* (Carlisle, Eng.: Paternoster Lifestyle, 2001), 895–901.

2. Steve Sang-Cheol Moon, "The Protestant Missionary Movement in Korea: Current Growth and Development," *International Bulletin of Missionary Research* 32, no. 2 (2008): 61.

country. In the years leading up to 2008, the number of Korean missionaries in Japan, Russia, Thailand, and India has risen.[3]

UNDERSTANDING KOREAN MISSIONARIES

Korean missionaries reflect characteristics of Korean society and the Korean church. These characteristics, highlighting both the advantages and the disadvantages of being Korean, work both positively and negatively with respect to current global trends. Slightly more than half (52.0 percent) of all Korean missionaries are women. Married missionaries outnumber singles by a ratio of almost nine to one. The percentage of single missionaries decreased from 20.2 percent in 1994 to 12.7 percent in 2000, and still further to 10.3 percent in 2008. The decreasing percentage of single missionaries can be traced to the gradual development of denominational mission agencies, whose members are mostly married seminary graduates, and also to large interdenominational agencies' preference for married members over singles.

By age, 69.6 percent of Korean missionaries are in their thirties and forties. The age distribution is related to the extent of ministry experience. The percentage of Korean missionaries with less than four years of experience is lower compared to previous surveys (39 percent in 2000; 68 percent in 1994), whereas the ratio of missionaries with over eight years' experience has increased (50.1 percent in 2008; 28 percent in 2000; only 8 percent in 1994). Though the number of veteran missionaries who are able to provide oversight of novice missionaries is increasing, more systematic efforts are needed to care for and support younger missionaries.

In level of education, 4.5 percent of Korean missionaries have completed only high school, 63.4 percent have an undergraduate degree as their highest degree, 27.3 percent have a master's as their highest degree, and 4.9 percent have completed doctorates. An increasing number of missionary personnel are educated at the doctoral level, many of them having pursued higher degrees in mission-related fields such as ethnology, management, and area studies. The high educational standard of

---

3. The Korean missionaries in the United States, Germany, and Canada are mostly involved in campus ministries.

Korean missionaries suggests that they are able to carry out highly specialized ministries, though nonformal and informal modes of education are also needed.

Nearly one-third of Korean missionaries are ordained pastors (32.1 percent). Pastors' wives and laypersons account for most others (67.9 percent). Since a majority of Korean missionaries have had theological education, we count on them to be effective in discipleship training, church planting, theological education, and, especially, leadership development. About one-fourth (24.2 percent) of Korean missionaries have secular jobs and can be categorized as tentmakers or bivocational missionaries. The Korean missionary movement has a strong inclination toward frontier missions, in which 41.0 percent of missionaries are involved. The proportion of Korean missionaries serving with international mission agencies is 21.8 percent.

In the 1970s and 1980s, the majority of Korean missionaries were involved in diaspora ministry; however, only a minority (8.2 percent) are currently involved in ministry to the Korean diaspora or in home ministries at headquarters. This percentage has slightly increased recently because mission agencies have accepted new members who are currently involved both in diaspora ministry and in reaching out to other people groups cross-culturally. Some mission agencies also have more home staff members than before. Most Korean mission agencies do not consider diaspora workers as missionaries, but if we were to include this number in the total number of missionaries, that figure would be much higher. Diaspora ministry is characteristic of a missionary movement with a monolingual and monocultural background.

Korean missionaries work within various religio-cultural blocs: Christian (24.3 percent of missionaries), Buddhist (13.1 percent), Islamic (23.2 percent), Communist (19.4 percent), animist (24.3 percent), Hindu (3.4 percent), and other (11.1 percent).

In terms of ministry focus, 78.2 percent of Korean missionaries are directly involved in evangelistic and spiritual work such as church planting, discipleship training, theological education, itinerant evangelism, and Bible translation. This engagement reflects the conservative theological orientation of the Korean church, but, while maintaining an evangelical understanding of missions, a more holistic concept of missions is desirable.

LEADERSHIP STRUCTURE AND ORGANIZATIONAL CULTURE

Korean mission executives consider leadership to be an important issue in missions.[4] Of the mission executives, 92.2 percent agree on the importance of leadership, and of this percentage, 51.9 percent replied that it is very important. In previous years KRIM's analyses have shown that Korean mission leaders are insufficiently equipped or trained to enable the maturation of the missionary movement. The mission executives have recognized the same thing, thereby confirming KRIM's analysis, for they also see a need for more trained leaders at all levels of the mission enterprise.

Servant leadership theories are not necessarily confined to nonprofit organizations but are relevant in missionary settings also. Over 90 percent of the respondents who are directors of mission agencies agreed that servant leadership models are of value for missionaries working in cross-cultural settings. Only 3.9 percent disagreed.

Mission executives also responded positively (88.3 percent) in their evaluation of the actual practice of servant leadership by field missionaries. Only 5.2 percent responded negatively. This aspect of missionary practice, as confirmed by personal conversations with Western missiologists such as Paul Hiebert, seems to be one of the brightest facets of Korean missions. Identification with local people is an area where Korean missionaries perform well, although there are always exceptions.

As for modeling leadership, mission leaders (32.5 percent), missionary trainers (27.3 percent), and fellow missionaries (26.0 percent) exercise significant influence, whereas pastors of home churches (11.7 percent), seminary professors (1.3 percent), and other people (6.5 percent) do not have as much influence. In this way mission leaders' influence is highlighted once again.

---

4. Of the 190 missionary sending agencies surveyed, 77 agencies responded organizationally, representing over 85 percent of all Korean missionaries. Logically, if not statistically, the findings may be assumed to be generalizable.

Missionary pre-field training centers are critical in terms of leadership formation. Half of the respondents (50.6 percent) point to pre-field training programs as a crucial element in leadership formation. Almost a quarter (23.4 percent) point to the influence of church and student fellowships, with continuing education (13.0 percent), seminary education (5.2 percent), and other factors (6.5 percent) trailing behind. Pre-field training centers cannot accommodate, however, the increasing number of missionary candidates; thus many missionaries depart for the field without proper training and preparation. Awareness of the need for increased training is an important issue that arises out of mission leaders' personal experience.

Most Korean mission leaders think that missionary leadership in the field should vary according to the context (77.9 percent). Only a small number of these leaders contend that leadership principles should be invariable, remaining the same despite differences in context. As an important contextual element for missionary leadership, the local cultural context is highlighted by half of the respondents (50.6 percent), with the remainder emphasizing the leadership styles of local church leaders (19.5 percent), missionaries' gifts (18.2 percent), the status of evangelization (9.1 percent), and other concerns (1.3 percent).

The majority of mission executives believe that missionary leadership structures should be democratic and horizontal rather than hierarchical (84.3 percent). They do not think that Korean missions should imitate Western models of leadership structure (78.2 percent). Finding a well-contextualized leadership structure is a key issue for Korean mission agencies. More concretely, lightly weighted leadership structures with flexibility and the ability for quick decision making are needed within the Korean context. The respondents indicate that important decisions regarding leadership structures should be made by field leaders (57.1 percent), field members (28.6 percent), home leaders (9.1 percent), leaders of supporting churches (1.3 percent), and others (2.6 percent). According to 92.2 percent of the respondents, leadership structure is important because it affects organizational culture. Therefore we need to study more closely the relationship between leadership structure and organizational culture.

Interestingly, on the question of influences on the missionaries' organizational culture, the number of respondents who list the influence of Korean church culture (33.8 percent) is slightly greater than the number who list local culture (31.2 percent). Respondents also indicated that Korean secular culture (15.6 percent) has more influence on missions' organizational culture than does theological orientation (14.3 percent). Even expatriate missionaries consider the traits of the home culture to be more influential than either local culture or a transcultural theological standpoint. Though this tendency can be found among multicultural groups, it is likely to be more strongly present among originally monocultural people. Since cultural isolation often entrenches a traditional cultural orientation among expatriate societies, a key issue is to transform the influence that the cultures of Korean society and the Korean church have on expatriate missionaries so that they become more flexible and horizontal.

Most of the mission leaders (67.5 percent) agree that the influx of new generations of missionaries from Korea is leading to adaptations in Korean missionary culture. Tensions and conflicts sometimes arise between different missionary generations due to different cultural norms. Younger generations are typically more horizontal in their way of thinking than older generations and thus are often misunderstood as being less orderly or even unspiritual. Also, cultural dynamics among missionaries on the mission field are complex, with a mix of contributions from local culture, local church culture, home culture, home church culture, generational culture, and global cultural climates.

Our survey asks related questions regarding the leadership experience of mission executives. Of the respondents 37.7 percent have been CEOs of mission organizations for less than five years, 26.0 percent for five to ten years, 7.8 percent for ten to fifteen years, 14.3 percent for fifteen to twenty years, and 13.0 percent for over twenty years. Most believe that an average leadership term of five to ten years is appropriate for a mission executive, with only 11.7 percent supporting the idea of a term of over twenty years. This view could be interpreted as short-sighted and unrealistic in light of the small leadership pool that is, in turn, a result of the short history of the Korean missionary movement. Korean agencies have adopted a democratic election system for their leadership positions, which has led to frequent leadership transitions. The accumulation of leadership expertise through continuity of personnel in leadership positions needs to be considered. Short leadership cycles, marked possibly by periods of trial and error, may undermine the stability of the missionary movement.

Personality and spirituality are listed as important qualifications for top leaders (75.3 percent). Missionary experience (11.7 percent), educational and training background (5.2 percent), fund-raising and administrative ability (5.2 percent), and other qualities (1.3 percent) follow. The importance placed on missionary experience has considerably decreased compared to previous surveys, while the importance of personality and spirituality has greatly increased. Basic spiritual health is emphasized because missionaries have similar needs. Missionary leaders are considered not as spiritual giants but rather as ordinary people with flaws and weaknesses. Mission leaders qualified in almost every way suggested above are not easy to find, an observation that points out the significant and urgent need to prepare mission leaders at different levels for the maturation of the Korean missionary movement.

The issues of leadership structure and organizational culture arise from complex cultural and organizational dynamics. We need to analyze these phenomena wisely to deepen our understanding of the cross-cultural dimensions of the Korean people and their ministries. Further qualitative research done by "insiders" is needed to flesh out an emic understanding of the facts and phenomena.

LEADERSHIP NEEDS

The continuing increase in the number of Korean missionaries in the 2000s requires careful thinking about leadership development for further growth in the 2010s and beyond. Unless good leaders are prepared, mission movements will not be able to move beyond the mere activism of inexperienced practitioners. Effective leadership requires a good sense of direction and a strategic mindset. To further both the quantitative and qualitative growth of mission activities, leadership in a variety of forms is needed. I highlight here several key areas of specialty.

First, to aid in its future growth, the Korean missionary movement needs good member-care specialists. Quality member care requires experts who can give professional care and counseling relevant for missionaries and cross-cultural expatriates. Member-care specialists should have personal experience of cross-cultural living, be trained in counseling, and possess a sound theological perspective. Specialists are needed in the subcategories of debriefing, short-term counseling, addiction therapy, and crisis counseling.

Second, the Korean missionary movement needs good field strategists. Field strategies should consider contextualization, globalization, and innovation and should exhibit a balance of theological reflection and practical application. Pragmatism alone cannot guide strategizing for field ministries, but field strategies should take field realities into account and should consider provision of member care after strategic assignments. Ministry strategies and member care should not be considered two separate facets of cross-cultural service but should coexist in creative tension. Subcategories of field specialists can include team leaders, country coordinators, area directors, and field directors (or directors of overseas ministry).

Third, the Korean missionary movement needs good home administrators. Home administration requires long-term stability and needs to constantly reflect the ethos of the mission community in policy making. Home administrators often work behind the scenes and thus are rarely in the spotlight, but they are an essential part of the ministry for the Kingdom of God. Mission agencies and local churches need to give due respect to mission administrators.

Fourth, the Korean missionary movement needs good mission mobilizers. The annual rate of growth in the number of missionary recruits decreased rapidly in the early 2000s, suggesting a need for good mobilizers who can recruit new candidates in creative ways. Recruitment should be reinforced not only among young adults but also among early retirees who as part of their life's journey are willing to go the extra mile for those in need in the mission fields. Mission training programs in churches should be optimally designed for the needs of different age groups.

Fifth, the Korean missionary movement needs good missiologists. Lack of field experience among Korean missiologists has been tackled in recent years through regular travel overseas. Nevertheless, there remains a significant need for Korean missiologists to focus narrowly and develop missiological expertise in one specific field of missiology, avoiding duplication of expertise. More mission historians, anthropologists, and area-study specialists are needed in the Korean missions circle.

Sixth, the Korean missionary movement needs good missionary trainers. Even with several missionary training centers now established in Korea, many Korean missionaries are still going out to the mission field without proper training. Additionally, existing pre-field programs should be upgraded with new insights based on awareness of ever-changing cultural climates. Continuing education and leadership development are intertwined. Pre-field training is not enough in and of itself. In many cases, when they must make strategic decisions for ministry, missionaries can call only on the knowledge they accumulated during the pre-field training period. Leadership skills need to be honed through continued learning in the field.

We can attempt to quantify the leadership needs for the further growth of the Korean missionary movement in the 2010s and beyond. In estimating numerical needs, we must remember that one leader can play multiple roles. In sum, approximately 2,000 team leaders, 1,000 country coordinators, 200 area directors, and 20 global leaders are urgently needed to strategize field ministries well and to provide effective member care for missionaries.[5] The need for home administrators is related to the size of mission agencies, but in total 233 home administrators who can serve long term as full members of a mission agency (not including paid staff workers in home offices) are required.[6]

---

5. The rationale for this estimate is as follows: mission agencies may need one team leader for every 10 members, one country coordinator for every 20 members, one area director for every 100 members, and one global leader for every 1,000 members.

6. In my estimation, the 89 mission agencies with a membership of less than 50 need one administrator each, the 15 agencies with a membership of 50–99 need two administrators, the 28 agencies with a membership of 100–499 need three administrators, the 5 agencies with a membership of 500–999 need four administrators, and the 2 agencies with over 1,000 members need at least five administrators.

Also, 100 mission mobilizers, 100 missionary trainers, 60 missiologists, and 60 counselors are needed for the strategic growth of the movement.[7]

From a qualitative standpoint a needs assessment would highlight competency in contextualizing leadership structures, in creating and managing organizational culture, and in providing innovative mission strategies through missional leadership. Although other leadership qualities also deserve close attention, the proper understanding of leadership structures and organizational culture that these proposals presuppose is urgently needed at this stage in the development of the Korean missionary movement. Frequent leadership transitions in many mission agencies suggest a need for focused attention on these issues. We need new leaders who are wise and innovative managers with creative minds to carry the torch passed on from earlier Korean visionaries who matured as leaders without any organizational support.

LEADERSHIP DEVELOPMENT

Leadership should develop organically. Nevertheless, we have a responsibility to be constantly making conscious efforts to nurture and develop leadership. Although leadership is not everything in missions, it has an important part to play in this movement.

Missional leadership needs to be contextualized in order to be effective in a cross-cultural setting. As the world is rapidly globalized, the need for globalized leadership also grows. Cultural issues are dynamically involved in both the contextualization and the globalization of missional leadership. The local cultural context, organizational cultural

---

7. One mobilizer is assumed to be needed for every 10 candidates, with the goal of 1,000 new missionaries per year. In total, 60 missiologists are needed based on the estimation that 3 missiologists are needed for each of the two agencies with over 1,000 members, 2 for each of the five agencies with a membership of 500–999, 1 for each of the twenty-eight agencies with a membership of 100–499, 0.5 for the fifteen agencies with a membership of 50–99, and 0.1 for each of the eighty-nine agencies with fewer than 50 members. The same scale is applied for counselor needs. The missiologists and counselors do not have to be internal resource persons; they may be external qualified experts employed on a contract.

background, and global cultural trends are all integral to promoting effective missional leadership in the field.

Leadership development can be pursued through the following processes.

Needs assessment of leadership in each organization. Korean mission agencies need to assess leadership needs on a long-term basis, pray for those needs, and invest in the significant work of God.

Profiling of leadership qualities. Each organization requires specific qualities and qualifications in its leadership. The purpose of profiling is not to set a leadership ideal but to identify people who most closely manifest the leadership qualities set forth by the organization. Both firmness and flexibility are necessary in the identification of the right type of leadership for each organization.

Defined procedures for leadership development. Defined procedures will not only identify the right persons but will also develop the leadership capabilities of missionaries. Every mission entity dedicated to excellence must design and run relevant programs for leadership development.

Investment in leadership development programs. Stakeholders should see participation in leadership development for the future of mission communities as a significant undertaking. Global companies invest in their future through leadership programs, and mission agencies need to learn from them and emulate their example by investing in missional leadership development.

Constant evaluation for further development in leadership. Rapid and drastic changes in the mission environment can bring disorder and chaos to the existing leadership. Past success more often than not gets in the way of continuing success, and therefore leadership programs must be re-evaluated in light of new categories and standards. Constant evaluation and real-life application will prepare us to make needed paradigm shifts in a timely but wise manner.

Effective leadership development requires conscious and constant effort by leaders to ensure that they are exercising their gifts in ways that are proper. Experienced mission leaders and administrators who are aware of the demands leadership involves should give focused attention to leadership development plans and programs. The mission statement of each mission entity should explicitly reflect the value of preparing leadership for the next generation.

Pastors of local churches should also play significant roles in developing missional leadership, by caring for missionaries and by encouraging them to pursue higher standards in spirituality and character formation. The burden of preparing mission leadership often falls on leaders of supporting churches, and pastors should therefore be able to make strategic decisions for their candidates' growth with a long-term perspective in mind. Pastors need to provide constant moral and emotional support for missionaries sent out from their congregation.

Missiologists and mission professors should provide know-how for leadership development. They should willingly become involved in preparing leaders for the next generation, using their expertise in different fields of missiology. Missionaries should consider leadership development an important part of their commitment because they need to grow in spirituality and leadership in order to serve others well. They also need to encourage one another to do well in this calling for growth.

Supporters and laypeople need to understand leadership development as part of their responsibility as caregivers for missionaries. Many supporters fail to see leadership development as one of the top priorities of effective missions. Such neglect should be addressed and be brought to the attention of mainstream supporters. Praying for leadership development and giving practically in its support should be considered a rewarding fruit of partnering in the kingdom of God.

CONCLUSION

At the end of 2008, churches in Korea were sending 18,035 missionaries through 190 mission agencies to 177 countries. The missionary movement keeps growing rapidly. Phenomenal growth within a short period has not allowed much time, however, for adequate qualitative maturation of Korean missions. Many problems that were foreseen are now becoming realities.

Planned growth would have moderated the speed of growth in Korean missions significantly. We need a deeper understanding of related phenomena if we are to galvanize the missionary movement continuously. Our actions need to be based on accurate understanding and knowledge, for otherwise the Korean chapter in mission history will be written in terms of both extreme positives and extreme negatives. We need to feed the strengths and starve the problems in order to manage the dynamics of growth to the best of our ability.

Leadership issues in Korean missions are significant. Missionaries have high expectations for missional leadership, but Korean mission agencies lack sufficient well-qualified leaders. Many people are well meaning, but missionary leadership requires performance and expertise that fluently crosses cultures, traditions, and boundaries. For the sake of the future of Korean missions, the churches in Korea need to invest in leadership development. The global church needs to pray that leadership structures and styles, organizational cultures and climates, and real people involved in Korean missions will mature to fulfill biblical and global standards in the years ahead. Amen!

8

MISSIONS FROM KOREA 2012:
Slowdown and Maturation

The Korean missionary movement is slowing down; the growth in the number of foreign missionaries is much reduced. In 2011 a total of 19,373 Korean missionaries were serving in countries outside South Korea.[1] Three years earlier, in 2008, there were 18,035 foreign missionaries, yielding a growth of only 1,338. In years past, it was common to add this many missionaries in a single year.

Since 2008, because of closures, mergers, and inactivity, the number of mission agencies has decreased from 190 to 168. In 2011 these 168 agencies included 119 sending agencies and 49 supporting agencies; 153 of the mission agencies were interdenominational, and only 15 were denominational. Security concerns make it increasingly difficult or unwise to identify the specific countries of service; overall, however, no big changes are evident. Korean missionaries are active in 177 countries.

About half of all Korean foreign missionaries are working in Asia (47.3 percent), and an additional quarter (24.3 percent) in countries

---

Originally published as "Missions from Korea 2012: Slowdown and Maturation," *International Bulletin of Missionary Research* 36, no. 2 (April 2012): 84–85, this chapter is reprinted by permission.

1. The total number of missionaries reported by Korean agencies for 2011 is 20,392. Of these, 1,019 are double counts, i.e., missionaries who appeared on the list of more than one agency, leaving a net total of 19,373. The data and observations in this chapter draw on a 2011 survey of Korean missions. Percentage breakdowns in paragraph 4 (beginning "The following describe") and in the table (sections 4 and 5, "Deployment" and "Personal data"), however, are drawn from a 2008 survey, one based on a larger data set that, overall, shows percentages quite comparable with those based on the 2011 survey.

that are majority Christian. The major receiving countries are China, United States, Japan, Philippines, Russia, Germany, Thailand, Indonesia, India, and Canada. A large majority of the foreign missionaries (90.7 percent) are pursuing traditional soul-winning ministries, namely, church planting (46.2 percent), discipleship training (23.7 percent), educational ministries (9.5 percent), theological education (5.3 percent), itinerant evangelism (4.2 percent), and Bible translation (1.8 percent). The rest (9.3 percent) are involved in medical service, humanitarian aid, community development, administrative work, or member care.

The following describe a majority of Korean missionaries:
- below age fifty (75.6 percent)
- less than eight years' experience in cross-cultural ministry (50.5 percent)
- an undergraduate or higher degree (95.5 percent)
- ordained or the spouse of one who is ordained (64.3 percent)
- members of an interdenominational mission agency (53.3 percent)
- members of a Korean (vs. an international) mission agency (78.2 percent)
- full-time career missionaries (75.8 percent)
- involved in cross-cultural ministries (91.8 percent)
- serve in "regular" mission fields, not "frontier" (59.0 percent)

Once we have observed early signs of stagnation—not merely statistically but also empirically, on the ground—we are obliged to reflect on the factors underlying this development. When people are too busy, there is little time for, or interest in, reflection. In preparing and digesting reports such as this one, we have the opportunity to ask deeper questions instead of relying on standard, predictable questions and answers. It seems now that we need to consider at least the following seven questions:

Question 1: Given the present context of stagnated church growth in Korea, what is an appropriate level of growth to expect in the Korean missionary movement? Many observers have noted that continued numerical growth in missions is not likely when church growth overall has stalled. This conclusion is tied to the observation that the Korean (or any?) missionary movement is a child of church revival.[2] It is important to set and promote realistic goals of missionary recruitment in light of the current level of church growth. (This is not to deny that there may be some value in trying to mobilize existing churches for greater involvement in missions.)

Question 2: Has numerical goal-setting in mission actually had the effect of undermining growth in the quality of our missionary work? Over the years, many mission agencies have been overly aggressive in seeking to increase the size of their missionary force, raising questions about the qualifications of missionaries sent out and about their performance in the field. Extravagant emphasis on numbers has had the negative effect of inhibiting growth in (1) the quality of missionary work and, long term, (2) the number of mission workers.

Question 3: What negative fruit have we seen in the aftermath of the rapid growth in Korean missions? Here we could mention insufficient attention being paid to (1) infrastructure development, (2) strategy for field ministries, (3) care of missionary families, (4) leadership development, (5) crisis management, and (6) preparation for missionary retirement. Though the last decade has seen significant progress in all these areas, an increasing number of problems in mission accountability have also been coming to light.[3]

Question 4: Have we recognized the positive side of missionary crises? For example, the abduction of twenty-three Korean Christians in Afghanistan in 2007 has had positive results, at least for improving crisis management and contingency planning in Korean missions, regardless of its negative impacts. Crisis can be a disguised blessing under God's sovereignty, which can be interpreted properly only with the advantage of thoughtful hindsight.

---

2. Andrew F. Walls, "Missionary Vocation and the Ministry: The First Generation," in *The Missionary Movement in Christian History: Studies in the Transmission of Faith* (Maryknoll, N.Y.: Orbis Books, 1996), 160.

3. Bahn Seok (Peter) Lee, "Accountability Issues Among Korean Missions Organizations," in *Accountability in Missions: Korean and Western Case Studies*, ed. Jonathan J. Bonk (Eugene, Ore.: Wipf & Stock, 2011), 181–83.

Question 5: In our mission work, do we rely more on "hard power" or on "soft power"? To depend inappropriately on hard power—military, material, financial, organizational, physical, and even mass media forces and equipment—may result in conveying worldviews that are non-Christian. The soft power of Christian love, in contrast, is unconditional, altruistic, nonnumerical, and immeasurable—but it transforms the world fundamentally. Only compassion for specific people motivates mission.[4] Korean missionaries, especially mission leaders, need to check their actual worldviews and, as needed, change them to harness missional soft power. Short-termism, obsession with visible results, and exporting prosperity myths are a few expressions of secular worldviews. Only the practice of incarnational mission can bring about changes at a deep level. There is a growing awareness of the importance of incarnational humility among mission communities and practitioners from Korea.

Question 6: How can member care for Korean missionaries be optimized so as to strengthen and consolidate Korea's missionary movement? It is encouraging to observe a number of Christian psychologists and counselors volunteering and joining hands in the common task of member care. There is growing awareness of the complex needs of missionary families, which has led, for example, to the development of MK hostels and camps. The Korean mission community has been slow in moving beyond stereotypes of the rugged, individualistic missionary or missionary family and truly grasping the significant needs member care addresses. In recent years we have seen impressive progress, especially in care for the children of missionaries, but enormous needs remain.

Question 7: How can we more fully value the place of research in missions? Empirical research itself is not a panacea, but we do need to cultivate an appreciation—and eagerness—for the empirical facts, wisdom, and insight that are available, both for our immediate, particular use and for accumulating and sharing across organizational boundaries and across generations. Empirical research, although limited, is a useful counterbalance to the activism common in many missional contexts.

---

4. Jonathan J. Bonk, "Mission by the Numbers," *International Bulletin of Missionary Research* 35, no. 1 (January 2011): 2.

We constantly need to remove blind spots in our missional research.[5] Evaluative studies, which are desirable in many areas, are best balanced by an attitude of appreciative reflection, not one that rushes to adopt a problem-solving mentality. It is encouraging to note that a few new mission research institutes have been established in recent years.

We possess fairly comprehensive statistics on the Korean missionary scene, which prompt questions such as the seven listed above. Overall, we can say that growth in Korea's missionary movement is slowing down but that we are seeing a corresponding maturation in reflection on mission. We trust that such reflection will initiate revitalization for further growth.[6]

---

5. David Greenlee, "Cookbooks, Firemen, Jazz Musicians, and Dairy Farmers: Strategy and Research for Twenty-first Century Missions," in *Global Passion: Marking George Verwer's Contribution to World Mission*, ed. David Greenlee (Carlisle, Eng.: Authentic Lifestyle, 2003), 167–69.

6. The data and observations in the following table draw on a 2011 survey of Korean missions. Percentage breakdowns in paragraph 4 above, beginning "The following describe," and in sections 4 and 5, "Deployment" and "Personal data," however, are drawn from a 2008 survey, one based on a larger data set that, overall, shows percentages quite comparable with those based on the 2011 survey.

Missionaries						19,373
Mission agencies						168
sending/supporting						119/49
interdenominational/denominational						153/15
Receiving countries						177
Deployment (percentage)						
by continent/region						
Asia	47.3	Latin America	5.8	Eastern Europe	2.0	
Eurasia/former USSR	14.6	Middle East	4.5	Other	2.0	
North America	9.3	Western Europe	3.9			
Africa	7.7	Oceania	2.9			
by religious/cultural bloc						
Christian	24.3	Buddhist	13.1	Other	11.1	
Islamic	23.2	Animist	5.5			
Communist	19.4	Hindu	3.4			
by ethnic/linguistic focus						
non-Korean	82.6					
ethnic Korean	8.2					
non-Korean and ethnic Korean	9.2					
Personal data (percentage)						
male/female						52.0/48.0
married/single						89.7/10.3
clergy (including spouses)/lay						64.0/36.0
full-time/bivocational						75.8/24.2
serve with interdenominational/denominational agency						53.3/46.7
serve with Korean/international agency						78.2/21.8
serve in "regular"/"frontier" mission field						59.0/41.0
age distribution						20s (6.0), 30s (26.9), 40s (42.7) 50s (19.4), 60s (4.9)
missionary experience						<4 years (28.1), 4–8 (21.9), 8–12 (21.3), 12–16 (14.8), >16 (14.0)
highest degree						doctorate (4.9), master's (27.3), bachelor's (63.4), high school (4.5)

Table 8.1. Korean missionary totals as of December 2011

9
MISSIONS FROM KOREA 2014:
Missionary Children

The education of missionary children (MKs) is an important responsibility for all who are involved in mission. If missionaries are to be successful in their overseas ministry, they must have access to a reasonable educational option for their children.

The information presented here is based on empirical research of two sorts: first, a quantitative survey I designed and processed with the help of staff at the Korea Research Institute for Mission (KRIM) in late December 2012, which has been updated with additional data gathered at the end of December 2013; second, qualitative research involving field-based interviews carried out in nine countries in which 176 members of the Korean mission community took part—missionaries (70), MKs (76), and MK educators (30)—during the period of October 2012 through April 2013.[1]

Originally published as "Missions from Korea 2014: Missionary Children," *International Bulletin of Missionary Research* 38, no. 2 (April 2012): 84–85, this chapter is reprinted by permission.

1. EunYong Cindy Kim carried out the interviews in the Philippines and Thailand. The remainder of the interviews in seven countries were carried out by Steve Moon with the assistance of Hee-Joo (Yoo) Moon and Jung Joo Lee. All are on the KRIM staff. In all but four instances the interviews were of individuals rather than of groups. The 176 interviews generated over 800 pages of field notes, which are now kept, along with recordings of the interviews, at KRIM.

Nine formal schools and two home schools in nine countries were covered by our research; two separate group interview sessions with a total of eight university students were added later. The schools covered by our research are Manila Hankuk (Korean) Academy, Manila, Philippines (principal: Segi Hong, www.mha.or.kr); Grace International School, Chiang Mai, Thailand (superintendent:

The results of the questionnaire survey administered in late December 2013 show that 20,085 Korean missionaries were working with 166 mission agencies in 171 countries. These missionaries had a total of 17,675 children, with the percentage of children at each educational level as follows: preschool (16.8), elementary school (22.9), middle school (13.4), high school (12.9), college or university (29.1), and employed or employable adults (4.9). For Korean missionary parents with children of primary or secondary school age, the type of schooling selected, by percentage, was as follows: local schools (35.9), international schools (28.6), schools in Korea (14.6), homeschooling (9.0), MK schools (8.9), and other options, including Korean overseas schools (3.0). Field studies suggest that each option has both advantages and disadvantages.

Many MKs feel that as a result of a decision made by their parents, they had to leave Korea suddenly and without sufficient opportunity to prepare. MKs who are unhappy in the field may begin to question God's goodness. Healthy spiritual relationships with God and parents should be consolidated before MKs reach adolescence.

Linguistic challenges are a hurdle in the education of MKs, especially during the first years in a new field. When MKs return to Korea on furlough, their Korean-language abilities are routinely tested by their grandparents and church members, and all too often the children are made to feel shame for their deficiencies. Yet at the same time teachers at international schools think that many Korean MKs need to give more effort to improving their English.

The emotional and psychological challenges for MKs are also substantial. MKs who attend boarding school may miss their parents and

---

Jennie Garcia, www.gisthailand.org); Black Forest Academy, Kandern, Germany (principal: Robert Shuman, www.bfacademy.com); Hanal Korean School in GDQ International Christian School, Tirana, Albania (director: Roger Pearce, www.gdqschool.org); Dakar Academy, Dakar, Senegal (director: Joseph Rosa, www.dakar-academy.org); Bourofaye Christian School, Dakar, Senegal (www.bcs-senegal.org); International Gateway Academy, Istanbul, Turkey (www.int-gateway.org); Glovill High School, Busan, Republic of Korea (principal: Kiyoung Shin, www.glovillhigh.hs.kr); Sejong Global School, Republic of Cheonan, Korea (director: EunHwa Chai, http://sejongglobalschool.org); and home schools in China and Myanmar.

siblings. Those who attend local schools often lack close friendships. An absence of peer bonding is particularly marked for children who are homeschooled. On all fronts, relational satisfaction seems very low, which can cause severe loneliness and depression.

MKs often struggle with their cultural identity, which is vitally related to one's sense of self and one's pattern of behavior. The quest for a singular cultural identity is increasingly challenging in our swiftly globalizing world. Identities are always in the process of becoming. MKs' multiple cultural identities surface especially on their reentry to their "home" or passport country.

Financial problems are experienced by almost all Korean missionary families. Only a small number of Korean missionaries have been able to afford education insurance or other plans that help parents prepare early for the high cost of a university education. The large majority of MKs whom we interviewed hoped eventually to earn a good salary, seeing such income as providing the opportunity to support their parents and contribute to the world. Interviews have led me to suggest that children of missionaries who have been securely supported by churches, fruitful in ministry, and respected by local Christians are more likely to see missionary service as a positive career path that they themselves might follow.

Currently, MKs may sense that they belong to neither the home culture "A" nor the host culture "B," but only to a third culture "C." When coined in the early 1950s, the term "third-culture kid" lacked its current positive connotations, which stress the child's intercultural adaptability and competence. Successful educational missionaries can help ensure that MKs belong to both the home culture "A" and the host culture "B," and thus in practice to a hybrid culture "AB." I suggest that such processes would allow us to replace the term "third-culture kid" with "hybrid-culture kid." Our understanding of the nature and mission of MK education should be updated along these lines.

Korean missionaries need to plan their children's education wisely by making informed decisions. A vague fideism among many Korean missionaries has sometimes hindered appropriate planning, effective preparation, and practical support for their children's education. Affordable best practice should guide decisions about MK education, which should be tailored to the situation of individual missionary families. Overall, despite many complicating factors, we should be confident that the complex goals of MK education can be achieved.

Missionary children need to understand and accept the realities of their lives and education and to appreciate what is available to them. An MK's spiritual heritage, cultural capital, and personal relationships are very rich and will provide him or her with opportunities later in life. Insofar as MKs internalize their identities and develop coping strategies, they develop psychological strengths and an emotional stability that will serve them well in unfamiliar situations.

A more nuanced approach will overcome the stereotypes of an idealized missionary life and will encourage Korean churches to upgrade their mission programs to take more fully into account the details of missionary life, including the realities for MKs. Because of factors often beyond their control, teachers, dorm parents/assistants, and administrators tend not to stay in this ministry for a long period of time, which inhibits the development and accumulation of expertise. Korean churches should set aside a portion of their mission giving as support for lay missionaries who work with MKs, for missionaries who do not focus on evangelism and church planting often have trouble raising support.

People who accept the lordship of God and desire the progress of his kingdom need to pay close attention to this often marginalized yet promising and often very talented group of people. God's mission is both cross-cultural and cross-generational. Korean MKs are God's covenantal people, but they are vulnerable as they stand with their parents on the front lines of the *missio Dei*.[2]

---

2. This summary report is based on a fuller report that was published as an addendum to *Family Accountability in Missions: Korean and Western Case Studies*, ed. Jonathan J. Bonk (New Haven: OMSC Publications, 2013), 243–58. The numbers for Korean missionaries and MKs have been updated to reflect the new data set gathered in December 2013.

3. In 2012 the average monthly educational cost per four-person Korean missionary family was ₩591,082 (US$ 555), ranging from a low of ₩200,000 ($188) to a high of ₩1,000,000 ($940). See Steve Sang-Cheol Moon, "Missions from Korea 2013: Microtrends and Finance," *International Bulletin of Missionary Research* 37, no. 2 (April 2013): 96.

Missionaries	20,085
annual growth rate (percentage)	1.4
Mission agencies	166
sending/supporting	124 / 42
interdenominational/denominational	150 / 16
Missionary children	17,675
Breakdown of MK population (percentage)	
by educational level	
preschool	16.8
elementary school	22.9
middle school	13.4
high school	12.9
college or university	29.1
employed or employable adults	4.9
by type of schooling (for primary or secondary education)	
local schools	35.9
international schools	28.6
schools in Korea	14.6
homeschooling	9.0
MK schools	8.9
Korean schools overseas/others	3.0
Other realities of MK education (approximate proportion/percentage)	
MKs' language preference in everyday life	
Korean 40 English 40 Local language/other	20
MKs' country preference for university education	
Korean 40 USA 40 Local universities/other	20
Korean MKs in international MK schools	
as proportion of total student body	7.2 to 18.0
MK educational cost as proportion	
of missionary families' expenditures[3]	19.2
MKs in MK schools considering a career	
in missionary service	21.7
Problems of Korean MKs (percentage)	
Serious adjustment problems in school	0.9
Professional counseling needs and mental health problems	0.6
Alternative schools	
Number of alternative schools in Korea[4]	230

Table 9.1. Korean missionary children totals as of December 2013

---

4. Alternative schools in Korea do not follow the pattern set out in the government's standard educational policies and curricula. They seek to overcome problems found in traditional public education by emphasizing differing educational goals and contexts. Overall, alternative schools are smaller in size, more experiential in teaching and learning, more individualized to accommodate different learning styles, and more likely to be based on a particular religious worldview than public schools.

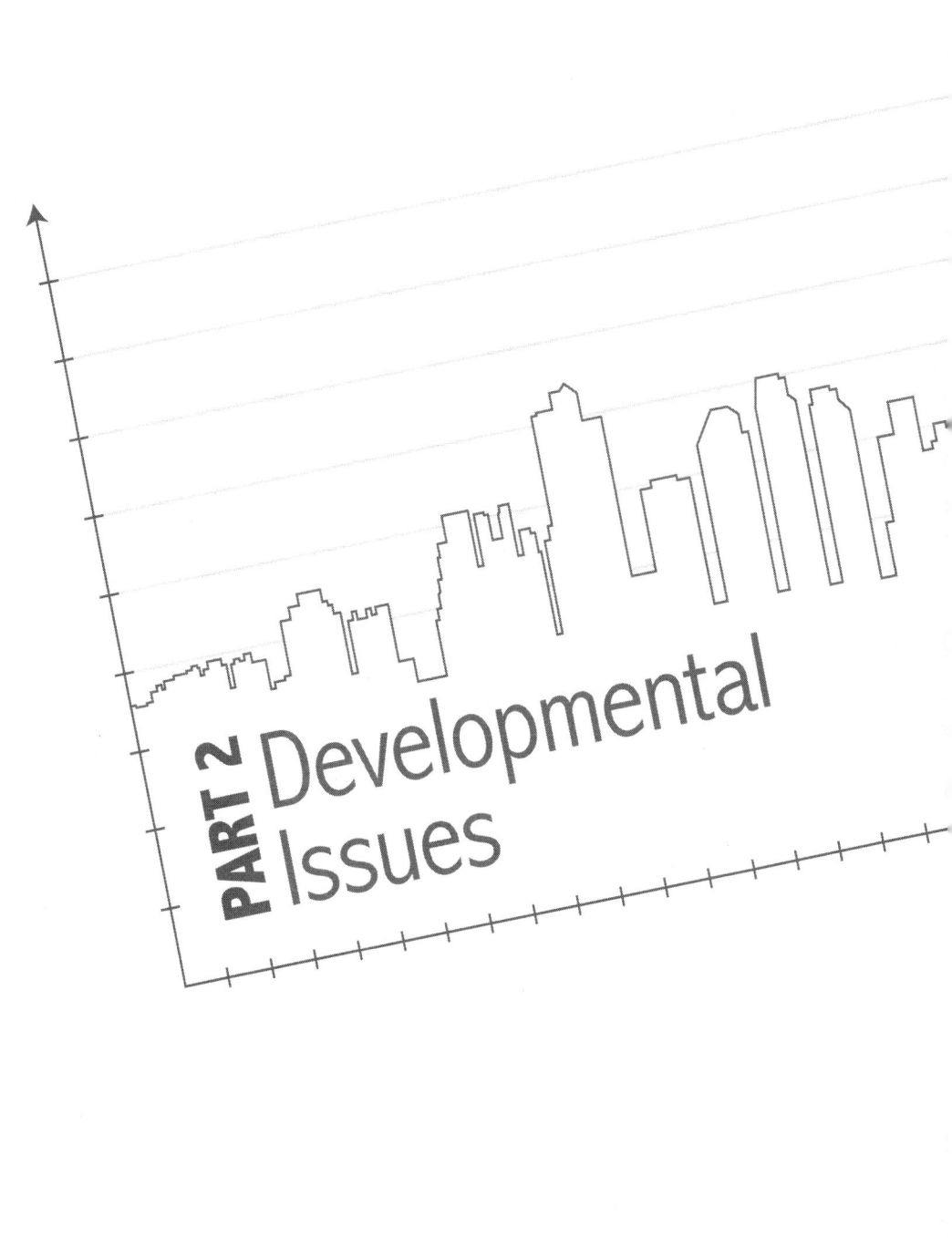

PART 2 Developmental Issues

10
MISSIONARY ATTRITION IN KOREA:
Opinions of Agency Executives

Missionary attrition is not a new problem. It is a problem that faced Paul's missionary band in the early church. Some members of the apostolic band such as Timothy, Titus, Luke, and Crescens remained faithful to the end (2 Tim. 4:10–11). Others on the team, however, were people like Demas, who later deserted Paul "because he loved this world" (2 Tim. 4:10). Mark, at an early point, also left the missionary team but was later recovered to the harvest force. The focus of attention in missionary attrition is not only to find ways to prevent attrition and recover some workers, but also to help the whole harvest force in our time to continue to serve the Lord effectively in the locations to which they have been called.

Missionary attrition is not merely a theoretical problem; it is a personal one as well. The thought uppermost in the minds of missionaries who return from the field may be to question the genuineness of their calling. Attrition, however, also has consequences that go beyond the individual missionary, involving overall loss of personnel and financial resources. Unlike most other missionaries from the Majority World, the majority of Korean missionaries serve beyond the nation's boundaries. For this reason, for a Korean missionary to leave the field is likely to mean, for the Korean churches, a larger loss of resources and investment. Missionary attrition undermines the emerging missionary movements present in the younger churches in many ways. A study of "the

---

Originally published in *Too Valuable to Lose: Exploring the Causes and Cures of Missionary Attrition*, ed. William D. Taylor (Pasadena, Calif.: William Carey Library, 1997), 129–42, this chapter has been edited and is reprinted by permission.

disappearing missionary" may serve to promote better missionary care, a matter that is most significant for the younger missionary movements.

REMAP IN KOREA

Korea Research Institute for Mission (KRIM)[1] conducted a survey of Korean missionary attrition as part of ReMAP (Reducing Missionary Attrition Project), a program carried out by the World Evangelical Fellowship Missions Commission. For the survey, a questionnaire prepared by the ReMAP team was translated into Korean and circulated by KRIM to Korean mission agencies in April 1995. The survey explored the extent of missionary attrition during the three-year period 1992–94. The questionnaires, which were mostly answered by mission executives, were received back by September 1995. Data processing and analysis took an additional six months, and the results are displayed in this report.[2]

During the course of the research process in Korea, limitations of the research design became apparent. That the survey did not ask for mission success stories posed a barrier to understanding, cooperation, and communication for some busy mission executives. At the time the questionnaire was designed, some of these barriers were foreseen,[3] but others were not detected until the data gathering process was under way. These weaknesses (detailed below) point to difficulties that are a part of carrying out an international research project.

---

1. KRIM is the research arm of Global Missionary Fellowship, an umbrella organization for nine different mission agencies.

2. Readers may note differences between the statistics presented in this chapter and those given in other chapters of *Too Valuable to Lose*, the book in which it originally appeared. Three reasons account for the variations. First, the calculations by Peter Brierley (chap. 6) were based on a first examination of the data. Second, Detlef Blöcher and Jonathan Lewis (chap. 7) had additional data from which to work. Also, they examined the data from a different perspective, asking different questions. Third, some of the statistics in the national case studies reflected new surveys and different ways of reading the numbers.

3. The author participated in the whole ReMAP process, beginning with the questionnaire design and continuing through the debriefing, and thus he shares responsibility for the weaknesses of ReMAP in terms of validity and reliability.

First, the research design was quantitative; it asked the mission administrators for numerical data. It may be desirable at some point to supplement this present study with a qualitative research project conducted through interviews and observation. The greater investment of resources and more extended commitment required would be offset by the possibilities for in-depth probing for the reasons for attrition the interview process would provide. During the process of interpreting the findings, I have drawn on my previous experience interviewing missionaries who have returned from the field in an attempt to compensate for the limitations of the quantitative research design.

Second, some questions were misunderstood and accordingly wrong answers were given. Part of the problem sprang from the questionnaire design. Busy people found it difficult to answer complex questions. Fortunately, answers to the most confusing item were supplemented by responses to a similar question. My familiarity with the mission agencies involved enabled me to clarify some of the ambiguous answers. To have carried out a pilot project preceding the main research project, however, would have provided more clarity and accuracy in data gathering.

Third, responses to the questionnaire made a potential danger—that of "impression management"—apparent, a danger that is not unique to any one culture. The response rate to the questionnaire was 78.1 percent, and the responses given could suggest a defensive mentality on the part of some of the agencies. This was so despite efforts to assure the respondents that individual answers would be treated with strict confidentiality.

Fourth, a convenience sample rather than a probability sample was used to gather the data. This approach precluded the use of statistical methods based on probability theory and the generalization of the findings to all mission agencies in Korea. Of the seventy-eight missionary sending agencies to which the survey questionnaire was sent, sixty-four agencies responded organizationally. These agencies represent over 90 percent of Korean missionaries. Logically, if not statistically, the findings may be assumed to be generalizable.

This report provides some background information about Korean missionaries and mission agencies, followed by a statistical summary of missionary attrition in Korea during the period 1992–94. An indepth analysis of the causes of attrition comes next, together with an attempt to interpret the various causes. After identifying the locus of the problem, the report suggests overall guidelines for remedies. Finally, a careful examination of the policies of mission agencies is presented.

MISSIONARY MOVEMENT IN KOREA

The issue of missionary attrition must be understood from within the context of each particular missionary movement. If a missionary movement is in decline, the problems raised by attrition become all the more acute. The Korean missionary movement maintains its vitality as the fastest growing missionary movement in the world, in spite of the presence of missionary attrition. In this section, ReMAP data have been augmented by up-to-date data from the 1996 edition of the *Korean Mission Handbook*.[4]

Missionary Expansion

According to the 1996 *Korean Mission Handbook*, the number of Korean missionaries in 1996 was 47.3 times what it had been in 1976. In 1996 at least 4,402 Korean missionaries were at work, scattered across 138 countries of the world.[5] See figures 10.1 and 10.2. In 1993 the churches in Korea sent more missionaries than did the churches in Australia (3,598) or Germany (3,524), following the lead of the United States (59,074), India (11,284), United Kingdom (7,012), and Canada (5,336).[6]

---

4. Steve Sang-Cheol Moon, ed., *Korean Mission Handbook* (Seoul, Korea: Global Missionary Press, 1996).

5. The number of missionaries was ascertained after eliminating duplicates. A couple was counted as two persons. See Steve Sang-Cheol Moon, "Acts of the Koreans: Status and Current Trends of the Missionary Movement in Korea," in Moon, *Korean Mission Handbook* (1996), i–ii.

6. The numbers of missionaries from other countries are for 1993, obtained from Patrick Johnstone, *Operation World* (Grand Rapids, Mich.: Zondervan, 1993), 643–49.

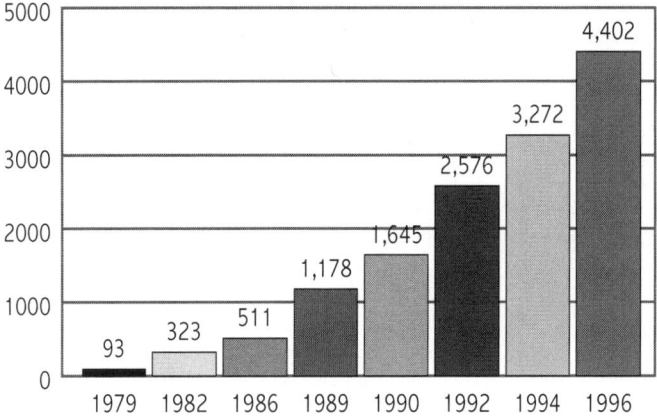

Figure 10.1. Number of Korean missionaries by year

In 1979, Korean missionaries were channeled through twenty-one agencies, but by 1994 that number had grown to 113 agencies. Of these 113 agencies, 78 were reported to have at least one member on the mission field. The number of mission agencies did not increase between 1994 and 1996. Existing mission agencies, however, rapidly expanded in size due to the addition of new members.

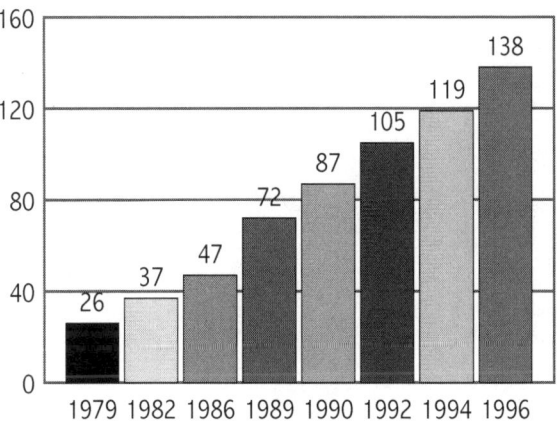

Figure 10.2. Countries with Korean missionaries by year

Mission Agencies

Though Korean mission agencies were growing in size, most of them were still small (see figure 10.3). Two agencies had over 500 members, and two more had between 201 and 500 members. I am aware of another twelve mission agencies with more than 100 missionaries. Overall though, 83.6 percent of Korean agencies have 100 or fewer members, and 69.9 percent have 50 or fewer. Approximately half (49.4 percent) of the mission agencies are small, having 25 or fewer member missionaries.[7]

Number of Members	Number of Agencies
1–10	18
11–25	18
26–50	15
51–100	10
101–200	8
201–500	2
>500	2
Total	73

Figure 10.3. Size of Korean mission agencies in 1996

For their size, the Korean mission agencies were younger in age than mission agencies from other countries. The ReMAP survey found that 71.9 percent of the Korean agencies were between one and ten years old, and 95.3 percent of them were twenty-five years old or younger.

Years in Operation	Number of Agencies
1–2	1
3–10	45
11–25	15
26–50	1
51–100	2
Total	64

Figure 10.4. Age of Korean mission agencies in 1996

---

7. Moon, "Acts of the Koreans," iii.

Only two agencies (both denominational) had been sending missionaries for over fifty years (see figure 10.4). Being young can be both a strength and a weakness, since the agency may be seen as being both energetic and immature at the same time.

Ministry of Korean Missionaries

During the early development of the Korean missionary movement, a majority of Korean missionaries worked among diaspora Koreans. Now 91.7 percent of Korean missionaries are involved in cross-cultural ministries in other countries, leaving only 3.9 percent in purely diaspora ministry.[8]

In their responses to the ReMAP survey, mission executives reconfirmed that a majority of Korean missionaries (79.7 percent) are involved in traditional types of ministry, including pioneer mission work among unreached people groups (45.3 percent), regular evangelism and church planting (26.6 percent), and helping the national church (7.8 percent). Eight agencies (12.5 percent of the responses) reported doing relief and development work, and five agencies (7.8 percent) were engaged in other service ministries in support of missions (see figure 10.5).

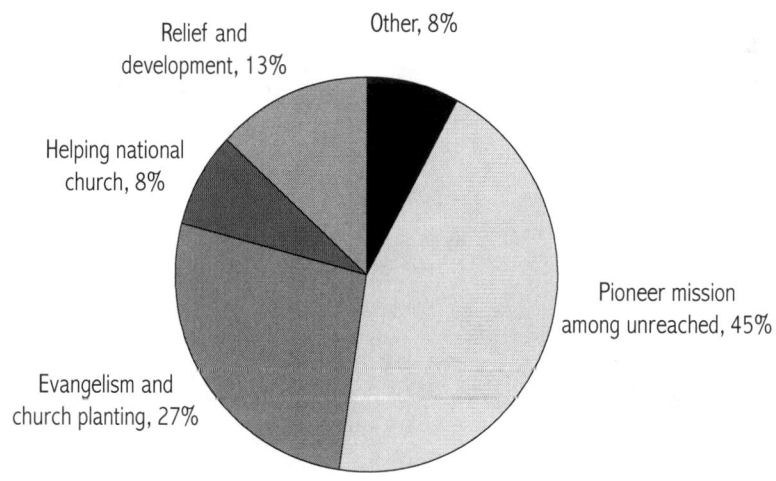

Figure 10.5. Types of ministry of Korean mission agencies

---

8. Ibid., iv.

Notably, 45.3 percent of the respondents stated that their missionaries were involved in pioneer mission work among unreached people groups. A 1996 survey for the *Korean Mission Handbook* produced a similar surprisingly high figure; in it 41.2 percent of the Korean missionaries were categorized as being engaged in frontier mission work among the unreached (see figure 10.6). Misconceptions about pioneer work and a tendency toward exaggeration possibly help to account for these high percentages. Another important facet of Korean missionary deployment is that 47.7 percent were serving in countries within the 10/40 window.[9] At the least these statistics show that pioneering work among the unreached was highly regarded among Korean missionaries. Recent emphasis on reaching unreached people groups seemed to be a dominant factor as missionaries and mission agencies selected areas of service.

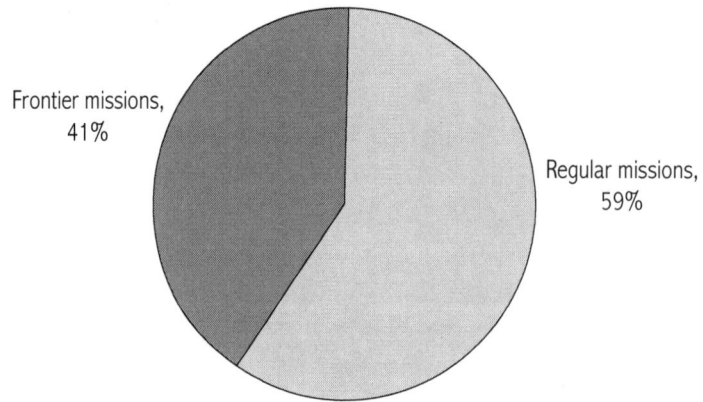

Figure 10.6. Regular vs. frontier missions

---

9. This figure is my calculation based on the 1996 *Korean Mission Handbook* data. The number of Korean missionaries in countries of the 10/40 Window was calculated according to the list by Luis Bush. The majority of Korean missionaries (49.3 percent) are in Asia. In addition, 13.1 percent are in Eurasia (mostly Central Asia), 7.9 percent in Africa, and 6.1 percent in the Middle East. The number of Korean missionaries in the two largest of the 10/40 Window countries—China (413 missionaries) and the former USSR (Russia, 339; Central Asian countries, 577)—together total 1,329. See Moon, "Acts of the Koreans," iv–v.

Overall, Korean missionaries are engaged in the difficult and demanding work of serving one of the most rapidly expanding mission thrusts in the history of Christianity. Koreans' characteristically never easygoing way may also possibly characterize both the Korean missionary movement and the movement's patterns of missionary attrition.

MISSIONARY ATTRITION IN KOREA

In this section the focus of attention is: How many missionaries left the mission field during the three-year period 1992–94, terminating their ministry earlier than expected? By looking at missions work in Korea overall, we can see the status of missionary attrition and spot trends.

Status of Missionary Attrition

In the two years of 1992 and 1993, additions to the Korean mission force equaled 696 persons.[10] An estimate for 1994 can be made by using the annual increase rate since 1994 of 16 percent, as reported in the 1996 *Korean Mission Handbook*.[11] This percentage enables us to estimate that the Korean missionary force increased by 523 in 1994. These figures indicate that an estimated 1,219 missionaries or 731 missionary units were added during the three-year period 1992–94.[12]

A summary of the attrition cases in Korean mission agencies is shown in figure 10.7. Thirty-five units (families or singles) terminated missionary work in 1992, followed by 71 cases in 1993 and 79 cases in 1994. Taken together, these numbers tentatively indicate that 185 families and singles left their mission agency for some reason during this period, but the findings must be adjusted to compensate for overlapping

---

10. Steve Sang-Cheol Moon, ed., *Korean Mission Handbook* (Seoul, Korea: Global Missionary Press, 1994).

11. Moon, "Acts of the Koreans," ii. This annual increase rate is derived from the biannual increase rate of 34.5 percent (1,130/3,272 x 100) for the two-year period 1994–95.

12. Since single missionaries make up 20.0 percent (656/3,272 x 100) of the total Korean missionary force, 243 of the 1,219 could be singles, and the remaining 976 missionaries or 488 units are married. The increase in units during this three-year period is then 731.

memberships in mission agencies and cases of transfer of membership from one mission agency to another.

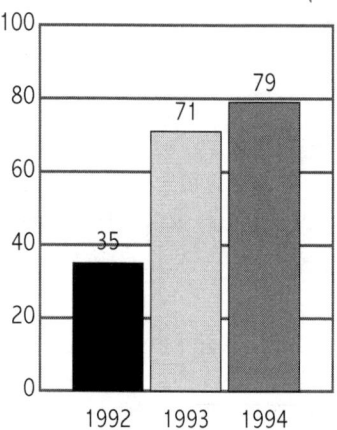

Figure 10.7. Missionary attrition by year

The 1994 *Korean Mission Handbook* reported an apparent overstatement of the number of missionaries due to dual memberships (239) and triple memberships (7) with the total cases of overlap equaling 253.[13] In other words, 7.7 percent of the total number of Korean missionaries overlapped. If we apply this percentage of duplication to the cases of attrition, we can estimate that 14 units (185 x 7.7/100) should be deducted from the total.

The number of cases of membership transfer is more difficult to estimate, since no question in the ReMAP survey addressed this particular concern directly. It is probable that about 10 percent (18 units) of attrition cases can be accounted for through membership transfer.[14] The total number of attrition cases for the years 1992–94 then becomes 153 units (185 -14 -18). When joined with the net increase of 731 missionary units given above, this figure of 153 units of attrition means that

---

13. Steve Sang-Cheol Moon, "Who Are the Korean Missionaries?," in Moon, *Korean Mission Handbook* (1994), 1–2.

14. This estimate is based on research by the author for the *Korean Mission Handbook*.

approximately 833 missionary units (731 +153 -51) went out during the years 1992–94.[15]

One question on the questionnaire sought to distinguish between preventable and unpreventable causes of attrition among missionaries; the percentage of unpreventable losses was found to be 34.1 percent (72/211 x 100). Thus, estimated preventable losses amounted to 101 cases (153 x 65.9/100).

This closer look at the reality of missionary attrition reveals several things. First, roughly 833 units (new families/singles) went to the mission field during the period 1992–94. Second, roughly 153 families/singles came back home during the same period. Third, roughly 101 units came back home for preventable reasons. This means that each mission agency lost an average of 2.4 missionary families (or singles) during that period. The attrition rate of 153 units out of the 833 units is 18.4 percent, implying that if 100 missionaries go out, eighteen will come back early. Twelve of these eighteen would come back for undesirable reasons.

If we estimate the annual loss of missionaries to be 65 units,[16] the estimated annual attrition rate for the year 1994 becomes 3.6 percent.[17]

Increasing Trends

A sobering aspect of the explosion of the missionary movement is that more and more missionaries are coming back home before the expected time, and more and more mission agencies are experiencing missionary attrition. In 1992, 23.4 percent of the mission agencies experienced missionary attrition. But that number grew to 42.9 percent and 43.7 percent in 1993 and 1994, respectively. Altogether, 37 mission agencies (58.7 percent of the responding missions) experienced at least one case of missionary attrition, for preventable or unpreventable reasons, during the period 1992–94.

---

15. This figure assumes that 102 units went out during the period and that 51 units that had been sent out before the period began left the field.

16. The annual loss of missionaries in 1994 equals 79/185 x 153, or 65.3.

17. The annual attrition rate equals the total loss of missionaries divided by the total number of missionaries times 100, or 65 units/3,272 x 100 = 117 persons/3,272 x 100 = 3.6 percent.

The rates of attrition vary for single female missionaries, single male missionaries, and missionary couples. Twenty-three mission agencies (35.9 percent) have experienced at least one case of single female missionary attrition during the last three-year period. Twelve mission agencies (18.7 percent) lost at least one single male missionary during the same period. In twenty-eight mission agencies (43.7 percent), at least one missionary couple left the mission field.

The attrition rate is higher among single missionaries than among missionary couples (see figures 10.8 and 10.9). In the years 1992–94, single missionaries accounted for 45.9 percent of total missionary attrition (78 out of 170). Attrition among single female missionaries is more likely than among single males (see figures 10.10 and 10.11). In Korea, 63.3 percent of the single missionaries are female, but they constitute 73.1 percent of the total of single missionaries leaving the field. Part of the reason for this disparity in attrition rate may be parental pressure toward marriage; such marriages may well fall outside of missionary commitment.[18] Overall, Korean mission agencies seem to lack specific policies for caring for single males and females.

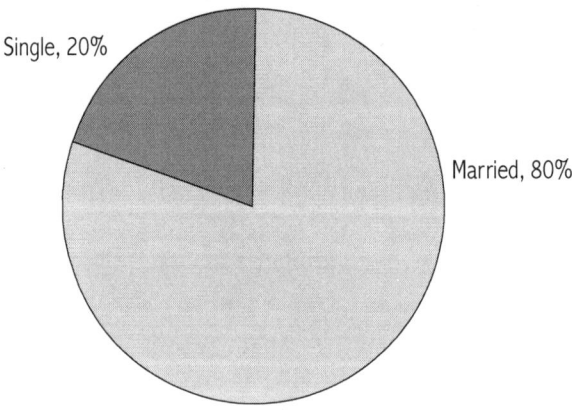

Figure 10.8. Proportion of mission force, single vs. married

---

18. In this interpretation, I am indebted to a suggestion by Lois McKinney. Her comments have been helpful in the whole process of data interpretation and writing.

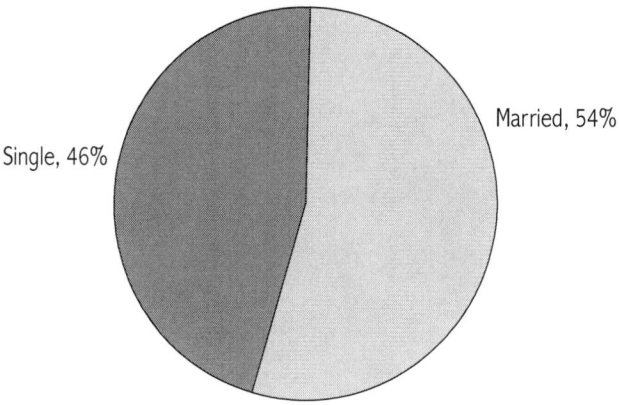

Figure 10.9. Proportion of missionary attrition, single vs. married

The older and larger agencies lost more missionaries than did smaller ones. This loss may indicate the need for more professional managerial skills and capacities within mission agencies as they grow rapidly.

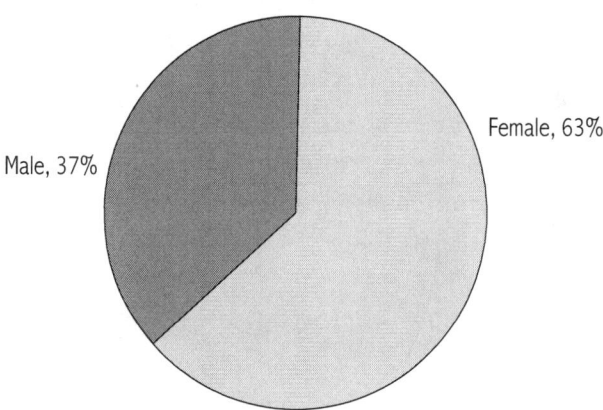

Figure 10.10. Proportion of single missionaries, female vs. male

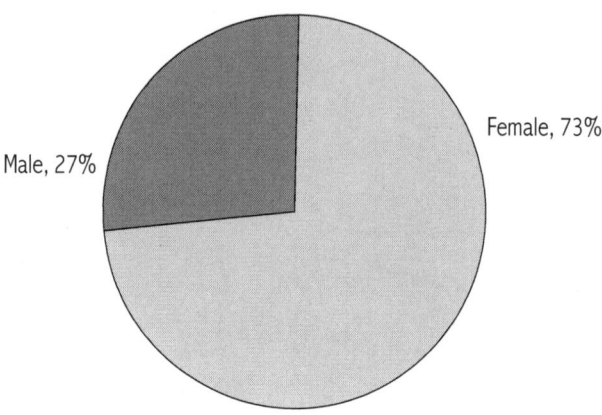

Figure 10.11. Proportion of single missionary attrition, female vs. male

International mission agencies reported a lower probability of attrition on the part of their Korean members, who represented 7.9 percent of the total attrition cases, even though roughly 12 percent of the total Korean missionaries were serving with international agencies.[19] Some factors contributing to the lower attrition rate may be (1) a more careful screening process, conducted in two steps (first by the home council office and then by the international office abroad); (2) systematic pre-field training; and (3) international agencies' expertise in member care. Such factors may have helped to overcome the additional burden of cultural adjustment Korean missionaries face in working within an English-speaking missionary society.

CAUSES OF MISSIONARY ATTRITION

The ReMAP survey also sought to identify reasons or causes of missionary attrition. To explore this issue, the survey first asked agency executives for their perceptions of the most important causes of attrition. Then the "real" reasons as opposed to "supposed" reasons as conjectured by executives for leaving the field were considered.

---

19. Moon, "Who Are the Korean Missionaries?," 7.

Perceived Reasons

From a list of twenty-six reasons for attrition, respondents were asked to select the seven most important items and to prioritize these according to their degree of importance. The major causes of attrition that emerged, as shown in figure 10.12, were (A) problems with fellow missionaries, (B) health problems, (C) change of job, (D) lack of call, (E) weak home support, (F) disagreement with sending agency, and (G) poor cultural adaptation.

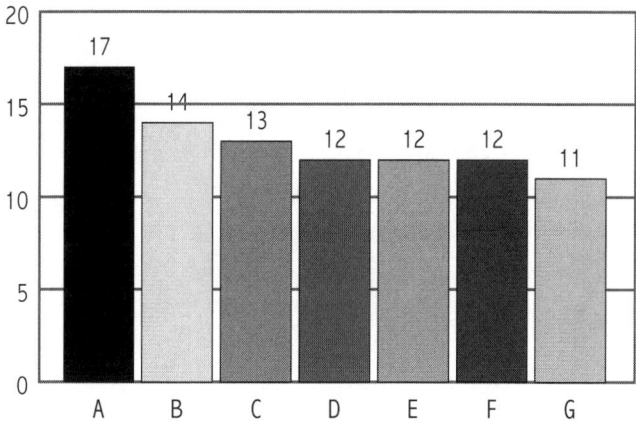

Figure 10.12. Seven most important reasons for missionary attrition

Of the seven items, responding agencies considered "problems with missionary peers" to be the most serious. Such conflict might occur, for example between a senior missionary and a junior missionary. A senior missionary has spent a longer time on the mission field but might be more traditional and authoritarian in his or her leadership style, whereas a junior missionary may favor a more independent spirit in missionary life and work. Such differences are likely to lead to conflicts within a relationship, which will need to be resolved if the two are to work together well.

Another important reason for attrition of Korean missionaries was "health problems." This rating may have arisen from the task orientation of Koreans, which is at the same time a strength and a weakness. The tendency of Koreans is to think that ill health should not be a problem if they are called by God; that tendency in itself may be part of the problem. Possibly Korean agencies do not pay as much attention to health issues at the time of screening as Western mission agencies do. Further, many if not most Korean missionaries are susceptible to feeling uncomfortable spending time and money on a vacation. Many health issues could be overcome with a better balance between work and rest.

"Change of job," "lack of call," and "weak home support" may reflect problems in the screening process. Koreans are perhaps somewhat emotional, not only in personal decisions, but also in their selection of missionaries. Missions zeal is a strength of Koreans, but it must not be allowed to override or subvert a careful selection process.

"Disagreement with sending agency" further indicates potential weaknesses in relational skills among Korean missionaries. It also reminds us of the importance of good interpersonal relationships as a prerequisite to intercultural competency. The problem of "poor cultural adaptation" underlines a potential weakness of which Koreans, who grow up in monocultural and monolingual backgrounds, need to be aware.

In summary, problems leading to missionary attrition appeared to be more relational than work-related. Interestingly, mission executives and administrators appeared to be fully aware of this weakness.

Categories of "Real" Reasons for Attrition

Figure 10.13 displays the breakdown of causal categories of attrition. The questionnaire responses revealed that 72 cases of attrition (34.1 percent) were for reasons that could not be prevented, including normal retirement, political crisis, death in service, marriage outside the mission, and change of job.[20] "Transfer to another agency" was often put in this category. "Marriage outside the mission," however, could be interpreted as a preventable rather than an unpreventable cause of attrition, depending on the specific case involved.

---

20. In answering the question in the ReMAP survey about the real reasons or categories of reasons for attrition, some respondents counted a couple as two units. Even though agencies were repeatedly reminded to count a couple as one unit, some adopted different ways of counting the total cases of attrition. Inaccurate answers might erode the reliability of the research to some degree. Additional steps were taken by the author, however, to correct and clarify the answers to the best of his knowledge about the individual agencies.

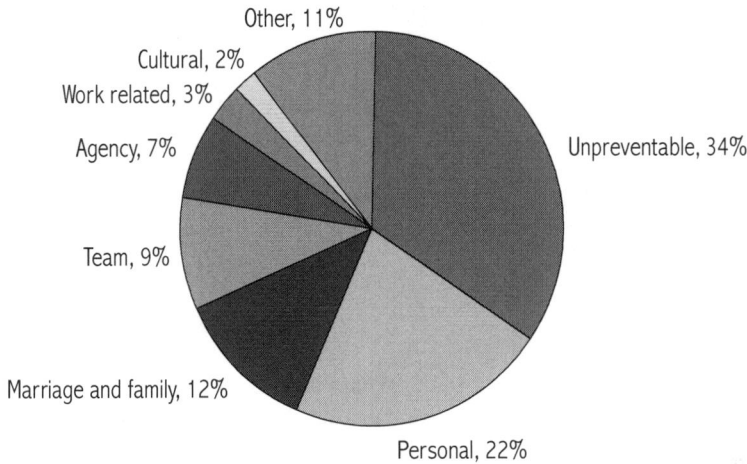

Figure 10.13. "Real" reasons for attrition by category

Personal reasons leading missionaries to leave the field included immature spiritual life, health problems, inadequate commitment, personal concerns, lack of call, immoral lifestyle, problems with peer missionaries, and problems with local leaders. In the perception of the mission administrators, 21.8 percent of 211 cases of attrition were because of weaknesses in this category.

Another large category of causes was "marriage and family problems" (11.8 percent). If the problem of "outside marriages"—single missionaries marrying non-missionary spouses—is included in this category, the attrition rate due to marriage and family issues becomes even higher.

Team reasons (9.0 percent) and mission agency reasons (6.6 percent) for attrition also confirm that the real problems lie at the relational level, rather than being work related (3.3 percent) or cultural (1.9 percent).

In summary, at least 49.2 percent of the attrition cases were caused by relational problems, including psychiatric or emotional problems, interpersonal relationships, and the missionaries' relationship with God, rather than by work-related issues. This percentage is probably even higher, since many "unpreventable" reasons were most probably preventable in actuality and so would fall into one of these relational categories. This summary of reasons given for attrition coincides with the mission executives' perception, given above, of the locus of the problem.

INVESTMENTS AND MISSION POLICIES

Missionary attrition is definitely related to an agency's willingness to care for its members. This willingness cannot be something abstract, but must find expression in actual investment. Willingness alone does not eradicate the problem. Agencies' policies should be examined carefully to find answers to the problem.

Investments of the Agencies

Korean mission agencies spend much time and financial resources on missionary care. Figure 10.14 shows that out of 64 mission agencies 35.9 percent spend over 30 percent of their financial resources on missionary care.

Financial Resources Invested in Member Care (%)	Number of Agencies
0	12
<1	2
1–5	7
6–10	10
11–20	8
21–30	2
>30	23
Total	64

Figure 10.14. Portion of finances Korean mission agencies invest in member care

The agencies' questionnaire responses, however, showed that they spent less of their time in caring for their missionaries than they did in investing funds (figure 10.15). Although 19 agencies (29.7 percent) indicated that they gave over 20 percent of their time to caring for their missionaries, no agency reported spending over 30 percent of its time on missionary care. Some agencies allocated less than 1 percent of their time for missionary care. It would appear that mission agencies were willing to spend money and time to care for their missionaries, but they did not know how.

Time Invested in Member Care (%)	Number of Agencies
0	12
<1	7
1–5	10
6–10	10
11–20	6
21–30	19
Total	64

Figure 10.15. Portion of time Korean mission agencies invest in member care

Problems of Mission Policies

Since mission agencies are willing to care for their missionaries, they may find that the problems leading to missionary attrition—and solutions to those problems—lie in policy making. As figure 10.16 shows, most of the agencies (82.5 percent, that is, 52 out of 64) provided (A) pastoral care through telephone calls or letters at least on a quarterly basis. Slightly over half of the mission agencies (54.0 percent) paid (B) a yearly visit to their missionaries and had (C) supportive team structures (52.4 percent) that could be used for missionary care. Supervision (D) by a field leader was available in 42.9 percent of the agencies.

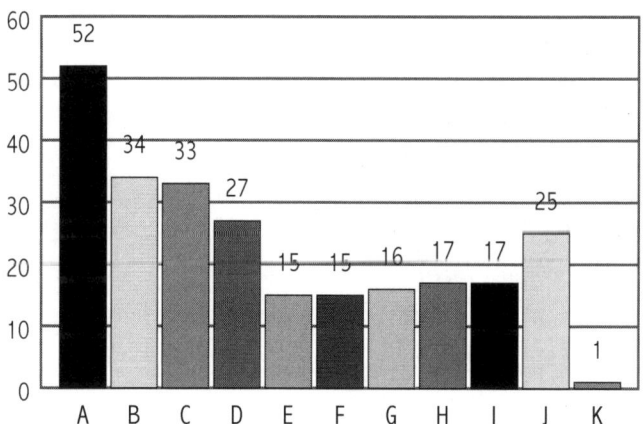

Figure 10.16. Means used for member care

Yet Korean agencies were weak in provision of (E) detailed job descriptions and of (F) annual leave/holidays (both 23.8 percent). Their offerings of (G) planned on-the-job training (25.4 percent); (H) pastoral oversight by someone other than a supervisor (27.0 percent); (I) schools, finances, or tutors for missionary children (MKs) (27.4 percent); and (J) local or area conferences for mission personnel (39.6 percent) were also weak. Provision for member care by (K) other means was minimal (1.0 percent).

Types of Training Required

Almost all of the Korean mission agencies required some sort of training prior to ministry in the mission field. Completion of theological or professional training (62.5 percent), intercultural orientation (57.8 percent), and the organization's own mission courses (51.6 percent), however, were emphasized more often than were nonformal missionary training programs (39.1 percent), nondegree programs in missiology (32.8 percent), and short-term intercultural experience (29.7 percent).

These data showed where missionary training programs needed to be strengthened. The importance of the informal and nonformal aspects of missionary education cannot be overemphasized.

Weak Areas of Screening

Mission executives have frequently pointed out that efforts to maintain quality control through pre-field training have often proven fruitless, because much of a person's character is determined much earlier in life.[21] So screening, more often than not, is of greater importance than pre-field training, because short-term training cannot suddenly transform the whole person.

Unfortunately, the screening process has seemed to be one of the weakest management areas for the Korean missionary movement. Of the agencies that responded, 63.5 percent (40 out of 63 valid answers) indicated that they did not require psychological and/or personality tests as part of the screening process. More than half of the agencies, 58.7 percent, did not consider the ages and number of children and other family

---

21. I am especially indebted to Dong-Hwa Kim, director of Global Missionary Fellowship, for this perspective. His valuable insights on quality control in Korean missions were extremely helpful.

constraints to be significant. A full 46.0 percent of the agencies did pursue the question of strong communication and relationship skills. Leadership and pastoral skills and the candidates' married or single status were not included among the factors considered important by 44.4 percent of the agencies. Experience in church work was not required for application to 41.3 percent of the agencies. Another extremely serious weakness of the screening process was that 39.7 percent of the agencies did not require personal character references for the missionary candidates. These findings indicate that qualitative concerns and emphases have been very weak or missing among many of the Korean mission agencies.

Neglected Elements of Missionary Care

In answer to a question about insignificant areas of missionary care, 25.0 percent of the agencies indicated that a supportive family or spouse is not significant. Another 25.0 percent considered "regular contact with friends, church, and partners" to be insignificant.

CONCLUSION

Not all missionaries should remain in the ministry. Some of them should not have been sent as part of the harvest force. But as in the early church, there are "Marks" who should be recovered. Our task is to do our best to prevent undesirable attrition and to maximize the manpower and womanpower of the harvest force in both a quantitative and a qualitative sense.

Analysis of the cases and causes of attrition provides us with some insights for policy making in missions, which need to be used at each level of a missionary society.

Marriage status and gender. Mission policies should be formulated to reduce missionary attrition resulting from marriage status or gender. Ways to maximize the opportunities of singleness should be suggested. Greater care is required in selecting and caring for single women missionaries.

Communication skills. Missionaries should be equipped with interpersonal communication skills before going to the mission field. The fact that problems were seen more often in the relational area rather than being related to the work suggests that interpersonal skills are needed even more desperately than is intercultural competency, although the areas are intimately connected.

Marriage and family issues. Marriage and family issues should be dealt with carefully. Awareness of the importance of family should be raised. Commitment to the ministry should not be an excuse for neglecting family concerns. Cultural norms surrounding this issue should be corrected in such a way that there can be a balanced emphasis on commitment to the task and on family care. Korean missionaries need to learn to take time to rest.

On-field care. Ongoing missionary care should be provided for missionaries in the field. To prevent conflict between senior and junior missionaries, detailed job descriptions and on-the-job training should be made available. Area conferences for mission personnel can be encouraged and promoted with the cooperation of mission agencies.

Education. Informal and nonformal aspects of education, not just formal theological education, must be stressed in missionary training. Because of Koreans' monocultural background, short-term intercultural experience is desirable.

Screening. More rigorous instruments need to be developed and applied in the screening process. Personal character references, psychological and/or personality tests, and tests of communication styles should be utilized.

Quality control. More than anything else, awareness of an ethos for exercising quality control in missions should be generated and elevated. Churches and agencies alike must be aware of the price that must be paid to maintain high quality in missionary work. Such efforts are needed not merely to prevent or reduce missionary attrition, but also to help all missionaries live and work fruitfully.

In wrapping up a lifetime in ministry, the apostle Paul stated, "I have fought the good fight, I have finished the race, I have kept the faith. Now there is in store for me the crown of righteousness, which the Lord, the righteous Judge, will award to me on that day." This glorious victory and prospect were promised "to all who have longed for his appearing" (2 Tim. 4:7 NIV). Let us strive to finish well in the task of reaching the world with the Gospel.

11
GLOCALIZING KOREAN MISSIONS (2007)

Globalization inevitably entails glocalization because globalization also raises the need for localization.[1] Missionary movements have a significant need for globalization as well as localization. The Korean missionary movement should grow according to global standards while maintaining reasonable local traditions. Contextualizing and globalizing the practical dimensions of Korean missions will enhance their performance. The dual focus is necessary because a national missionary movement is part of the global missionary movement. This line of thought also recognizes the need to reflect the realities of the mission field in doing missions.

This research paper evaluates the glocalization of Korean missions. Three questions have driven the investigation: How glocalized are Korean missions? What areas should be glocalized? How can we promote the glocalization of Korean missions? The questions raised and the analysis of the answers received are a response to the need to diagnose and evaluate the overall health of the Korean missionary movement.

The scope of this study includes synchronic analysis and evaluation of the present practice of Korean missions and an inquiry into alternative ways of doing missions. The study's approach is limited in that it only reflects insiders' perspectives and evaluations; different criteria might lead to different assessments. Despite this limitation, this empirical research,

---

This chapter appears in print in this volume for the first time.

1. See Rolland Robertson, *Globalization: Social Theory and Global Culture* (London: SAGE Publications, 1992), 173–74.

based on a survey by questionnaire, casts useful light on developmental issues faced by Korean missions.

RESEARCH METHOD

This study of the glocalization of the Korean missionary movement reports on a quantitative questionnaire survey administered in 2007. Responses to the survey's twenty questions required scaling, selecting, and free answers, and queries that covered levels, areas, and methods of glocalization in Korean missions. The questionnaire forms were circulated among 150 Korean missionaries who were serving in Turkey during an annual conference held near Istanbul, Turkey, in August 2007. Only 71 survey forms were completed. Though this level of response was disappointing, the data was still imported for analysis in view of the small size of the research population.

Respondents to the survey included 29 members of Korean denominational mission agencies, 33 members of interdenominational Korean mission agencies, and 9 members of international mission agencies from a Western background. By age group, 8.5 percent were in their 20s, 39.4 percent in their 30s, 38.0 percent in their 40s, 11.3 percent in their 50s, and 2.8 percent in their 60s. By the respondents' highest qualification, 9.9 percent were high school graduates, 50.7 percent had completed an undergraduate degree, 35.2 percent held a master's degree, and 4.2 percent had a doctoral degree. In sum, 39.4 percent of the respondents had completed some level of graduate education.

The answers to the survey were encoded in SPSS for statistical analysis and generalization. The author's previous fieldwork in Turkey helped to deepen the qualitative analysis and interpretation of the data. The analysis tells of one facet of Korean missions in a particular field situation.

DATA ANALYSIS

The analysis of the data follows the order of the three research questions and that of the questions in the questionnaire, centering on the check of mean scores.

How localized (or contextualized) are Korean missions in the Korean cultural context, that is, do Korean missions feel authentically Korean rather than seeming to be copies of older missions from the West? The average score for the responses was 6.8 on a scale of 10, which is lower than a realistically acceptable level of 8. (The score of 8 that is taken throughout as realistically acceptable is lower than the ideal point of 10, but is deemed acceptable in light of the variety of conditions encountered in different fields.) A majority of the respondents (67.6 percent) gave a figure lower than 7, which points to the need for more effort to be given to contextualizing the mission movement within the Korean cultural context. The low level of contextualization within Korean missions seems to be connected to the low level of contextualization in church ministries in Korea. If Korean missions were to be connected more strongly to Korean traditions and cultural characteristics could generate greater creativity, an area in which Korean missions overall are weak.

At an average of 6.4 on a scale of 10, the respondents scored the globalization of Korean missions, as shown in adapting to global standards, lower than the score for localization. Slightly more than eight out of ten people (80.3 percent) gave a score of less than 7. These responses emphasize the need for Korean missions, as a new missionary sending force, to follow global standards accepted in international missions circles. This need was highlighted not only by members of international mission agencies, but also by members of indigenous Korean mission agencies. An important consideration in interpreting the data is that Turkey is a mission field where Korean missionaries can work advantageously due to the linguistic and cultural proximity between Turkey and Korea.

How much does Korea's monocultural background constrain the ministries of Korean missionaries? A majority of respondents answered "very significantly" (22.5 percent) or "significantly" (50.7 percent); 21.1 percent indicated "not so significantly" and 5.6 percent "minimally." That a large majority of the missionaries in Turkey (73.2 percent) acknowledged the potential constraints occasioned by being Korean but working in a cross-cultural setting indicates their high level of awareness but also identifies an obstacle for field ministries. These indicators support the theoretical observation that monoculturality imposes limitations.

Armed with this shared insight, Korean missions can plans ways to tackle this problem.

A related question dealt with ethnocentrism in the practice of missions. A significant majority of the respondents (64.8 percent) stated that ethnocentric tendencies can create obstructions for Korean missions in Turkey. Among respondents, 19.7 percent said that ethnocentrism worked very negatively, 45.1 percent negatively, 26.8 percent not so negatively, and 8.5 percent minimally. That fewer respondents pointed out the danger of ethnocentrism than identified the danger occasioned by a monocultural orientation could imply a denial of personal intentionality while acknowledging a potential weakness in cultural orientation.

To the open-ended question of what areas should be glocalized in doing missions, 17 answers addressed cross-cultural understanding (27.0 percent), 14 addressed education (22.2 percent), 9 addressed leadership (14.3 percent), 3 addressed the Korean church (4.8 percent), and 20 addressed other areas (31.7 percent). The significant number of responses for "other areas" is indicative of the diversity of the areas that can be addressed. Overall, the emphasis fell on understanding the cross-cultural nature of missions in more detail, providing a direction for future research and education.

When asked to identify the areas in most urgent need of being changed in light of global standards, respondents specified ministry structure and system (45.1 percent), leadership (26.8 percent), strategy (15.5 percent), infrastructure (7.0 percent), missiology (1.4 percent), and others/no answer (4.2 percent). This emphasis on the need to change ministry structures and systems gives us cause to ponder the relevance of existing field structures and systems. Are the structures and systems found in international mission agencies relevant? Are the team structures and member care systems provided by Korean mission agencies relevant? Such questions could stimulate healthy and constructive discussion at a number of levels.

With the average level of leadership in large international mission agencies assigned a value of 100, the Korean missionaries were asked to evaluate their mission in terms of excellence in leadership. The average score of 76.1 was lower than the level set as appropriate by the researcher after considering many factors and conditions. A majority of the respondents (66.1 percent) gave an answer lower than 80, with many of them giving very low ratings in their answers, and only 22.5 percent gave a score higher than 100, which would have indicated that Korean mission leadership outperforms that of large international missions.

Respondents evaluated the level of ministry structures and systems found in Korean mission agencies at 71.8 percent of that of large international mission agencies, lower than the score for Korean mission agencies' leadership. Almost half of the respondents (49.3 percent) gave a number lower than 80, again with many of them assigning very low ratings in their answers. These answers are consonant with the answers to the earlier question that asked for identification of the area most urgently in need of change. One explanation for the weakness of Korean missionaries in this area lies in their individualistic tendencies. Teams as well as individuals need to be evaluated and then supported accordingly.

Strategizing in Korean mission agencies was evaluated at 83.6 percent of that found in major international mission agencies. The answer indicates a certain level of confidence among Korean missionaries, at least in Turkey. Rapid learning and the updating of mission strategies within the Korean missions circle contributed to this result. At the same time, many Korean missionaries identified a need for creative devising of new methods.

At only 67.9 percent, the survey responses ranked Korean mission agencies' infrastructure much lower than that of major international mission agencies. The score is lower than in the other areas under comparison. In general, the respondents thought that the weaker infrastructure was problematic but did not think that it needed to be given urgent priority. Korean mission agencies should not feel obliged to build infrastructure up to the Western level, but they do need to build it to a level of operational adequacy. So that they can better support mission agencies and teams, Korean churches need to be made aware of this significant need.

Respondents placed the level of missiology among Korean mission agencies at 83.4 percent of that found within major international mission agencies. A minority of respondents (28.2 percent) claimed that the Korean level exceeded 100 percent. Unsurprisingly since the two points are intertwined, the responses for missiology are similar to the responses for mission strategies. Together they indicate the desirability of additional missiological effort on the part of missionaries and of more holistic support from churches. As I pointed out in my 2007 report on Korean missions, missiology needs to keep in step with mission strategy to help ensure that Korean missiology is sufficiently practical.[2] Harnessing empirical research methods is critical for this significant yet often neglected task of missions.[3]

Asked directly about ways to glocalize Korean missions, 49 respondents pointed to method and strategy (18 cases), followed by education (13), leadership (5), mission structure and system (5), cross-cultural issues (4), and Korean church issues (4). The answers to this open-ended question disclose a comparative weakness within Korean missions: their methodological and strategic expertise lags behind their passionate and purpose-driven orientation.

The respondents highlighted that the best way to glocalize Korean missions is to invest in developing experts in diverse fields (33.8 percent). The glocalization of prefield training programs (29.6 percent) and the provision of continuing education programs for missionaries (16.9 percent) were also stressed. Korean churches tend to emphasize investment in the construction of church buildings and facilities in the mission field, while missionaries place emphasis on investing in the people engaged in doing missions. Investment in people is evidence of a long-term perspective. Their personal experience has made Korean missionaries keenly aware of this need.

Who should take the initiative for developing experts in missions? In answering this practical question, 45.1 percent of the respondents accented the role of mission agencies. Others emphasized the part played by local churches (22.5 percent) and mission associations (21.1 percent). Regardless of the tough realities Korean mission agencies face, missionaries believe that the agencies should initiate and support the

---

2. Steve Sang-Cheol Moon, "Hankuk Gidokgyo Seonkyowoondongeu Donghyangkwa Kwaje" [The trends and tasks of the Korean Christian missionary movement], *Pabalma* (a weekly news bulletin published by KRIM) 192 (September 10, 2007). *Pabalma* refers to the horses used to carry urgent news in traditional Korean societies hundreds of years ago.

3. Ibid.

development of expertise among their missionary members. A desirable pattern would be for mission agencies to take the initiative in expertise development with support from churches and mission associations. Especially mission agencies and local churches need to be on the same page about the importance of this issue.

Who should take the initiative in seeking to develop international cooperation and partnership? Respondents looked to both mission agencies (46.5 percent) and mission associations (33.8 percent) to assume this task. These entities share a common goal; but for mission agencies, addressing urgent practical issues through cooperation and partnership has primacy, while mission associations are better fitted to address overarching international agendas. Korean missionaries are well aware of the distinction between these two types of structure.

Responding to the issue of quality versus quantity for field missionaries, a majority of the Korean missionaries in Turkey (67.6 percent) maintained that mission agencies need to screen missionary candidates critically, overriding a minority opinion (22.5 percent) suggesting that standards should be lowered so that as many missionaries as possible can be sent. The ratio indicates a preference for qualitative maturation over quantitative growth at this stage in the development of the Korean missionary movement. The reality, however, is that missionary recruitment in Korea shows the opposite tendency. Mission mobilizers do not examine the sense of calling of missionary applicants and candidates as much as they did in the past. If candidates' sense of calling is not fully verified, we will not be able to avoid the secularization of missionary service. When a missionary career becomes a fallback option for those who have failed to find a ministry opportunity within Korea, the divine dimension of calling is ignored.

When asked to suggest a good way to glocalize pre–field training programs, the respondents mentioned the need to design curricula that are Korean yet global in style (38.0 percent), to run the whole or part of the training program overseas (22.5 percent), to cooperate with missionary training centers in other countries (22.5 percent), and to recruit faculty members who have worked in a cross-cultural setting (15.5 percent). Such emphases underscore the need for changes in the operation of training programs, but to date few alterations have been made in curricula or the way programs are run. New realities both in the mission field and in the sending base require new approaches to training. In view of the increasing complexity of this ever-globalizing world, a wider range of course selections need to be offered so that trainees can select courses that better fit their purpose and situation.

Respondents mentioned that for the sake of leadership development, curricula should be designed with the needs of missionaries in mind (60.6 percent). Other considerations were that programs be run in nearby locations (15.5 percent), faculty members with expertise be found (15.5 percent), scholarships be provided (5.6 percent), and degree-level study be made feasible (just 1.4 percent). Here, again, curriculum design was emphasized. Concern about curricula is general in theological education in Korea. In Korean seminaries, curriculum design is all too often based on what the teachers can teach instead of what the students need to learn. Missionaries show more interest in learning what will be helpful for their ministry than in simply earning a degree, which reflects well on their motivation for seeking ongoing education.

A majority of the Korean missionaries working in Turkey highlighted methodological and strategic issues in doing missions because they saw weaknesses in those areas. While maintaining its passion for missions, the Korean missionary movement needs to be reinforced in these respects. Ongoing missiological research should be directed to that end.

RESEARCH FINDINGS

The issue of glocalization has been clarified through analyses of answers to selective and open-ended questions. Korean missions can advance by engaging both localization and globalization. This study has addressed levels, areas, and methods of glocalization, showing how to compensate for weak areas in Korean missions.

The overall level of glocalization was seen to be lower than the cutoff point that the researcher arbitrarily set as a realistically acceptable standard and was much lower than the ideal standard. The main factors working against glocalization are a monocultural orientation and ethnocentrism. But Korean missionaries' awareness of this problem gives hope for the future.

Among many areas of concern, Korean missions' weakness in ministry structures and systems deserves attention and calls for more effort and investment. Cross-cultural research conducted on the mission field is essential. Leadership, strategy, infrastructure, and missiology would also all benefit from creative development.

With the support of the Korean church, mission agencies must enable glocalization by consciously and intentionally seeking to develop experts who have both knowledge and mission experience. Mission agencies and mission associations should also take the initiative in building international partnerships. Korean mission agencies need to screen missionary candidates more thoroughly. Curricula designed according to the needs of the trainees will enhance missionary training and field ministry.

As Korean missionaries are well aware, the Korean missionary movement is still at a developmental stage in terms of its localization and globalization. This type of empirical research needs also to be conducted in other ministry contexts elsewhere in the world. Methodologically, the perspectives of those to whom missionary service is addressed and of other mission forces need to be reflected in future studies.

12

THE PERFORMANCE LEVEL OF KOREAN MISSIONARIES IN TURKEY (2007)

It is meaningless for churches to send out large numbers of missionaries unless those missionaries' activities bear fruit in the mission field. Creative ministries carried out even by a small number of missionaries, however, are pleasing to God and to his church. How fruitful are the ministries of Korean missionaries? While guarding against a short-term perspective that expects that fruit to ripen too quickly, we still need to ask this question and listen carefully to all answers. The ultimate purpose of such inquiry is to stimulate further development of the Korean missionary movement.

This chapter reports on an empirical study conducted during the annual conference of Korean missionaries in Turkey held near Istanbul in August 2007. Participants were asked to fill out and return a questionnaire containing twenty-nine questions. The research was designed to enable the missionaries to provide an evaluation of their own performance. The research question was: "In your perception, how high is the performance level of Korean missionaries as measured against an ideal level and the U.S. level?" One hundred and fifty missionaries participated in the conference each of whom received one survey form, and seventy-one questionnaires were returned, for a response rate of slightly below 50 percent.

The research population for this study consisted of the 250 Korean missionaries then serving in Turkey. The data gathered did not allow for probability sampling since it was drawn from the 150 participants at the conference who voluntarily cooperated with the survey. The analyses

---

This chapter appears in print in this volume for the first time.

and findings of this study have only limited generalizability, but they could well serve as the basis for a case study. Insights drawn from such a case study would need to be checked carefully before being extrapolated to other contexts.

This evaluation focuses mainly on categories in which the performance of Korean missionaries might differ from that of nationals or missionaries from other countries. Clearly a single research project cannot address all issues or reflect all perspectives and categories. Still, self-evaluations are worthwhile even though they are to some degree subjective. The main purpose of the study was to identify the strengths and weaknesses of Korean missionaries in a real situation so that these strengths might be enhanced and these weaknesses complemented.

LITERATURE REVIEW

This research-based evaluation of the performance level of Korean missionaries in a real situation is the first study of its kind. Up to now little has been done to evaluate the ministry performance of Korean missionaries, though the biannual research reports on the status of Korean missions—begun by Marlin Nelson in 1979 and continued, since 1990, by me—have addressed important issues. The 1995 study of Korean missionary attrition that I conducted as part of the World Evangelical Alliance Mission Commission's ReMap (Reducing Missionary Attrition Project) also had an evaluative dimension.[1]

Other research related to evaluation, attrition, or retention includes Paul Hyung Keun Choi's 2000 Ph.D. dissertation on the effectiveness of Korean missionaries and missionary training programs, Hark Yoo Kim's 2001 Ph.D. dissertation on retention factors found in the long-term ministry of some Korean missionaries, and two master's level research projects, by Soo Jung Kim and Young Ran Yang, that I directed, which focused on factors present in the successful ministries of

---

1. Steve Sang-Cheol Moon, "Missionary Attrition in Korea: Opinions of Mission Executives," in *Too Valuable to Lose: Exploring the Causes and Cures of Missionary Attrition*, ed. William D. Taylor (Pasadena, Calif.: William Carey Library, 1995), 129–42.

Korean missionaries.[2] That the literature on the performance of Korean missionaries is so sparse points to the need to encourage field-based empirical research for the sake of advancing Korean missions.

RESEARCH METHOD AND PROCEDURE

Though the research question could be addressed either qualitatively or quantitatively, a quantitative approach was selected for this study because it offered numerical measurability. The questionnaire consisted of twenty-nine questions, four addressing the missionaries' proficiency in the field language (Turkish), four on family care, four on the system of field ministry, four on relations with local people, four on relations with leaders at the home office, four on relations with supporting churches, four on direct ministry performance, and one that was comprehensive. An additional nine questions sought information about the respondents themselves.

Survey forms were circulated to participants during a session and returned by them during meeting breaks. Efforts were made to retrieve more questionnaire forms after the conference, but with few additional results. The research team encoded and analyzed the data statistically using SPSS.

Three of the four questions in each domain were analyzed on a 10-point scale in which 10 is considered ideal and 8 acceptable. The ideal point of 10 was briefly explained to the respondents in the survey form, but the realistically acceptable point of 8 is an arbitrary cut-off point set by the researcher after considering related factors and conditions. The remaining question in each domain compared the performance of

---

2. Hyung-Keun Choi, "Preparing Korean Missionaries for Cross-Cultural Effectiveness" (Ph.D. diss., Asbury Theological Seminary, 2000); Hark Yoo Kim, "The Retention Factors among Korean Missionaries to Japan" (Ph.D. diss., Trinity International University, 2001); Soo Jung Kim, "Seonkyosaeu Seongkongjeokin Sayeok Yoine Daehan Yeonku: Egypt Seonkyosareul Jungsimeuro" [A study of the factors for successful ministries: The case of Korean missionaries in Egypt] (M.Div. thesis, Hapdong Theological Seminary, 2003); Young Ran Yang, "Jungkuk Jujae Hankuk Sconkyosaeu Seongkongjeakin Jangkisayeoke Daehan Yeonku" [A study on the factors of successful ministries of Korean missionaries in China] (Th.M. thesis, Hapdong Theological Seminary, 2006).

Korean missionaries to that of U.S. missionaries using a 100-point scale. The responses were analyzed to obtain the mean score for the group.

DATA ANALYSIS

The data analysis provided the following breakdown of the missionaries' self-evaluation.

Language proficiency. The Korean missionaries' average level of proficiency in Turkish, the field language, was 7.2 on a 10-point scale, lower than the acceptable level of 8. For evangelism their language proficiency declined to 6.6, lower than for everyday conversation. The missionaries' language proficiency for preaching and lecturing was much lower, scoring 5.9.

Overall the language proficiency of the Korean missionaries in Turkey is disappointing since Koreans have an advantage in learning Turkish, for Korean and Turkish belong to the same Ural-Altaic language group. The field language proficiency of Korean missionaries in countries with less linguistic proximity is likely even lower than was found in Turkey. An extenuating circumstance, however, is that at the time of the survey many of the respondents had not lived in Turkey long enough to have learned the language well.

A positive note is struck with the realization that the average level of proficiency in Turkish of the Korean missionaries was estimated to be 106.2 percent of the average level of U.S. missionaries. Still, this comparative level does not appear to reflect the full advantage Koreans have for learning Turkish, raising concerns again about Korean missionaries' performance in countries where the field language does not have linguistic proximity with Korean.

Family care. Under family care, the respondents were asked to evaluate health care for families, trust within family relationships, and the practice of the family's vision. Although in health care the average level was 7.4 on a 10-point scale, which was lower than acceptable, the average trust level within family relationships was 9.0, and the average level in practice of the family's vision was 9.6. These averages may be indicative of a task orientation among Korean missionaries, who work hard to realize their vision and mission but do not give adequate attention to their health.

In comparison with U.S. missionaries, Korean missionaries estimated their level of family care as 86.6 percent, indicating a need for them to give greater emphasis to family care and to prioritize their family life.

Field system. The questions addressing the category of "field system" covered relationships and cooperation within the mission staff and mission community. The questions dealt with basic relationship satisfaction in ordinary life, communicational effectiveness, and strategtic teamwork to achieve common goals in team structures. The mean score for basic relationship satisfaction within the field system was 8.2 on a 10-point scale. The level of communicational effectiveness was estimated to be 8.0, not ideal but acceptable. The score of 7.0 for strategic teamwork to achieve common goals was much lower than the acceptable level. This score indicates that in working together to achieve goals Korean missionaries do not meet their own expectations. In their basic relationship satisfaction, they evaluated themselves more favorably. One possible conclusion is that Korean missionaries relate well with other Korean missionaries but are less successful in developing working relationships for the purpose of reaching common goals.

Overall, the responses of the Korean missionaries in this category indicate that they believe that they reach 90.8 percent of the level achieved by U.S. missionaries. One difference to be noted is that Korean missionaries receive less training as preparation for working within a field system than do U.S. missionaries, training that would help them overcome personal, dispositional, cultural, and theological differences. Korean missions need to place more emphasis on competence in working together regardless of differences, an achievement that is a sign of maturity. Flexibility in working relationships should be emphasized more strongly earlier in the process, during pre-field theological education and missionary training. Missionary candidates will then develop an ability to accept difference while maintaining, in a balanced way, their own identity and standpoint.

Relations with local people. Within the category of relations with local people, the survey considered basic relationship satisfaction with the local populace, effectiveness in communicating with the local populace overcoming differences, and working together in a team structure with the local populace to achieve goals selected in common with them. The missionaries evaluated basic relationship satisfaction as reaching 9.1 on the 10-point scale, higher than the level of simple acceptability. At 7.7, communicational effectiveness scored below basic relationship satisfaction. The level for working together to reach common goals fell lower still, to 7.2.

In summary, Korean missionaries tend to get along well with local people but have problems in working together with them to accomplish joint tasks. This phenomenon is due to the fact that Korean missionaries view local people as objects of evangelism and ministry but not as coworkers in ministry. In this area, the average score given by Korean missionaries to their relations with local people was 106.9 percent of the level achieved by U.S. missionaries. In other words, they perceive their working relationship with local Christians to be somewhat weak but better than that of U.S. missionaries.

Relations with the home office. Missionary relations with the home office were evaluated in terms of basic relationship satisfaction, communicational effectiveness, and strategic teamwork to reach common goals. The respondents scored their basic relationship satisfaction with their home office with 8.1 of the possible 10 points. They scored communicational effectiveness at 7.9, just below the acceptable level. At 7.6, the score for strategic teamwork to achieve common goals was lower. These scores disclose weakness in working relations between field missionaries and home leaders, an issue of concern to both parties. Home-office leaders, especially, need to exert more effort to understand the field-oriented outlook characteristic of field missionaries. Improvement in this area is a matter that Korean missions as a whole should pursue.

In their relationship with their home office, the Korean missionaries estimated that they stood at 85.1 percent of the U.S. level. This gap might be attributable to the presence within U.S. missions of a higher percentage of outstanding home leaders who have had field experience. As new leaders with field experience move into home-office roles, Korean missions can expect to see momentum for change in the relationship between the home office and the mission field. We must ask how such new leaders can be helped to acquire a global outlook and to enlarge their vision beyond a perspective rooted in a particular set of field experiences. As well as in breadth of outlook, new leaders need to grow in depth of understanding, adding worldview-level insight to their cross-cultural understanding.

Relations with supporting churches. The missionaries were asked to evaluate their relations with supporting churches in the areas of basic relationship satisfaction, communicational effectiveness, and strategic teamwork to reach common goals. They scored basic relationship satisfaction as 8.0 on a 10-point scale. The score for communicational effectiveness fell to 7.5, the same score as for strategic teamwork to reach common goals. These scores suggest that, as I indicated in a previous report, relations between Korean missionaries and their support base are weak.[3] The missionaries wrote that they felt difficulty in sharing their vision and in working together with their supporting churches to achieve their aspirations. To overcome this weakness, Korean missionaries need to clarify their vision and share it persuasively. Their presentation needs to be concrete and to include good examples of mission success stories. With such positive and grounded accounts, Korean missionaries can motivate churches to support missions actively and avoid potential fatigue.

The Korean missionaries ranked their performance level as 85.6 percent of that of the U.S. missionaries. This score indicates that the Korean missionaries perceive a weakness in their relationship to their support base.

The preceding six categories, while not direct measurements of missionary performance, cover components that enable missionaries to perform their ministries. The analysis was intended as a means of comprehensive evaluation, with its scope not limited to direct field performance. The final category addresses ministry performance directly while maintaining this comprehensive outlook.

Direct ministry. Under the category of direct ministry, the missionaries' performance was evaluated in three areas: evangelism, discipleship

---

3. Steve Sang-Cheol Moon, "Hankuk Kidokkyo Seonkyoundongeu Donghyangkwa Kwaje" [The trends and tasks of the Korean missionary movement], *Pabalma* (News bulletin [Korea Research Institute for Mission]) 192 (2007).

and nurturing, and church planting and growth. For evangelism, the average performance level was 6.2 on the 10-point scale, lower than in the other categories. Considering the importance of evangelism in missionary service, this negative evaluation is a serious issue. Missionaries should perform this core ministry well, and yet their own evaluation of their performance is lower than the expected level. In discipleship and nurturing they scored their performance at 6.7, a little higher, but still not satisfactory. For church ministries the score was 7.1, again higher, but still below the acceptable level.

Overall, Korean missionaries evaluate their ministry performance as not meeting their own expectations. They estimated their level of performance to be 103.5 percent of that of U.S. missionaries, however. Further research is needed on ways to compensate for perceived weaknesses in performance.

Viewed comprehensively, that is, taking into account all the direct and indirect categories and elements related to ministry performance, Korean missionaries estimate their performance level to be 105.1 percent of that of U.S. missionaries, although the assessment varies by area of concern and Korean missionaries do not always come out ahead. U.S. missionaries and local people might assess performance differently, but no comparable research evaluations are available.

RESEARCH FINDINGS

In summary, according to the analysis of the data, Korean missionaries tend to be weak in health care, but perform well in other areas of family life. Their team ministries received rather positive evaluations, although there are some areas of concern. Their overall evaluation, however, is lower than the acceptable level in terms of language proficiency, cooperating relations with local people, relations with the home office, relations with supporting churches, and direct ministry performance. The low levels of language proficiency and direct ministry performance would seem to be interrelated.

In a perceptional comparison with U.S. missionaries, the performance level of Korean missionaries is a little higher than that of U.S. missionaries in several key categories, although lower in others. Korean missionaries perceive themselves as performing better in language acquisition, relations with local people, and direct ministry, but worse in family care, field system, relations with the home office, and relations with supporting churches. This self-evaluation helps us to understand some strengths and weaknesses of Korean missions.

For the sake of comparison further research is needed on the perspectives and self-evaluations of missionaries from other cultural backgrounds, as well as on the perspectives of local Christians in the mission fields. Qualitative research could also deepen the analysis and enrich understanding. May this study stimulate more creative research that will further strengthen the Korean missionary movement.

13
THE LEADERSHIP STYLES OF KOREAN MISSIONARIES

Leadership plays an important role in competency for cross-cultural ministry. When missionaries become good leaders, their ministries are able to bear fruit naturally. Therefore, more research needs to be conducted on missionary leadership. Leadership characteristics essential in a cross-cultural setting may be different from skills acquired through years of training in the home country. The cross-cultural dimension of leadership needs to be addressed if we are to deal well with the practical dimensions of missionary leadership.

RESEARCH PROBLEM

If we are to avoid armchair argumentation, study of missionary leadership needs to be based on empirical research. Otherwise, leadership theories may not reflect leadership realities "on the ground." To set an ideal standard is important, but the practical dimensions of leadership also deserve attention. Good missional leadership demands a proper understanding of both leadership principles and field realities.

Three research questions drive this study of the leadership styles of Korean missionaries: What are the leadership virtues of Korean missionaries? What are the main leadership styles of Korean missionaries? How do Korean missionaries perceive their own leadership qualities?

Two preexisting questionnaire forms (one translated from English into Korean) were utilized to address the first two research questions, and the author's own questionnaire form addressed the third question.

This chapter was first presented at the Fifth Bangkok Forum held in Bangkok, Thailand, January 21–25, 2008; translated, edited, and reprinted by permission.

The questionnaires were distributed to a set of Korean missionaries; their responses were gathered by e-mail during the period December 20, 2007, through January 14, 2008. The two preexisting questionnaires had their own methods of data analysis, and their data sets were analyzed accordingly. The third questionnaire's data set was analyzed with SPSS.

This study was conducted with the cooperation of two large mission agencies respected as being leading Korean mission organizations, one denominational and the other interdenominational. The results of the data analysis, therefore, are valid for large Korean mission agencies in particular, that is, those with over 500 missionaries, and cannot be generalized. Additional research is needed to disclose the leadership virtues, styles, and self-awareness tendencies among members of small- to medium-sized mission agencies. Future inquiry should also examine correlations between mission leadership characteristics and denominational background.

This study seeks to facilitate creative discussion. If they are to help enhance and strengthen mission leadership, mission leaders, missiologists, missionary trainers, and church leaders need to pay attention to the practices of mission leaders in the field.

LITERATURE REVIEW AND ANALYTICAL MODELS

Among the multitude of books on leadership are a large number that deal with leadership style. Not many, however, provide models of research designed for or relevant to the leadership characteristics of missionaries. Two research models—Jeffrey Glanz's analytical model of leadership virtues and the analytical model of leadership styles by Toshikazu Watanabe and Mitsunori Miyake—seem to hold promise, however, and were used to gather data for the first two questions in this study. The two analytical models differentiate between questions of virtue and questions of style in leadership. Glanz's model originally focused on educators to determine their leadership virtues, and Watanabe and Miyake's model was originally designed to study the leadership styles of managers in companies.

Leadership virtues that Glanz looks for in educators include courage, impartiality, empathy, judgment, enthusiasm, humility, and imagination.¹ Because of the similarities in the roles of educators and missionaries, missionary leadership demands similar qualities. Leaders in every domain should embody these qualities to some degree, but not every leader can practice all of these virtues with excellence. The question is which leadership qualities need to be explicitly present in missionary leadership. Cases in which two or more items scored the same points were aggregated as a mixed type, the ratio of which was also checked.

The analytical model of Watanabe and Miyake purposes to strengthen the performance of companies at the division level. This model basically divides leadership styles into six types—directive, visionary, affiliative, participative, pacesetting, and coaching.² The authors of this model presuppose the need for situational leadership that depends on context, implying that leaders are expected to adjust their leadership style as situations and contexts vary. In order to be able to adapt to a context, a leader is supposed to know his or her dominant leadership style well.

RESEARCH METHODS AND PROCEDURES

The identification of relevant analytical models and the subsequent preparation of research instruments (questionnaires) formed the first steps in the research process. The research instrument developed by Watanabe and Miyake was available in Korean, but I translated Glanz's instrument into Korean so that it could be distributed among Korean missionaries. These two instruments consisted of fifty-six questions and twenty-three questions, respectively, and eight more questions were added to explore Korean missionaries' perceptions of their leadership realities. Altogether, eighty-seven questions were included in the instrument for data gathering and analysis.

---

1. Jeffrey Glanz, *Finding Your Leadership Style: A Guide for Educators* (Alexandria, Va.: Association for Supervision and Curriculum Development, 2002), 85–138.
2. Toshikazu Watanabe and Mitsunori Miyake, *Performance Leadership*, trans. Sin-Il Kang (Seoul: Sigma Insight, 2003 [2002]), 66–86.

The total number of respondents for this questionnaire survey was 101 persons; 74 percent were members of the Global Missionary Society (the sending arm of the Presbyterian Hapdong denomination) and 26 percent members of the Global Missionary Fellowship (an interdenominational mission agency). The pool of respondents consisted of 83.2 percent men and 16.8 percent women. By age group, none were in their twenties, 14.9 percent were in their thirties, 44.5 percent in their forties, 36.6 percent in their fifties, and 4.0 percent in their sixties or older. By ministry experience, 11.9 percent had been in ministry for less than 4 years, 12.9 percent for 4–8 years, 25.7 percent for 8–12 years, 20.8 percent for 12–16 years, 27.7 percent for over 16 years, and 1.0 percent for another period. The educational standards of these two mission agencies are much higher than those of other Korean mission agencies. Respondents with a doctorate as their final degree came to 19.8 percent, master's degree 66.3 percent, bachelor's degree 13.9 percent, and none had only a high school diploma. Singles composed 14.9 percent; 85.1 percent were married. The denominational background was predominantly Presbyterian Hapdong (73.1 percent), which means the sample represents male Hapdong missionaries better than it does other groups.

The first two data sets were imported and, following the frameworks suggested by the original researchers, were analyzed to determine the dominant leadership type and style of each respondent. In cases of equal scores in more than two items, mixed types and styles were used, which were analyzed again in more detail to see if any particular combinations appeared to be dominant. The dominant leadership virtues and styles were also analyzed according to age, ministry experience, and educational level. The responses to the eight supplemental questions were analyzed as a means of assessing the missionaries' self-awareness concerning their characteristic leadership style and their understanding of their needs. The whole of the survey project focused on drawing out implications for ministry.

DATA ANALYSES

The data analyses focused on leadership virtues, leadership styles, and self-awareness of leadership realities on the part of missionaries.

Analysis of Leadership Virtues

Jeffrey Glanz suggested seven leadership virtues. In the survey results, empathy emerged as the dominant virtue for 22 of the 101 respondents (21.8 percent). The six other leadership virtues trailed far behind: impartiality (7 persons, 6.9 percent), judgment (5 persons, 5.0 percent), enthusiasm (5 persons, 5.0 percent), humility (4 persons, 4.0 percent), courage (1 person, 1.0 percent), and imagination (0 persons).

The number of respondents with mixed types, that is, ones who recorded the same score for more than two items of virtue, was 57 persons (56.4 percent). The mixed type "empathy and enthusiasm" was the most common, with 9 cases. The tendency to lean toward the virtue of empathy fits with our expectations that missionaries will serve people in general well. It also fits with the fact that the majority of Korean missionaries are ordained ministers or their spouses.

The lack of diversity in the mission leaders' dominant leadership virtue is noticeable, underscored by the absence of any leaders characterized by the virtue of imagination. This facet of Korean missional leadership may be tied to cultural characteristics found in the Korean church. Weakness in or absence of imaginative leadership among Korean missionaries presents a potential lack of creativity in the cross-cultural ministries carried out by Korean missionaries. How should the Korean missions movement seek to address this issue?

Viewed by age group, of respondents in their thirties, 40 percent were of the empathy type, 33.3 percent of the mixed type, 13.3 percent of the enthusiasm type, 6.7 percent each of the judgment and the humility types, and none of the impartiality, courage, or imagination types. Respondents in their forties were 55.6 percent mixed type, with 24.4 percent for empathy, 11.1 percent for impartiality, 6.7 percent for judgment, 2.2 percent for enthusiasm, and none for humility, courage, or imagination. Respondents in their fifties were 64.9 percent mixed type, with 13.5 percent for empathy, 5.4 percent for judgment, 2.7 percent each for courage, impartiality, and enthusiasm, and none for either humility or imagination. The breakdown for respondents in their sixties was 50.0 percent mixed type, 25.0 percent each for empathy and enthusiasm, and none for impartiality, judgment, humility, or imagination.

There were, however, only four respondents in their sixties, a number too small to allow for meaningful distribution across the seven types.

The percentage of mixed types is slightly higher among female respondents (58.8 percent) than among male respondents (54.7 percent). The percentage who identified with the humility type is significantly higher among female respondents (11.8 percent) than among male respondents (2.4 percent).

Length of ministry experience correlates with identification as a mixed type. The longer the ministry experience, the more cases of mixed type. The percentage of mixed types for respondents with less than 4 years' ministry experience was 41.7 percent, those with 4–8 years' experience 46.2 percent, 8–12 years 51.6 percent, 12–16 years 60.0 percent, and over 16 years 67.9 percent. This progression shows that as missionaries spend more years working in a cross-cultural setting, they grow in flexibility of leadership type.

The leadership virtues present among Korean missionaries are those of people who are devoted to serving other people in a cross-cultural setting. The need for diversity in leadership type within the pool of mission leaders, however, still remains.

Analysis of Leadership Style

Watanabe and Miyake's typology suggests six styles of leadership—directive, visionary, affiliative, participative, pacesetting, and coaching. Of the 101 respondents to the survey, 26 (26.7 percent) were of the participative style, 14 (13.9 percent) coaching, 11 (9.9 percent) visionary, 6 (5.9 percent) affiliative, 2 (2.0 percent) pacesetting, and none were of the directive style. A total of 42 persons (40.6 percent) had a mixed style, and of these, 13 were a combination of the participative and coaching styles.

The predominance of combined styles can play a positive role in mission leadership since it suggests potentially higher adaptability in fluid situations. That the participative style is well represented fits with the fact that a majority of Korean missionaries are involved in leading church ministries, interacting with other members of the ministry team and the church community. The coaching style matches well with the ministries of discipleship in which many Korean missionaries are involved. The virtual absence of the pacesetting and directive styles among the respondents seems characteristic of leadership in voluntary organizations. The absence of certain styles within a leadership team, however, could prove a hindrance to organizations that wish for their organizational culture to reflect diversity.

A higher percentage of men (42.9 percent) than women (35.3 percent) identified their leadership style as being mixed. This contrasts with the greater frequency among women (58.8 percent) than among men (54.7 percent) of mixed types of basic leadership virtues, as was seen earlier. According to this analysis, women might be expected to display more flexibility of personality type, but men to be more flexible in working style. The presence of the coaching style is much higher among women (23.5 percent) than among men (11.9 percent).

Viewed by age group, missionaries in their forties checked the participative style with greater frequency than did missionaries in the other age groups. At the same time, the percentage of mixed styles is lower among the missionaries in their forties than in other age groups. The frequency of the visionary style increases in proportion to length of ministry experience, with the exception of respondents in cross-cultural ministries for over 16 years. The participative style is found more frequently in the group with ministry experience of 8–12 years than in other groups.

Sorting for leadership style in relation to educational level yields the following observations. Missionaries' educational level is proportional to the percentage of mixed styles, but educational level is inversely proportional to the affiliative style and the participative style. Half of the missionaries with doctorates are of mixed styles (50.0 percent), a higher percentage than among those with master's degrees (40.9 percent) or bachelor's degrees (28.6 percent).

Mixed styles of leadership are observed more frequently among more highly educated male missionaries in their forties. We can say that a good missionary leadership team will include diverse styles of leadership and will nurture creativity.

Analysis of Self-Awareness

Most respondents to this survey were aware of the need for leadership development, and 98.0 percent identified it as an important task. Fewer than half (45.5 percent) saw a pronounced difference between exercising leadership in a cross-cultural setting and doing so in a home-country setting. A 54.5 percent majority stated that the essence of ministry remains the same whatever the ministry context. Both perspectives contain an element of truth about the nature of leadership in cross-cultural ministries.

A large majority of respondents (82.2 percent) believed that they were well aware of their own leadership styles. When asked, however, about the type of leadership they were supposed to exercise for their particular ministries, the percentage of respondents (75.3 percent) who indicated confident awareness was lower. In other words, a significant number of missionaries knew their own preferred leadership style, but were less certain that it was the style of leadership called for in a given ministerial situation.

A majority of the respondents (64.4 percent) indicated that they were making specific efforts to enhance their leadership capability, but only 34.7 percent knew of any training programs that could help them polish their skills. At the personal level, missionaries are making an effort to advance their leadership abilities, but they lack systematic organizational support. Eight out of ten respondents (80.2 percent) also indicated a desire for professional assistance in nurturing their missional leadership capabilities. A large majority of the respondents (88.1 percent) also identified a need for empirical research, such as this survey, on leadership styles.

This analysis of the missionaries' self-awareness in relation to styles and demands of leadership points to the need for informally nurturing missionaries' leadership skills, for leadership training programs, and for systematic and professional assistance in the development of mission leaders.

RESEARCH FINDINGS AND IMPLICATIONS

The above analyses highlight the need to know both one's own leadership characteristics and the leadership needs in the field. Korean missionaries need to identify their types and styles of leadership so that they can meet the leadership needs in their ministry contexts.

The analysis of leadership virtues shows a dominance of mixed types and a lack of the imagination type among Korean mission leaders. The need for diversity in leadership virtues is a matter to which the mission community should give attention. The exercise of leadership must be sensitive to context, and therefore missional leadership in the field must be flexible and adaptable. These points all have to do with maturity. Maturity enables leaders to compensate for their deficiencies or even set aside their personal preference among the different types of leadership.

The analysis of leadership styles also shows a dominance of mixed styles, with the participative style ranking second. The participative style tends to emphasize the commitment of followers, but is only applicable when the leaders are independent, capable, and highly motivated. The coaching style requires a long-term perspective, for it presupposes high motivation for learning on the part of followers. The increasing dominance of the visionary style as length of missionary service increases seems to reflect the need for transformation in the mission field.[3]

One conclusion to be drawn from the analyses is that Korean missionaries tend to be idealistic in their understanding and defining of missional leadership in their contexts. They are sensitive to the ideal standard of leadership required for their ministry and seek to adjust the character of their leadership to the expectations set by their followers. They need to express their frustration and sense of vulnerability more candidly. Qualitative research could address this aspect in more detail.

Finally, Korean missionaries need good training programs and trainers who can help them in figuring out ways to develop their leadership abilities in the mission field. These needs are real and important, and Korean churches and mission agencies must acknowledge and address them. Leadership matters in the maturation of a missionary movement.

---

3. Ibid., 58.

14

PARTNERSHIP IN KOREAN MISSIONS (2010)

For the sake of the global church, parochialism within any sector of the church worldwide must be overcome through partnerships formed with other parts of the body of Christ. The history of the Korean missionary movement records examples of various mission leaders who have sought to connect it with the global missionary movement. Lessons accumulated through this process need to be shared for the benefit of mission leaders of the present and future.

The definition of partnership offered by William Taylor, "using mutual gifts to accomplish tasks," does not limit partnership to joint ventures or strategic alliances, but includes multiple models—for example, mother/daughter, parachurch establishment/entrepreneurial, national support, nationals-on-the-team, paternal network, secondment, empowerment, and multinational church network enablement. Partnerships need to be pursued at multiple levels, in various ministerial contexts, and within diverse relationships.[1]

Among the many people who have contributed to the advancement of partnership in Korean missions, I focus here on the contributions of six mission leaders: Chan Young Choi, David Dong Jin Cho, Chun Chae Ok, Bong Rin Ro, Sung-Sam Samuel Kang, and David Taiwoong Lee. All are still living, though they are retired from active field service.

This chapter was first presented in Korean at the Fifth National Consultation on World Evangelization held in Sungnam, Korea in June 2010; translated, edited, and reprinted by permission.

1. William D. Taylor, ed., *Kingdom Partnerships for Synergy in Missions* (Pasadena, Calif.: William Carey Library, 1994), 244–46.

This essay addresses three questions: How did these mission leaders contribute to the advancement of Korean mission partnership? What did they learn from their partnership experience? What are their expectations as future mission leaders seek to lead partnership ministries? The research process consisted of a literature review plus interviews with the six mission leaders through meetings, e-mails, and telephone calls. Analysis and generalization of the data gathered form the basis for this chapter.

HISTORY OF KOREAN MISSION PARTNERSHIP

Significant steps taken in Korean mission partnership can be recounted by highlighting the roles key leaders have played in international settings while being careful not to neglect other developments at the grassroots level. Contributions the six leaders made to the advancement of partnership will be summarized in the order in which they began their respective cross-cultural ministries.

Chan Young Choi (b. 1927)

Chan Young Choi graduated in 1951 from Presbyterian Theological Seminary, Seoul, Korea, and was ordained. Four years later he and his wife were appointed by the Presbyterian General Assembly as missionaries to Thailand, beginning their ministry in 1956. Choi became pastor of the Second Thai Church in Bangkok and also served as chaplain at Bangkok Christian Hospital.

Following graduation from Pittsburgh Theological Seminary, Pittsburg, Pennsylvania, in 1962, Choi served as general secretary of the Thailand Bible Society and the Laos Bible Society. He continued in the ministry of Bible distribution while based in Manila, Philippines, from 1974 to 1978, where he became the regional director of the Asia Pacific Bible Society, and in Hong Kong from 1978 through 1992. He also spoke at various consultations and conventions, both in the Asia Pacific region and in other parts of the world. One of his most important contributions to Bible distribution in the Asia Pacific region was the establishment in 1987 of a large facility for printing Bibles in Nanjing, China.[2]

---

2. This information is based on Chan Young Choi's autobiography, *Choi Chan Young Iyagi* [The story of Choi Chan Young] (Seoul: Joy Press, 1995), Appendix.

When he retired from field ministry in 1992, at age sixty-five, Choi was appointed as a lifetime member of the American Bible Society. In 1992 he began to teach at Fuller Theological Seminary, Pasadena, California, starting a Korean studies program. He received an honorary doctorate in education from South Korea's Jeon Ju University; was appointed in 2005 as professor and endowed chair at Torch Trinity Graduate University, Seoul, Korea; and since 2009 has been serving as general director of GEDA International, based in Los Angeles, California.

Choi filled significant leadership roles at the United Bible Societies for thirty years (1962–92), representing the Asia Pacific region and contributing to the globalization of the organization. His ministry as a speaker in mission consultations and conventions served to bridge between the Korean church and other parts of the global church. The Korean studies program at Fuller is evidence of the Korean church's increased stature in missions and of a hope that Korea will contribute to missiological advance. Choi's multifaceted ministry to a younger generation is still in progress.

David Dong Jin Cho (b. 1924)

David Dong Jin Cho was born in Yongcheon, North Korea, in 1924, into the family of an independence activist. He publicly confessed his Christian faith at age seventeen, and went to Chosun Theological Seminary, in Seoul. He also attended Presbyterian Theological Seminary, graduating in 1949, and was ordained in 1950. For a time he served as an evangelist in a dangerous Communist region, where he was the means of salvation for many.

In 1956 Cho went to the United States for further studies at Barrington College (Barrington, Rhode Island), WEC Missionary Training Center (Fort Washington, Pennsylvania), Bethany Mission College (Minneapolis, Minnesota), and Asbury Theological Seminary (Wilmore, Kentucky), from which he received a Th.M. in missions. From 1960 through 1978 he pastored Huam Presbyterian Church in Seoul, where he led a mission-oriented church ministry. He began to teach missions at Presbyterian Theological Seminary in 1961. In 1968 he started the Korea Evangelistic Inter-Mission Alliance (KEIMA), which in 1970 changed its name to Korea International Mission (KIM).

He also taught missions at Presbyterian Theological Seminary, Methodist Theological Seminary (Seoul, Korea), and Seoul Theological Seminary of the Holiness Church. He received a Ph.D. in international development from William Carey International University (Pasadena, California) in 1993.[3]

In 1973 Cho made a major contribution to the advancement of international partnership by hosting the first All-Asia Mission Consultation, held in Seoul. Not only Asian mission leaders but also Western mission leaders participated in this significant event. The Asian Missions Association held a conference in Seoul in 1975, where the Seoul Declaration on Christian Mission was issued.

Cho's international ministry includes the paper on innovation in world mission structures that he presented at the 1974 Lausanne Congress on World Evangelization. He also contributed to the formation of the World Evangelical Alliance's Mission Commission at the Seoul conference in 1975. Furthermore, he taught missions at William Carey International University, Western Seminary (Portland, Oregon), and Fuller Theological Seminary. The climax of Cho's international leadership was his election as founding chair of the Third World Missions Association in 1989, in which position he continued until 1995.[4]

In the period 1989–2000, Cho traveled to North Korea twenty-four times to teach as a visiting professor of religious studies at Kim Il-sung University in Pyongyang. He also preached at Bongsu Church and Chilgol Church there, and taught regularly at Pyongyang Seminary. From 2000 to 2003, he was involved in theological education for Russian pastors in Moscow, and in 2004 he established the David Cho Missiological Institute (Hwasung, Korea) to further missiological research in Korea.[5]

David Cho has exercised global leadership as a mission-oriented pastor, a mission leader, a missiologist, and a missionary trainer,

---

3. This biographical information is based on David Dong Jin Cho, "Naeu Somyeong, Naeu Seonkyohaengjeon" [My calling, my mission acts], in *Somyeong: Naega Yeogi Itnaida, Nareul Bonesoseo* [Calling: Here I am! Send me!], ed. Timothy Kiho Park and Wonsuk Ma (Seoul: Qumran, 2010), 48–52.

4. Ibid., 53–58.

5. Ibid., 59–60.

representing the Korean church in international arenas for many years. His main contribution to the advance of Korean missions was his establishment of a faith mission agency in the Korean context. His efforts to facilitate partnership in global missions were systematic and long-term, involving many mission leaders globally.

Chun Chae Ok (b. 1938)

Chun Chae Ok was born in Gangreung, Korea, in 1938. She graduated from Seoul's Ewha Woman's University in 1960 and was sent to Pakistan as a missionary in 1961. There she worked as a missionary from 1961 to 1965 while studying Urdu at Murree Language School. Afterward, she studied at All Nations Christian College (Hertfordshire, United Kingdom; 1965–66), at London Bible College and at the University of London (1966–69), and at Fuller Theological Seminary's School of World Mission (1974–77), where she earned Th.M. and D.Miss. degrees.

Beginning in 1970, Chun taught at Ewha Woman's University, serving as department chair from 1984 through 1993 and as dean of the divinity school from 2000 through 2004. Ordained as a pastor in 2002, she also served as general secretary of Darakbang (Upper Room) Evangelism Fellowship which belongs to Ewah Woman's University. Since 2004, Chun has been serving both as professor emerita at Ewha and as founding chair of the Institute of Islamic Studies, Seoul, Korea. She was appointed as professor and endowed chair at Korea University of International Studies in Seoul in 2006 and has been director of Torch Trinity's Institute of Islamic Studies since 2007.

Chun Chae Ok has served many Christian organizations in Korea: as a board member of Darakbang Evangelism Fellowship, Overseas Missionary Fellowship Korea, Korea InterVarsity Christian Fellowship, Global Missionary Training Center, Torch Foundation, and Torch Trinity Graduate University; as a member of the central council of Korea Evangelical Fellowship; as chair of the Korea Evangelical Missiological Association and Korea Missiological Association; as a consultant for Korea Interserve; as an advisor to SIM Korea; and also as vice chair and later co-chair of the Korea World Mission Association.

Chun's international leadership roles include executive secretary of the World Evangelical Alliance Mission Commission (1976–79), central council member of the same organization (1979–89), central council member of the Lausanne Committee for World Evangelization, visiting professor at the Centre for the Study of Christianity in the Non-Western World at the University of Edinburgh, president of the International Association for Mission Studies (IAMS; 1996–2000), executive member and later vice president of the International Fellowship of Evangelical Students, research fellow at Yale Divinity School (New Haven, Connecticut), senior mission scholar at the Overseas Ministries Study Center (New Haven, Connecticut), and visiting professor at Midwest Theological Seminary. In 2010 she received an honorary doctorate from Torch Trinity Graduate University.

Chun's missionary career was the result of an international partnership between the churches of Korea and Pakistan. As a missiologist and mission leader, she was very active in connecting the Korean church with other parts of the global church. Serving as a spokesperson for the Korean missions circle in international arenas, she facilitated mutual understanding and exchange. Another important role she played was that of caregiver for women missionaries and mission leaders. Her founding of the Institute of Islamic Studies was a pioneering step that advanced Korean missiological research related to Islam. As president of IAMS she raised the level of the Korean missiological contribution. In the course of her career, Chun Chae Ok was a rare instance of someone from Korea combining the identities of single, female, missionary, and missiologist in one person.

Bong Rin Ro (b. 1935)

Bong Rin Ro was born in Seoncheon, North Korea, in 1935. After graduating from Seoul National University, he studied at Columbia Bible College (Columbia, South Carolina; 1956–60; B.A.), Covenant Seminary (St. Louis, Missouri, 1960–61), Wheaton College (Wheaton, Illinois; 1961–62; B.A.), and Concordia Seminary (St. Louis, Missouri), where he earned an S.T.M. and a Th.D. in church history (1969).

In 1970 Ro was commissioned as a missionary to Singapore, serving with Overseas Missionary Fellowship (OMF). His teaching ministries extended from Singapore (1970–74) to Taiwan (1975–89) to Korea (1990–2000). He taught missions in Korea's Asian Center for Theological Studies and Mission (1990–97) and at Torch Trinity Graduate University (1997–2000), before retiring. His ministry roles in Korea include serving as executive director of Torch Mission Center and general secretary of the AD2000 and Beyond movement in Korea.

While working in Taiwan and following his election as field director and a field council member, Ro exercised leadership for eighty OMF missionaries. He also served as executive secretary of the Asia Theological Association (1970–90) and as international director of the World Evangelical Alliance's Theological Commission (1990–96).

The founding, under Ro's leadership, of the Asia Theological Association (ATA) enabled the accreditation of sixty-seven seminaries and Bible colleges during the period 1975 through 1990, a figure that grew to 136 by 2010. In 1984 Ro was instrumental in establishing the Asia Graduate School of Theology (AGST) in Manila, Philippines in 1984 and served as its first president, running the Th.M., D.Min., Ed.D., and Ph.D. degree programs. Through ATA, he published ten books on theology and missiology.[6]

After retiring in 2000 from thirty years of missionary service in East Asia, Ro continued teaching but at Hawaii Theological Seminary, in Honolulu, serving as president and professor of church history and missiology.

Having been educated in the English-speaking world, Bong Rin Ro was able to contribute to the advancement of partnership between the Asian church and the global church. His ministry in theological education and educational administration in East Asia raised the level of partnership both inside and outside Asia. Though born in North Korea, through his publications he is most widely known in the English-speaking world as an Asian American missiologist.

Sung-Sam Samuel Kang (b. 1941)

Sung-Sam Samuel Kang was born in Osaka, Japan, in 1941. After graduating from Dankook University in Seoul, he worked as an English

---

6. For more detailed biographical information, see Bong Rin Ro, "Sunkyosaro burcombateun chukbok" [The blessing of being called as a missionary], in *Somyeong: Naega Yeogi Itnaida, Nareul Bonesoseo* [Calling: Here I am! Send me!], Park and Ma, 86–97.

teacher before studying theology at Chongshin Theological University, also in Seoul (1976–78; M.Div.). He was ordained as a pastor and became a missionary.

In 1979 Kang and his wife, Sarah, began missionary service in Nigeria that continued until 1991. Their main ministry responsibilities included theological education (Billiri Theological College; he was academic dean), missionary training (Nigeria Evangelical Mission Institute; he again was academic dean), and church planting.

Kang served with a multicultural team and was a team leader for many years. His ministry took place within a partnership between the Global Missionary Society (GMS), a Korean mission agency, and SIM International, an international mission agency. He and his wife were pioneers for Korea of service within an international partnership model for missions; they were the first Korean missionary couple to have dual membership in two mission agencies.

Kang studied at Columbia International University, leading to an M.A. in 1984. He earned a Ph.D. in intercultural studies at Trinity International University, Deerfield, Illinois, in 1995.

After completing missiological studies in the United States, Kang served as general secretary of GMS (1991–97). His leadership positions included associate general secretary and then general secretary of the Korea World Mission Association (KWMA; 2001–2010), which he continues to serve as chairman. His efforts resulted in 2002 in the enrollment of KWMA as a legal body. He was also instrumental in establishing the graduate school of missions at Chongshin Theological University, serving as the founding dean, and he continues to work as president of Chongshin International Graduate School.

An international mission leader, Kang has served as an associate member of the World Evangelical Alliance Mission Commission since 1993, as executive member of the Asia Theological Association since 1998, and as executive board member of the International Council for Higher Education and chairman of its Commission for Globalization and Education since 2000.

Through his field experience in theological education and church planting ministries, Samuel Kang has contributed to the development of the Korean missionary movement. From its beginning, his ministry has had a glocal dimension, incorporating Korean and global perspectives. Especially in his leadership roles in KWMA, he tried to reflect the different backgrounds and standpoints of member mission agencies in a harmonious way.

David Taiwoong Lee (b. 1940)

David Taiwoong Lee was born in Seoul in 1940. After graduating from Seoul's Hanyang University in 1969, he worked in a discipleship training ministry as a layman. He served full-time with Joy Mission for the period 1972–79 and later became the mission's president. In 1976, he studied theology at Southern Baptist Theological Seminary (Louisville, Kentucky) for one year. Later, he did further studies in theology and missiology at Trinity Evangelical Divinity School (Deerfield, Illinois; 1980–83), leading to M.Div. and D.Miss. degrees.

Returning to Korea, Lee launched the Global Missionary Training Center (GMTC) in 1986, serving as director for twenty-one years. His pioneering work included establishing the Global Missionary Fellowship (GMF) in 1987. His vision was to set up a mission community with a Korean background that offered a full array of missionary services and operated on a global standard. GMF grew to function as an umbrella organization for nine ministries—three missionary sending agencies, two missionary training centers, one arm for research, one arm for educating missionary children, one arm for leadership training for experienced missionaries, and one arm for legal affairs and organizational coordination. Lee served as chair of GMF's board until 2008, also twenty-one years. Over the years he acted as a consultant for several international mission agencies as they sought to establish a base in Korea.

Lee pursued a gentle yet efficient partnership with such international mission agencies as Wycliffe Global Alliance, Overseas Missionary Fellowship, and Frontiers. Neither exhibiting a nationalistic sentiment nor walking in Western footsteps, he set an example of missional partnership based on mutual respect and formed GMF into a Korean mission community open to various ways of working together with other entities active in mission. Top leaders of international mission agencies as well as missionaries in the field welcomed this open stance that promoted purpose-driven partnerships.

Lee contributed to the development of the World Evangelical Alliance Mission Commission as an executive member for thirty years, beginning in 1987, and especially as chairman for the period 1994–2002. His responsibilities included those of missionary trainer, mission administrator, and missiologist. He placed emphasis on reflecting the perspectives and voices of the Majority World in international mission circles. As cochair of the committee that drafted the Iguassu Affirmation issued by the Iguassu Missiological Consultation in 1999, he provided a sense of balance from his rich experiences as missionary trainer and member-care specialist. As a missiologist, his extensive reading insured that he was always up-to-date.

Lee contributed to leadership development at multiple levels, mentoring missionaries in a focused way. He continues to be a source of encouragement for many Korean mission leaders and experts.

LESSONS LEARNED FROM THE HISTORY OF PARTNERSHIP

What have Korean mission leaders learned from their partnership experiences? What lessons do they want to pass on to following generations? From interviews conducted by the author with these six leaders, four issues stand out.

Spiritual Fundamentals

Spiritual fundamentals are important in practicing international leadership for intercultural ministries. As a prerequisite for global leadership, good character cannot be overemphasized. By adhering to values that are consistently based on biblical norms, leaders will be equipped with values that are compatible with the values of other leaders. Though many outward differences due to differing cultural backgrounds are evident among leaders, the presence of internal norms and values can bring about a sense of united purpose among them. Conscious effort should be made to that end.

Personal maturity can strengthen trust across cultural and organizational boundaries. Though not wholly distinct from personality, diverse cultural characteristics require sensitivity on the part of leaders. Maturity in cultural sensitivity deepens mutual understanding and allegiance between leaders.[7] Indeed, missional judgment and insight presuppose sensitivity and maturity in the cultural realm. These leadership qualities are of greater importance than language proficiency. Language proficiency (often in English) is significant, but of greater importance is an understanding of and sensitivity to the fundamental intentions and character of other human beings. Regrettably, some people, while excellent at communicating in English, lack spiritual maturity and cultural sensitivity.

As David Lee pointed out, showing oneself to be a reliable and respectable person is very important in international relations. Genuine friendship is required if leaders are to work together well. Therefore, coordinating or merging the leadership of international organizations takes a long time. Global partnership is strengthened by the tests of time. Spiritual maturity and integrity are the foundation of global leadership and partnership.

Ministerial Expertise

Mission leaders should build up their intercultural competence, including the ability to communicate, insight into field ministries, and skills in performance evaluation, and should cultivate a humble yet bold attitude. Individuals need to develop their ministerial expertise fully if they are to be recognized as resource persons in the international missions circle. Without expertise in at least one appropriate field, leaders will find it hard to influence others. Chun Chae Ok emphasized the need to develop ministerial expertise if one is to contribute to the accumulation of missional knowledge.

Ministerial expertise demands field experience, missiological insight, and long-term experience in mastering a specific subject field. Without such qualifications, one can only influence others superficially. Taking an official position if one lacks proper preparation, competence, and expertise is dangerous. Both soundness of fundamental character

---

7. Yun Taek Yim identifies Chan Young Choi as a fraternal worker to the Thai church. In its early years of sending missionaries, the Korean church cooperated with the receiving church. See Yun Taek Yim, *Haebang Hu Choechoeu Seonkyosa Cheheomgi* [The biography of the first missionary after independence] (Seoul: Duranno Press, 2009), 252–64.

and expertise are required; it cannot be a matter of either/or. When these two leadership qualities—sound fundamental character and expertise—are combined, the potential is present for high performance within a ministry partnership.

Each of the six Korean leaders introduced above has his or her own story of faith and ministry. Whatever their differences, they possess in common a high level of spiritual maturity and capability as mission leaders. Without forgetting these foundational qualifications, the next generation of mission leaders will need to build on the work of this generation of leaders so as to develop greater expertise in various fields.

Teachability

The six mission leaders remained teachable. They studied missions at Western theological institutions and learned the practicalities of missions by interacting with international mission agencies. This attitude of being a learner is an essential component of global leadership and of global partnership. Unless one is willing to learn from one's partner, one cannot cooperate well with that partner. When the partner's strength complements one's own weakness, the synergies potentially present in partnership can be truly experienced.

Bong Rin Ro emphasizes learning from Western missions since they have a longer history and richer know-how than do Korean missions. The Korean missionary movement will be enriched by knowledge gleaned from the West's accumulated experience and expertise, enabling the movement to be global rather than parochial in outlook. Korean missions should also have on their agenda learning from other new missionary movements from the Majority World. Active learning across traditional cultural boundaries needs to be a crucial emphasis in Korean missions.

Korean missionaries must recognize the importance of analyzing and understanding mission fields, mission strategies, and mission personnel. Being informed on their field of service is essential for field-oriented missionaries, and research on mission strategies is crucial for effective field ministry. Research focused on mission personnel is essential for in-depth member care for the harvest force. The accumulation of expertise in these fields will contribute to advancing Korean missions. Instead of being satisfied simply with growth in the number of Korean missionaries, we need to strive to bear fruit in the field, which is our real goal. Learning is crucial if effectiveness and efficiency in mission are to be enhanced.

Kingdom Mind

Lack of unity among Korean churches and organizations, these Korean mission leaders stated, undermines partnership among Korean missionaries in the mission field. The shortcomings of the Korean churches impede partnering among Korean mission agencies and teams. Korean churches and organizations need to promote synergistic kingdom partnership, first among themselves, next with Western organizations, and then also with churches and organizations in the mission fields.

As in the case of Bong Rin Ro, who was elected as field leader by the members of a multinational organization, Korean missionaries need to be supported by others with different cultural backgrounds. A "horizontal" cooperative outlook can be consolidated and expressed by developing concrete working relationships. Many mission leaders point out that Korean missionaries tend to be simultaneously independent in a positive sense, but solitary and isolated in a negative sense. Having the ability to cross organizational boundaries and to work with other organizations is an important asset for an organization to possess.

The presence of a cooperative mind-set is appreciated by other purpose-driven leaders. A partnership mind-set that is fixed on accomplishing God's purposes will place a higher value on the expansion of the kingdom of God than on the growth of one's own organization. Holding onto this higher value helps to overcome the constant demands imposed by organizational interests, so as to cultivate the practice of kingdom synergy. The art of coordinating the demands of different organizational interests is an essential component of good missional leadership.

As Samuel Kang astutely observed, partnership is impossible unless some of the interests of a leader's denomination or organization are sacrificed. In pursuit of biblical ecumenism for the sake of the kingdom of God, we need to increase our practice of fellowship, sharing, and servanthood. Serving with one's strengths will benefit other entities that are also part of the kingdom of God. According to Kang, partnership is not a matter of need, but of faith, conscience, and prayer.

ISSUES OF FUTURE DEVELOPMENT

The partnership experiences of the six Korean missional leaders reviewed have provided wisdom and insight. Further reflections on directions that must be pursued in the future are summarized below.

Cooperation among Korean Mission Leaders

These six leaders expended much energy on building international partnerships, working at different levels. Much of the globalization of Korean missions can be attributed to their efforts. Moreover, through their contributions the global church was able to understand the Korean church and missions movement more fully. In this way these leaders played a bridging role.

A question that arose, however, was, what level of intimacy and effectiveness in partnership was achieved within the circle of Korean mission leaders itself? In the global missions arena each leader played his or her part well, but what synergy did they create among themselves through working together? Unless the character of partnership within the national missionary movement is monitored, that partnership may become self-centered and a veneer, and be "partnership" in name only. It would seem desirable to practice partnerships at the national level as well as pursuing them at the global level. Mission organizations should reflect the value of partnership in their core vision and philosophy.

Korean mission leaders would benefit from getting together more often and sharing more with each other at the level of companionship. They need to serve one another more. Companionship and sharing do not necessarily happen automatically; their achievement may require conscious effort and concrete steps. This concern should be prominent on the agenda for the future development for the Korean missionary movement.

Competition can work against genuine partnership. Mission agencies too often compete over which can be the largest, have the fastest membership growth rate, report the greatest number of conversions, or lay claim to the most resources. They must combat such a human-centered mentality and perspective. They should make every effort to avoid duplication and competition in their investments in the mission fields and instead look for creative ways to bring about synergy between their ministries.

The six leaders have served their times well, but now the leaders of the next generation need to gear up and labor toward forming fully functioning partnerships that work both locally and globally. Leaders of the present and the future need to pursue forms of team leadership that are truly glocal.

Developing Leadership Pools

Although missional leadership cannot be developed through human effort alone, churches and missions must still make conscious efforts to raise up leaders. Up to the present, Korean mission leaders have not emerged as the result of intentional nurturing. They have been self-made leaders. A more desirable way is for leaders to be fostered through intentional and consistent investment in their growth. As in the case of Paul with Timothy, senior leaders must cultivate the leadership abilities of promising junior personnel.

Many Korean mission agencies are going through leadership transitions in the 2010s, but they do not seem to be well prepared for such significant organizational change. Systems for electing new leaders are in place, but the new leaders are not well prepared for their new roles. The more important the leadership role, the longer the period of preparation should be.

Samuel Kang and David Lee suggest that Korean missions need to develop leadership "pools." Senior Korean mission leaders should play an active role in leadership development. Instead of a wildflower model of leadership development—plucking flowers that happen to emerge on their own—active nurturing of new leaders is needed so as to develop a plentiful supply. This proposal does not mean, however, adoption of a uniform centralized system; different development models can be tried out. A leader's worth should be measured not by the positions he or she has occupied, but by the results of his or her influence. One standard for evaluating a leader's contribution is the number of additional leaders he or she has nurtured.

Systems for seconding personnel between organizations are vital to leadership development. Korean mission leaders need the experience of having worked beyond their organizational boundaries. They need to be seconded to international organizations for the benefit of the entire global missions circle.

One problem affecting the process of mission leadership development is the low awareness of this issue on the part of local churches in Korea. Many churches decide to stop supporting missionaries who return to the home country to take leadership positions. The churches need to change their perspective and to continue to support missionaries in leadership roles. Unless sending churches are fully supportive of new leaders, transitions between missionary roles cannot be made smoothly.

Korean seminaries need to design specially run degree programs that focus on leadership development for missionaries, and their mission programs should be evaluated accordingly. Seminaries, churches, and mission agencies must work together to address this significant requirement.

Division of Roles in International Missions

In the past, Korean mission leaders occupied various roles in the arena of international missions, often acting as mission administrator and missiologist at the same time. Their areas of specialty included missionary training, member care, partnership/networking, and research. Doubling up of leadership roles still characterizes Majority World missions. In the case of Korean missions, however, dividing roles according to areas of expertise is now necessary. Unless the roles are reasonably divided, the development of expertise cannot be secured.

The knowledge fields of mission administration, member care, missionary training, continuing education, leadership development, research, crisis management, mission mobilization, and networking/partnership among others can usefully be segmented. To facilitate the maturation of these fields, Korean leaders need to limit themselves to developing expertise at depth in one or two particular areas. Then mission leaders from other parts of the world will be able to identify Korean leaders who are experts in specific areas and to build relationships with them.

As the level of expertise in particular areas increases within Korean missions, Korean leaders must consider needs in other countries that either send or receive missionaries. Especially, Korea's experience in missionary mobilization and training can be shared with mission leaders of other countries. The network of Korean leaders active in Korea in the area of mission research and development could eventually contribute to advancing mission research and development at the global level.

As Korean leaders work together in the arena of international mission, they need to take leadership transition into consideration. Senior leaders need to mentor junior leaders through on-the-job training. International cooperation requires not only expertise but also a certain level of diplomatic capability. Experienced leaders should encourage younger leaders to upgrade their skills step by step, intentionally crossing organizational and denominational boundaries together in that process.

Toward a Global Model of Partnership

Mission partnership must overcome the dichotomic view of the West versus the non-Western world and also leave behind the vestiges of Western dominance. What does it mean to be global in mission partnership? We need to remember that global mission partnership embraces different entities and perspectives. The Korean missionary movement is only one stream of the global missionary movement.

An essential precondition for international mission partnering is the cultivation of a truly global mindset that is considerate of minority groups. Korean mission leaders of the future must pay close attention to the voices of leaders from minority backgrounds. In field ministries, Korean missionaries should consult with local church leaders before making important decisions. In international mission agencies, Korean missionaries need to consider the situation faced by members from the Majority World. A mindset attuned to building up global partnership requires humility. Challenges in communication as well as differences of perspective can too easily be allowed to become barriers to genuine unity in Christ. Humility overcomes misunderstanding and miscommunication because even across cultural boundaries people easily discern a humble attitude.

International mission consultations need to be planned more functionally and as smaller-scale gatherings that focus on particular agenda items such as missions in the Buddhist world, reaching the unreached people groups in the Islamic world, missional business by regional blocs, sending missionaries from China, and re-evangelizing Europe. There are too many conventions or consultations for leaders to be able to attend them all. Wisdom and orchestrated effort need to be given to planning large-scale conventions so as to prevent duplication.

CONCLUSION

Partnership in missions must be based on biblical principles. The vision of the universal church described in Revelation 5–7 sets the direction for global mission partnership. Crossing boundaries of cultures, generations, and backgrounds, the body of Christ must embody and express genuine unity. The churches of the world need to work together voluntarily toward the same vision.

The Korean church nurtured Chan Young Choi, David Dong Jin Cho, Chun Chae Ok, Bong Rin Ro, Sung-Sam Samuel Kang, and David Taiwoong Lee. Through them God made both Korean missions and world missions more global. Korean mission leaders of the next generation must remember the lessons learned through past experiences of partnership.

The global missionary movement needs global leaders who are strong in their spiritual fundamentals, highly specialized, committed to learning, and firmly committed to pursuing synergistic kingdom partnership. Korean mission leaders need to cooperate more among themselves, build leadership pools, divide roles in international settings, and pursue a global model of kingdom partnership. May God continue to call forth leaders who are willing and capable to do this! May God continue to provide helping hands for such leaders! Amen!

15
MULTIFACETED GLOBAL PARTNERSHIP:
The Case of the Korea Research Institute for Mission

The Korea Research Institute for Mission (KRIM) was started in 1990 to help Korean churches and mission agencies by conducting missionary research and carrying out education on intercultural ministry for world evangelization. KRIM has the following purposes:
1. To contribute to the Korean missionary movement by conducting research related to the mission field, mission force, and mission strategies
2. To assist Korean churches, mission agencies, and missioners by providing relevant information and strategic education needed for intercultural ministry
3. To mobilize, educate, and assist Korean churches for their effective participation in world evangelization
4. To facilitate cooperation and partnership among Korean mission agencies and missioners

PARTNERSHIP WITH LOCAL CHURCHES IN KOREA

The churches supporting KRIM agree with what we are trying to do as an RDD (research, development, and delivery) community dedicated to world evangelization. Only a small number of churches, however, support our ministries; so KRIM's ministry offers an example of the contribution made by a few dedicated churches enabling benefit to be provided to many churches.

Originally published in *Church Partnerships in Asia: A Singapore Conversation*, ed. Michael Nai-Chiu Poon (Singapore: Genesis and Trinity Theological College, 2011), 154–67, this chapter has been edited and is reprinted by permission.

In 2007 KRIM began to hold open forums four times yearly to facilitate church-missions partnership in Korea. These forums or "Network of Local Churches for Missions" are intended for people who are involved directly in making policies and decisions as members of their local church foreign missions committees. We have attracted from fifty to seventy participants each time. For us, these forums were a down-to-earth approach as we tried as a service organization to meet the neglected but felt needs of local churches through lectures, presentations, and resource materials.

PARTNERSHIP WITH LOCAL MISSIONS IN KOREA

KRIM functions independently and autonomously but is part of the umbrella organization Global Missionary Fellowship (GMF).[1] GMF is a partnership of like-minded mission organizations that share the vision of establishing a "glocal" missions community based in Korea. While the other agencies in GMF have supported our ministry faithfully from the beginning, the proportion of financial support KRIM receives from them has decreased, since KRIM has sought to be self-supporting. KRIM serves the wider missions community, which is not necessarily aware of our relationship to GMF organizationally, as we are not confined to the boundaries of GMF's scope of activities. KRIM adheres to the organizational concept of "boundarylessness." This concept is useful for promoting an active exchange and cooperation among mission agencies. The concept does not deny the existence of organizational boundaries, but it encourages and facilitates free movement and exchange across the boundaries.[2]

As a research institute KRIM maintains a database of Korean missionaries and publishes the *Korean Mission Handbook* every two years.

---

1. Under GMF, there are three sending agencies (Global Bible Translators, Global Missions Pioneers, and HOPE), two training centers (Global Missionary Training Center and Global Professionals' Training Institute), and three supporting ministries (MK NEST, Legal Affairs Ministry, and KRIM).

2. See Ron Ashkenas, "The Organization's New Clothes," in *The Organization of the Future*, ed. Frances Hesselbein, Marshall Goldsmith, and Richard Beckhard (San Francisco: Jossey-Bass, 1997), 104.

It also conducts research projects with specific themes such as leadership styles of Korean missionaries. Korean mission agencies cooperate willingly since they eventually benefit from these research endeavors. As a think tank we try to help local missions grow as a community of "reflective practitioners" in a symbiotic relationship.[3]

GLOBAL PARTNERSHIP WITH OTHER RESEARCH CENTERS

KRIM is modeled after other mission research centers in the United States. Our networking has helped us maintain the quality of our research. KRIM's ministry partners include Global Mapping International (GMI), the Overseas Ministries Study Center (OMSC), the U.S. Center for World Mission (mobilization division), and Operation World.

GMI and KRIM co-host workshops on mapping and training in research methods, share information, and implement staff exchange programs. KRIM tries to emulate the academic quality of the *International Bulletin of Missionary Research* (*IBMR*) that is published by OMSC. Another source of encouragement has been sharing and learning through participation in the network of the World Evangelical Alliance Mission Commission. More recently, our partnership with Middle East Concern has enriched our ministry. Without this kind of network and partnership we would not be able to maintain the quality of our research.

KRIM has had to deal with several challenges in its twenty-five years of partnership with global research centers as well as within its own local churches and local missions.

GLOBAL VISION FOR PARTNERSHIP

The catalyst that motivates partnership among organizations with different histories, backgrounds, and philosophies is a shared global vision. The vision, however, must be pure and authentic; the purer the vision,

---

3. William Taylor, ed., *Global Missiology for the Twenty-First Century: The Iguassu Dialogue* (Grand Rapids: Baker, 2000), 3.

the stronger the bond. A blurred vision may lead to achieving short-term goals but doing so at the expense of disappointment and dissatisfaction.

Our mission is not about the expansion of organizational boundaries but about the expansion of the kingdom of God. We need, therefore, to recover the catholic nature of our communities in our philosophy and vision before we embark on the practicalities of partnership. The localness of churches and missions are realities of the universal church, and parochialism is a big problem that we need to overcome.

SYMBIOTIC RELATIONSHIP

The interdependent nature of partnership is to nurture and benefit both parties, leading to a win-win relationship.[4] The life of the partnership is dependent on the strength of this symbiotic interdependency.

One development that works against the mutually beneficial nature of a partnership is dependency. When one party is dependent on the other, the relationship cannot last, since the other will lose interest in the partnership as time goes by. At the opposite extreme, independence and a self-sufficient spirit can lead partnerships to self-destruct, as organizations which pursue self-sufficiency are not interested in partnership.

PARTNERSHIP, NOT PATERNALISM

On the one hand, although people talk about partnership, they may have paternalism in mind—the kind of relationship found between a superior and an inferior, with one dominating and the other subordinate. In many cases, Western mission agencies seeking partnerships are actually looking for branch offices. This kind of mentality is imperialistic in its nature. We need to make sure that we are pursuing partnership, not paternalism.

On the other hand, many mission agencies in the Majority World use the term "partnership" to raise financial support. To them, partnership is a euphemism for an unsound dependent-codependent relationship.

---

4. Andrew F. Walls, *The Cross-Cultural Process in Christian History* (Maryknoll, N.Y.: Orbis, 2002), 70.

An antidote against this kind of misuse of partnership is for churches to commit themselves to the four-self principles of being self-governing, self-supporting, self-propagating, and self-theologizing.[5] Interdependency without independent grounding is actually dependency. Churches and organizations need independence prior to interdependency. Again, we need to make sure that we are pursuing partnership, not paternalism.

KNOW-WHO AND KNOW-WHERE

Knowing one another comes before working together, so relationship or "know-who" matters in partnership. Our history of partnership with other organizations over the years has shown us the importance of consistent personal interaction and dialogue with the leaders of our partner organizations. We know about their likes and dislikes, their excitement and frustration, and their praises and prayers.

As a research institute, we focus on "know-where" over "know-what." It is unrealistic for us to put together data and information resources on one database. It is more realistic to be updated on the "know-where" of mission information and knowledge, making it vital to establish a global network of mission knowledge and expertise. This effort also facilitates both decentralization and centralization as mission information and knowledge are both gathered and widely distributed.[6]

STEP-BY-STEP UPGRADE

I have found that the step-by-step approach to partnership is a right and wise approach. I have seen cases of mismatched partnership due to insufficient compatibility, inadequate preparation, or impure motivation.

Partnership development is much like friendship; sufficient time is needed to make both a friend and a partner. I have seen organizations fail in finding the right partner organizations because they were in too

---

5. Paul G. Hiebert, *Anthropological Reflections on Missiological Issues* (Grand Rapids: Baker Books, 1994), 96–97.

6. Larry D. Pate, "The Changing Balance in Global Mission," *International Bulletin of Missionary Research* 15, no. 2 (1991): 56–61.

much of a hurry and did not invest enough time in the search. For example, I was once urgently asked to nominate a Korean representative for the Korean branch of a Western agency. Most churches and missions in the Majority World, however, are chronically short of manpower, and thus it is not easy to find a well-prepared leader who can commit to a foreign organization on short notice.

ECUMENICITY AS A REQUIREMENT OF GLOBAL LEADERSHIP

A characteristic of global leadership is ecumenicity. Even denominational leadership needs a certain degree of ecumenical spirit. The nature and characteristics of missionary leadership require an ecumenical spirit even more in this ever-globalizing world. Divisions among denominations in Korea have to be dealt with before embarking on fostering sincere partnerships at a deeper level on the global scale. Ecumenicity here does not mean blurring the boundaries of one's denominational or theological tradition or conviction, but it means crossing personal ecclesial boundaries while remaining loyal.

TOWARD A THEOLOGY OF IVY

The life of the ivy lies in the fact that as a creeping plant its leaves and branches can grow to cover the walls of a whole building. Like ivy, we need to cover our fragmented and compartmentalized missions, churches, theologies, and lives according to the biblical image of the holy community described in Revelation 5 and 7.

The word partnership has limitations because it fails to cover the fundamental nature of a relationship which is created by the blood of Christ. "Blood is richer than water," a Korean saying goes, which means that mission partnership is a blood relationship that is dedicated to covering the whole world with the Gospel of the blood. When we are committed to this kind of relationship, we are true bearers of a Christian worldview, centered upon the Lamb of God, who is both unique and universal. Thus, the worldview we live by and live for is an ivy worldview. Let us "ivy" one another in the *missio Dei*.

UNDERSTANDING KOREAN MISSIONARIES

Partnership requires mutual understanding if it is to be meaningful. I believe understanding Koreanness is important for advancement in intercultural partnership. As an ethnographer, I will try to be as neutral as possible in describing ten strengths and ten weaknesses of Korean missionaries.

Ten Strengths

1. The conviction of Korean missionaries about the authority of the Bible and its inerrancy reinforces their commitment to missions. This factor has contributed more than other sociocultural factors to the phenomenal growth of the missionary movement in Korea.
2. Korean missionaries emphasize prayer as an important component of spiritual life. They are often disappointed by Western leaders who plan without proper emphasis on prayer. The power of prayer maintains the vitality of the missionaries' service.
3. Koreans believe in the three-self principles (self-governing, self-supporting, and self-propagating) as important guidelines for church planting and church growth. They are convinced that the phenomenal growth of the Korean church has been the result of the Nevius principle, which drives them to apply the same principle in the mission field. Emphasis on interdependency should not reinforce dependency on the part of the receiving party, they argue.
4. Koreans maintain a high view of church and pastoral leadership. This perspective causes them to be uncomfortable with overly casual worship styles. It also draws both young and older Korean Christians to enter seminaries in order to become missionaries. The resulting surplus of seminary graduates has further contributed to the growth in mission activities.
5. Korean missionaries maintain a narrow definition of mission, with an emphasis on church planting and discipleship;

39.1 percent of missionaries are involved in church planting and 21.5 percent in discipleship training.[7] Korean missionaries do not like the idea of expanding the concept of mission to include transforming society and politics. This may be both a strength and a weakness.

6. Koreans firmly believe that a commitment to God's service requires a true understanding of God's Word. This characteristic is another driving force for seeking seminary education in Korea. Many seminarians forsake opportunities in the secular world in order to gain more systematic knowledge of the Bible. Many Korean missionaries would feel more satisfied and would be more cooperative if they met leaders who displayed a deep understanding of biblical principles, as opposed to leadership that is hemmed in by the organizational styles of Western cultures.

7. Koreans believe that diligence is an essential part of faithfulness. This trait causes the missionary to appear shortsighted in the eyes of Westerners, while the Korean feels uncomfortable with the amount of time Western missionaries spend on vacation. Korean missionaries often think that they should stay on the mission field regardless of whatever difficulty may arise, since missionary attrition is considered shameful. Diligence works positively, however, when balanced with patience and waiting.

8. Most Koreans understand effectiveness as being equal to completing a task speedily, which becomes a weakness if there is no assurance of quality. In general, they work well with tasks that require speed; thus it is important to understand the agonies of Korean missionaries in Islamic countries since that context requires endurance and patience.

---

7. Steve Sang-Cheol Moon, "The Protestant Missionary Movement in Korea: Current Growth and Development," *International Bulletin of Missionary Research* 32, no. 2 (2008): 59–64.

9. Koreans generally consider collective goals more important than individual goals. Missionaries who are members of international mission agencies have a stronger sense of belonging if collective goals shared among the members are made more concrete. Missionary service tends to be individualistic when it is not guided by a clear corporate vision and goals; thus international mission agencies with regional or professional foci are more convincing to Korean Christians.
10. Korean missionaries take pride in their history as a country—for example, that Korea has never invaded other countries. For this reason, Korean missionaries have an advantage in countries that have been colonized by a Western power, as they can easily empathize and mingle with the local people. Paradoxically, the lack of historical baggage and national guilt tends to cause them to be more aggressive in their approach on the mission field.

While these ten strengths may also be weaknesses, we can highlight ten weaknesses among Korean missionaries.

Ten Weaknesses

1. Korean missionaries come from a traditionally monocultural background. They have little understanding of cultural diversity when they join an intercultural community, as they have a tendency to assume that people from other cultural backgrounds are just like them. Such a limitation may not cause conflict with local people on the field, because the Korean culture and the host culture are often similar. It can be more serious, however, in relationships with Western counterparts. The Korean monocultural orientation is improving significantly with adequate pre-field missionary training and because of the ever-diversifying society.
2. Koreans come from a traditionally monolingual background. They are often misunderstood as being immature when they have a problem acquiring a new language.

Often, however, Korean missionaries are more fluent in the languages of the mission field than they are in the English language. Fortunately, in some Altaic language blocs, Korean missionaries seem to perform better than Western missionaries in terms of an early acquisition of language. Younger generations of Korean missionaries are often more fluent in both English and the field languages.

3. Korean missionaries are willing to observe the main principles of communities and organizations, but are also flexible enough to disregard unnecessary and unreasonable regulations for the sake of relationship. This trait may be seen by some as a weakness, for they do not seem to observe laws and regulations as well as Westerners do. They assign different levels of importance to boundaries that guide the way human beings may relate.[8]

4. Koreans are task-oriented and workaholic, often lacking a balance between work and rest, considering rest to be selfish and unproductive. Many need to acquire a theology of rest, to rediscover rest as an important component of Christian spirituality. More specific rules and regulations regarding home assignments for Korean missionaries are needed, with more flexible ways of taking a sabbatical.

5. Korean missionaries are often short-sighted. Short-term goals are emphasized over long-term goals. They tend to be hasty in many cases and are vulnerable before the threat of burnout. They actively emphasize strategy but do not emphasize history enough. Unfortunately, mission campaigns initiated by Western mission leaders have all the more encouraged mission myopia, at least in Korea. Our mission should be not only to do our work well in this generation, but also to prepare the next generation to do their job better.

---

8. Hiebert, *Anthropological Reflections*, 110–36. See also Paul G. Hiebert, *Transforming Worldviews: An Anthropological Understanding of How People Change* (Grand Rapids: Baker Books, 2009), 36.

6. The independence of Korean missionaries means they do not easily partner with other entities and organizations. Korean megachurches also have an effect on overseas missions. An independent spirit may be considered a strength, but parochialism stands in the way of true global partnership in the body of Christ. The "self spirit" in the three-self principles needs to be upgraded to the "together spirit" of globalism.[9]
7. Korean missionaries are not very sensitive about minority issues. Discrimination against minority groups can be found in Korean organizations. Sometimes laymen and women and the educationally and economically disadvantaged are not treated fairly. In many countries, Korean missionaries are strategically concentrated in capital cities to the neglect of small cities; they are less concerned for the spiritual status of the underprivileged of the earth.
8. The narrow definition and understanding of mission held by Korean missionaries may hinder engaging in holistic mission. A balance between broad and narrow understandings about the nature of mission—a kingdom perspective—is needed. This balanced perspective will lead to restoring the fullness and wholeness of our community.
9. Koreans are overly sensitive to group pressure, often at the expense of personal freedom and creativity. Group pressure is a stumbling block that inhibits creative missionary service. Old-timers on the mission field sometimes play the role of Cinderella's stepmother, blocking the birth of new ideas among Korean missionaries. The danger of syncretism cannot be ignored, however. A balance is needed between theological orthodoxy and practical creativity in missionary service to allow the pursuit of contextualization.

---

9. Walls, *Cross-Cultural Process*, 77.

10. Korean missionaries tend to overvalue formal education as opposed to informal and nonformal aspects of education. This blind spot is borne out in my research, which indicates that 4.4 percent of Korean missionaries hold a doctoral degree and 30.1 percent have a master's degree as their highest degree.[10] A formal educational background is good, but it can become a problem when adequate attention is not given to informal and nonformal modes of education.

CONCLUSION

Partnership is important, but not easy. Wisdom and purity are needed, and deepening the level of partnership requires a bigger picture of the global church. The ideal of unconditional but mutually beneficial church relationships across cultural and organizational boundaries needs to be recovered.

Multifaceted partnership models need to be both realistic and biblical. This type of partnership must be pursued among mission organizations all the more in this ever-globalizing world. Rigid and exclusive partnerships are outdated. In order to facilitate strategic partnerships at greater depth, we need to be intentional about understanding one another at a deeper level, including the strengths and weaknesses of our partners. Then mutual understanding and the fostering of partnerships above and beyond boundaries can be facilitated.

---

10. Steve Sang-Cheol Moon, "The Protestant Missionary Movement in Korea," 59–64.

16
MISSIONAL ACCOUNTABILITY IN KOREAN CONTEXTS

Accountability is a sign of healthiness in many spheres of social life. Missions are not an exception. Accountability consolidates missional activities and gives them added stature. Attention to the issue of accountability is rather new in the Korean missions circle, although the concept itself has been present from the start since missions have a systematic or organizational aspect. But if the truth were to be told, too often the history of mission has been composed of the stories of lone rangers. In relation to missional accountability, the norms and realities clash with one another.

This chapter focuses on a brief history of recent Korean discussions of missional accountability, followed by an analysis of mission agencies' policies regarding missional accountability. Our review and analysis will enable us to identify areas of weakness which need to be reinforced to achieve best practices in missional accountability.

A HISTORY OF RECENT DISCUSSIONS

Two recent forums focused on the issue of accountability in relation to the Korean mission community: the Second Bangkok Mission Forum, in 2005, and the Korean Global Mission Leadership Forum, in 2011.

Originally published in *Hapshin Theological Review* no. 1 (November 2012): 137–49, the English language journal of Hapdong Theological Seminary, Suwon, Korea, this chapter has been edited and is reprinted by permission.

Second Bangkok Mission Forum

The Second Bangkok Mission Forum, held in Bangkok, Thailand, in 2005, focused on missional accountability. Over thirty Korean mission leaders, missionaries, and pastors met together to deal with the issue, with twenty-five presentations and responses. For the meeting the steering committee divided the main topic into two parts, financial accountability and ministerial accountability. Min-Young Jung gave focus to the discussion by relating accountability to maturity in leadership.[1] He also suggested looking to the future by building accountability structures that will ensure accountability in Korean missional contexts.[2]

In dealing with the twin issues of financial transparency and financial accountability, the forum both paid attention to the needs of mission agencies' financial systems and supplied guidelines that are useful for individual missionaries who are raising support. The presenters and respondents had sufficient experience in this field to be able to make concrete suggestions for future development. Chang Nam Sohn, in particular, presented the need for use of standard report forms, double entry bookkeeping, common financial principles, auditing system, and credit evaluations. He further encouraged training for bookkeepers and building a network of Christian professional accountants.[3] Caleb Shin's presentation fleshed out the details of creating policies to govern personal support raising by missionaries and provided guidelines for contributors providing support.[4]

The forum dealt with accountability issues in cross-cultural ministry, covering the missionary receiving system, the field administration

---

1. Min-Young Jung, "Seonkyowa Chaekmu" [Mission and accountability], in *Mission and Accountability* (in Korean), edited by Bangkok Mission Forum Steering Committee (Chunan, Korea: Hebon, 2005), 21.

2. Ibid., 33.

3. Chang-Nam Sohn, "Seonkyo Danche Jaejung System: Hyegye Gijun" [The financial system of mission agencies: Accounting standard], in *Mission and Accountability*, Bangkok Mission Forum Steering Committee, 94–100.

4. Caleb Shin, "Mogeum Wonchikkwa Huwon Guideline: Seonkyodanche Ipjang" [Principles of fund-raising and guidelines for support: A mission agency perspective], in *Mission and Accountability*, Bangkok Mission Forum Steering Committee, 166–80.

system, member care in the field, strategic planning and review, member care on the part of sending churches, and partnership with receiving churches. The presentations, responses, and follow-up discussion sessions were effectively summarized. Practical issues of missional accountability, starting from cultural understanding and adaptation and carrying through to ministry reporting, were ably summarized by Dae Heung Kang, who also offered related recommendations. Both presenters and respondents recognized that building mentoring systems must be included within the issue of accountability.[5]

The latter part of the Second Bangkok Mission Forum was devoted to the issue of a missions accreditation system. Samuel Kang's presentation identified specific categories for evaluation and offered suggestions for carrying out evaluations. The impressive appendix to Kang's presentation was both concrete and exhaustive. The final presentation, by Paul Hahn, provided a case study of the Adopt-A-People movement in Korea. The presentation began as a chronological report of the movement and ended with the suggestion of investing in research and development so as to advance Korean missions. The declaration drafted by the forum was short, yet it effectively expressed the significance of missional accountability and a commitment to accountability in missions.

Korean Global Mission Leadership Forum

The Korean Global Mission Leadership Forum (KGMLF hereafter)—held at the Overseas Ministries Study Center, New Haven, Connecticut, USA, in February 2011—focused on the topic of accountability in missions. The rationale for the forum was that cross-cultural comparison helps us both to see inherent weaknesses and to identify strengths of some particular culture, tradition, or movement. Comparison also helps us to refine our procedures and goals and to find ways to move toward maturity in missional accountability. Mutual learning across cultures and traditions was the main intention of the forum. Forty-two mission

---

5. In Sik Jang, "Seonkyohyunji Haengjeong System: Response to 'Receiving Entity System'" [Administration system in mission fields: Response to "Receiving entity system"], in *Mission and Accountability*, Bangkok Mission Forum Steering Committee, 251.

leaders and missiologists participated in this forum, with ten plenary presentations and responses, two Bible studies, three gatherings for small-group discussion, and four prayer sessions.

Geoffrey Hahn's response to Timothy Park's position paper emphasized a partnership of equals characterized by grace, concluding that grace is necessary in every sphere of partnership.[6] The position paper presented by Stanley Green warned against accountability myopias and promoted a kingdom-oriented approach.[7] By way of response, Nam Yong Sung emphasized cultivation of a *coram Deo* consciousness.[8] Larry Fullerton provided an inspiring case study, introducing Black Rock Congregational Church's accountability structures and policies which included concrete suggestions such as use of the church's Mission Covenant and its annual missions conference.[9] A negative diagnosis of the exercise of accountability within Korean missions came from Ban Seok (Peter) Lee, that is to say that he finds the concept of accountability, separate from relationships, to still be foreign to many Korean mission organizations and their leaders.[10] Hunter Farrell discussed cases of sexual abuse in a missions community. His argument was that the self-understanding of the Reformed church as always being reformed is reinforced through the course of confession and healing.[11] In a case study of the Korea Presbyterian Mission (KPM Kosin), Shin Chul Lee highlighted several specific suggestions and solutions to improve

---

6. Geoffrey W. Hahn, "Response to Kiho (Timothy) Park, 'The big picture,'" in *Accountability in Missions: Korean and Western Case Studies*, edited by Jonathan J. Bonk (Eugene, Ore.: Wipf & Stock, 2011), 70.

7. Stanley W. Green, "Mission, Missionary, and Church Accountability That Counts: Implications for Integrity, Strategy, and Dynamic Continuity," in *Accountability in Missions*, Bonk, 77–78.

8. Nam Yong Sung, "Response to Stanley W. Green, 'Mission, Missionary, and Church Accountability as a Case Study,'" in *Accountability in Missions*, Bonk, 83.

9. Larry Fullerton, "Accountability in Mission: Black Rock Congregational Church as a Case Study," in *Accountability in Missions*, Bonk, 149–76.

10. Ban Seok (Peter) Lee, "Accountability Issues among Korean Missions Organizations," in *Accountability in Missions*, Bonk, 186.

11. B. Hunter Farrell, "Broken Trust: Sexual Abuse in the Mission Community: A Case Study in Mission Accountability," in *Accountability in Missions*, Bonk, 215.

accountability in KPM.¹² Min-Young Jung dealt with strategic accountability within Wycliffe Global Alliance, suggesting that the Korean church needs multilateral strategic accountability.¹³ Other presentations and responses were also well focused and constructive, based on the participants' long-time experience in leadership and field ministry.

Participants felt that one of the most significant areas of weakness in the Korean missionary movement—namely, underdeveloped expectations and structures for accountability—was helpfully addressed through the forum's process of cross-cultural learning and discussion. In order for the arguments to bear fruit as good practices in missions, however, much follow-up is needed.

Three points highlight the KGMLF meeting's historical significance. First, it was an intercultural learning community that meaningfully crossed cultural and organizational boundaries. Listening to and responding to one another across cultures and boundaries went both ways; this model of two-way traffic provided a good learning experience for both sides. Second, the participants were open and made themselves vulnerable as they discussed missional accountability, especially during the case studies. Cases of failure in accountability were constructive, giving lessons and insights for future development and maturation in diverse fields. Third, differences between the Korean and Western cultures and worldviews were made vivid by Scott Moreau's semantic analysis. Despite their differences, the commonalities stimulated the participants to learn, during the Bible studies led by Christopher Wright, from biblical models of accountability such as Samuel in the Old Testament and the apostle Paul in the New Testament. Models hold up common goals for all, and case studies show us the reality of differences and shortcomings.

---

12. Sin Chul Lee, "Accountability in Mission: A Case Study of Korean Presbyterian Mission (Kosin)," in *Accountability in Missions*, Bonk, 222–39.

13. Jung, Min-Young. "Strategic Accountability: God's Mission in God's Way," in *Accountability in Missions*, Bonk, 267–77.

A SURVEY OF THE ISSUE

In a survey conducted by the Korea Research Institute for Mission (directed by Steve Sang-Cheol Moon) at the end of December 2011, a series of questions about accountability were directed to mission executives. Altogether, sixty-one mission executives (representing eight denominational agencies and fifty-three interdenominational agencies) responded to the questionnaire.

A majority (96.7 percent) of the respondents thought that accountability was currently an important issue among Korean mission agencies; 57.4 percent thought it was very important, 39.3 percent considered it important, and only 3.3 percent were negative in their responses.

Important areas of accountability identified were ministry (47.8 percent), finance (22.4 percent), strategy (14.9 percent), property (3.0 percent), and others (11.9 percent). Many respondents seemed to think that these areas of accountability were interrelated in practical ways. They can be spoken of as loci of problems concerning accountability.

Some 73.8 percent of the respondents answered that their organizations were conducting some form of an audit; 37.7 percent reported that they conduct internal audits through an appointed nonprofessional accountant, 24.6 percent through internally appointed professional accountants, and 11.5 percent through external auditing. A not insignificant proportion (8.2 percent) have no auditing system in place at all.

Out of the mission agencies that have an auditing system in place, a majority (83.0 percent) reported conducting audits once or twice per year, with 52.5 percent doing them once a year, and 30.5 percent conducting audits twice a year.

Control of mission properties in the field is a matter of contention, and property related disputes are a cause for dismay. Sixty-one mission agencies reported forty-four cases of dispute about property. Rumors exist of Korean missionaries in the fields inappropriately exercising property ownership; these rumors have been verified in a number of cases. Since the reports we have represent only sixty-one mission agencies, the number of property dispute cases is certainly larger than forty-four. With reports from additional mission agencies, more such cases are likely to come to light.

Officially final decisions related to property are made by the following: home councils (56.7 percent), missionaries (11.7 percent), field structures (10.0 percent), other bodies including supporting churches (5.0 percent), and others (16.7 percent). Mission executives think that decisions related to property should be made by home councils (56.9 percent), field structures (19.6 percent), other bodies including supporting churches (19.6 percent), and individual missionaries (3.9 percent). The opinions of field leaders and supporting churches need to be reflected more in making decisions related to property.

Diverse opinions exist about who should exercise ministerial and strategic accountability; 35.9 percent specified home director and staff, 21.9 percent field leaders, 17.2 percent home councils, 6.3 percent no specific entity, and 18.8 percent others.

Many concrete suggestions and detailed opinions were provided in answer to open-ended questions that asked respondents to identify important issues in missional accountability. These responses can be summarized in nine points.

First, mission executives emphasized the importance of pre-field training as an effective means of preventing serious failures. Failures of accountability cause serious damage to missions and efforts toward prevention are worthwhile.

Second, in the case of some mission agencies minimal accountability structures can be a realistic alternative. Structures in themselves cannot guarantee the level of accountability, and in mission contexts accountability is not so much a matter of organizational control as of voluntary submission to one another. The voluntary spirit that embraces mutual submission can enhance accountability exercised through simple but effective accountability structures.

Third, respecting and practicing biblical principles are important foundations for accountability; they should be widely applied in mission practice. This point is not an abstract argument; it is a call for reflection on the issue of accountability under the illumination of the Spirit. It resonates well with the spirit of *coram Deo* that was mentioned previously.

Fourth, as a diagnostic tool, accountability checklists should be made and used to identify problems. Efforts of this type come from a humble mind-set that acknowledges that nobody is immune to failures in accountability and integrity. Checklists can be used personally for self-evaluation and reinforcement. Sometimes checklists can also be used to evaluate organizational practices internally. Use of checklists may serve to enhance personal/spiritual health and organizational best practice.

Fifth, mission agencies need good financial accounting systems. Double entry bookkeeping enabled financial assets to be better managed, thereby enhancing accountability. About ten years ago the Korea Research Institute for Mission developed an accounting system called M-Account. The M-Account system, however, needs significant upgrading in light of changes in OS versions. In order to advance and for innovation to continue, constant investment in this kind of detail is needed on the part of Korean missions.

Sixth, recognition is needed that spiritual life is the foundation of ministerial accountability. These two are not separate things; they are intimately connected. This perspective contrasts sharply with a secular perspective that conceives of accountability in terms of formal logic and regulations. Spiritual life should be expressed in the observation of regulations for accountability.

Seventh, respondents to the survey warned missionaries against indulging in frequent visits to their home country. In this globalized world, the need to visit home countries does arise, but in the eyes of mission executives, visits that are too frequent become a serious problem. Cautious review should be made of this phenomenon so as to learn the level of awareness that local supporters have of this phenomenon. Inevitably, there will be cases of visits to the home country because of health problems, visa extensions, home assignments, and other urgent matters, and such visits must be recognized as valid.

Eighth, systems should be established that call for periodic reports. Various observers report that Korean missionaries, especially those serving in indigenous Korean mission agencies, do not clearly understand or follow through on their responsibility to submit reports. As people who were officially sent, missionaries need to report to the mission agencies and churches, providing information on their activities, ministries, and plans. Too often reports are vague and need to be more informative.

Ninth, positive models of missional accountability need to be given recognition. Models that offer a good example can raise the general level of accountability. In this area as in others, provision of positive examples is more persuasive and productive than recitation of negative approaches. Examples of good practices of missional accountability on the part of individual missionaries, teams, mission agencies, and inter-organizational partnerships can be gathered and then shared in the missions circle for challenge and encouragement.

USING KEY INFORMANTS TO ENHANCE THE REFLECTION PROCESS

Reflection is not necessarily a private matter; it can be done as a corporate thought process. Key informant interviews can guide and provide systematic grounding for the reflection process. In addition to the points made and opinions shared via the survey conducted in December 2011, key informant interviews were conducted, up to the end of July 2012, before and while this chapter was being written. The key informants (ten persons altogether) were mission executives and senior missionaries with extensive experience. The interview questions focused on solutions to issues of missional accountability, considering both the contextual phenomena and the supracultural norms.

Different Perspectives

Key informants' answers to questions about missional accountability reflect different understandings and perspectives. The points of interest and emphasis for them differed. Field missionaries on home assignment tended to view accountability within a more comprehensive missional framework. They were more sympathetic with missionaries who have weaknesses in accountability than were mission executives. Field missionaries attribute failures in accountability (such as disputes over property) to systematic problems, including insufficient support from the home office and churches. Mission executives and administrators are more oriented toward policies and regulations. To them, many of the problems related to accountability are problems of integrity. These two perspectives clash with each other.

The differences between the outlook of field missionaries and the perspective of executives and administrators seem to be rooted in the two groups' different ministry positions and experience. Mission executives, not surprisingly, can be seen as gravitating toward bounded-set thinking, whereas missionaries are oriented toward centered-set thinking.[14] Missionaries are more relational, whereas mission executives are more policy-oriented. A focus on policy seems to be even more pronounced among executives of international mission agencies. Here a growing recognition among international mission agencies of the importance of integration and holistic views is encouraging. At first blush, people with a bounded-set worldview might seem to pursue accountability more rigorously, but at a deeper level people with a centered-set worldview often practice accountability with greater willingness of spirit. Both worldviews, however, have challenges—namely, the bounded-set worldview can devolve into legalism, while the centered-set worldview may be challenged by idolatry.[15] When properly understood these differences can become blessings. Emphasis on policies and regulations should not be allowed to fall into the pit of a judgmental spirit. Emphasis on relational aspects should not fall into the pit of loss of integrity.

Mission accountability is a mutual responsibility and should be undertaken reciprocally by each stake holder. We have considered missionaries' obligation to give account of their activities to their mission agencies, but mission agencies should also be accountable both to their member missionaries and to their supporting churches. Consideration

---

14. As noted in chapter 2, the cognitive category of bounded sets points to clear boundaries demarcating homogeneous groups. Bounded-set thinking, a cultural orientation characteristic of Westerners, can emphasize integrity but at the same time raises the potential for problems of legalism. Orientation of life and outlook by reference to a central value or person, which defines the cognitive category of centered sets, characterizes the cultural orientation of many Asian peoples, including the Korean people. People with a centered-set outlook tend to emphasize relationships. For the Korean people the concept of a boundary is not absent, but a person's relationship with the center has overriding importance. These cultural differences should be neither exaggerated nor underestimated. Both outlooks have strengths and weaknesses. Awareness among missiologists of the important distinction between bounded sets and centered sets is especially indebted to Paul Hiebert; see his *Anthropological Reflections on Missiological Issues* (Grand Rapids: Baker Books, 1994), 130–31.

15. Ibid., 115, 129.

of accountability should carry all the way through to include discussion of missionary exit strategy and how missionaries will be supported after retirement.

In order to establish a sound basis for mutual understanding, mission agencies need to set up good orientation programs at the very beginning. Orientation programs need to specify in detail the rights and obligations of member missionaries concerning certain assets, properties, projects, and ministries. Senior members need another kind of orientation before retirement. They must not be left to feel that they will not have anything to do, not have any place to stay, or not receive any support after retirement.

Gaps come to light when Korean missionaries work with foreign missionaries from other countries. They need to be addressed appropriately. What issues are cultural matters, and which are problems of integrity? Discernment is needed. Personal issues should not be vaguely passed over as being cultural characteristics. Teams need to check and review these types of things patiently and in a nonthreatening way. Cultural differences should be neither exaggerated nor underestimated.

When different perspectives intersect, we recognize our own limits and are led to invite divine intervention and orchestration by the Holy Spirit. In that sense accountability is not a purely systematic or organizational matter, but a spiritual matter. With the mediation of the Spirit, we can expect a harmonized perspective on common ground.

Common Ground

Key informants share a common recognition that the Korean missionary movement is shifting from passion to structure. The attention being given to accountability arises from concern to stabilize the movement through strengthening its structures. Structure for its own sake is not their overriding point of focus, but it is an important area of concern. Key informants evaluate the discussions that have taken place up to now very positively, considering them to be a necessary stage of the development of the missionary movement in Korea. To them, accountability is a hallmark of maturity.

Although systematic improvement through policies and protocols is important, voluntary pursuit of accountability is a more desirable and more realistic approach for voluntary organizations such as mission agencies. The foundation for a voluntary approach to accountability is integrity or cultivation of a *coram Deo* consciousness. A perfect system to secure transparency and accountability does not exist, but the motivation supplied by a desire for integrity can cause people to be accountable before God and other people. Our relationship with God and his people should propel us toward accountability. Seen in this light, the relational aspect of accountability is not always negative; it can work positively as well. Genuine Christian spirituality finds normative expression in integrity and accountability.

Gaps exist between ideals and practices surrounding children's education, nationality, home schooling, and other areas, but good prioritizing can assist in overcoming these differences. Having a true sense of order and putting first things first enables us to overcome chaos and confusion. Through our efforts to establish priorities, we can experience clarification and purification on our pilgrimage. Our children's education is important, but it is not the top priority. On the mission field, adjustments to a different national school system and a different language of instruction at times present problems of which we need to be aware. When the local school system is inadequate, home schooling can offer a good alternative, but resorting to home schooling is questionable if other good schooling options are available. This issue and many others are actually issues of priority. To missionaries, ministry is the highest priority and comes first before other things, not the other way around. When we prioritize well, we can overcome temptations.

Another area of common ground in our understandings about accountability is the importance of communal missiological reflection. The term "communal" is important and is in line with Hiebert's notion of an international hermeneutical community.[16] By being communal, we can enjoy the richness of missiological reflection. Corporate reflection helps us to measure our life and ministry against ideal standards and to focus our practices. The expression "missiological reflection" assumes the need for an integrative effort through which we can find the right places where our fragmentary knowledge related to missional life and work

---

16. Ibid., 30.

fits together. Reflection is an all-inclusive process of thinking toward best practices in ministry. Reflection and practice should be synergistic, working hand in hand.

Through the process of education, many opposing views can be drawn into harmony and conflicts resolved. Continuing education is a great need so as to improve ministries in the fields. Though pre-field training covers many things, it is not enough. Higher-level educational programs are necessary to meet the need for leadership development. From a long-term perspective, it is important that missionaries' experiences be theorized, that is, that they be used as building blocks for the creation of instructive mission theories. For these purposes, continuing education programs are helpful. A significant educational need is to teach pastors and church leaders to understand better the changed realities of global missions, so that they can partner fruitfully with their missionaries. At present, pastors' low level of missiological knowledge is a hindrance to the maturation of the missions movement in Korea. It may be the same with theologians in other fields.[17] Missionaries need to help to educate leaders who make important decisions regarding mission assignments and activities but lack proper missiological knowledge and a humble spirit.

Practical Solutions

True reflection on missiological issues should find expression in concrete practical suggestions. Considering both the differences and commonalities in understanding that we have seen, how can we flesh out practical solutions for accountability issues? Though not every problem can be resolved at once, some important issues should be dealt with at this stage in the growth of the Korean missions movement.

A first-order need is to redefine and normalize the function of the boards of mission agencies. In many cases, mission agency boards consist of pastors and church leaders who became involved because of a

---

17. As Andrew Walls well states, one is tempted to suggest that the missionary movement affected every department of scholarship—except theology. See Andrew F. Walls, *The Cross-Cultural Process in Christian History* (Maryknoll, N.Y.: Orbis Books, 2002), 42.

prior personal relationship with the agency leader. Often such boards lack expertise in missions and unsurprisingly are passive in the decision making process. Persons who possess differences in expertise and background make boards more robust. Many Korean mission agency boards do not have enough female members. Sometimes boards are too large; they have too many members to allow different voices to be heard in the meetings.

Good procedures are necessary for evaluating megaprojects such as universities, hospitals, or other projects requiring construction on the field. Too many times a mission project is the innovation of one visionary with everyone else expected to follow along and support the project. Such a management style is not healthy. During the process of planning, experts who know the situation well should be consulted. Unexamined projects often are ineffective and inefficient in relation to their cost. When megaprojects are launched by megachurches, these needs become even greater; church leaders need to invite mission leaders from outside to serve as consultants. A needs assessment should be included in the pre-project evaluation process; this step can be carried out by a third party if objective internal evaluation is not available. In Korea, these needs—of evaluation, needs assessment, and consulting—are, unfortunately, too often neglected by mission agencies and churches.

Overall, the field structures established by indigenous Korean mission agencies seem weak. Too often missionaries are not assigned as a team, but according to individual preferences. They often have minimal supervision, which impairs their ability to form and properly operate intense field structures. Korean mission agencies need to adopt thoroughgoing use of team structures in place of their present practice of sporadic dispersion of their missionaries in the field. Teams may not necessarily be tightly-knit—with common vision, purposes, and activities—but at least strategic frameworks of ministry should be shared. Korean missionaries serving in international mission agencies face different issues, such as adapting to the organizational culture of an international team. They need to learn to practice bounded-set thinking in order to play their roles within Western-dominant organizations.

Key informants emphasized that field-oriented communication between missionaries and home leaders is necessary, a point they illustrated by citing cases of frustration. Younger missionaries are impatient with one-way communication, which they consider outmoded and outdated; they want to be heard by the leaders. Mission executives are always mindful of overall policies, regulations, and agreements, but field missionaries have in view their concrete case, their people, and the reality of their ministry. The two groups need to expend effort to understand each other. For two-way traffic in communication to occur, leaders' listening ears are more important than anything else. Intergenerational issues are involved here, too, but mutual respect will open up channels of communication and keep them open.

Regarding property ownership, missionaries and mission agencies need to understand and communicate the terms and conditions clearly from the beginning. Drawing up a contract or memorandum of understanding is a realistic way of preventing possible misunderstandings. For the sake of accountability within the organization, mission agency boards need to examine and oversee these important procedures. When disputes arise between a missionary and the agency, the board must exercise ultimate authority or delegate its decision to other units, such as a subcommittee. Instead of showing a judgmental spirit, mediators need to patiently and wisely facilitate honest conversation and to seek for win-win solutions.

Disputes over property ownership are not a stand-alone issue; they are intertwined with missionaries' fears and anxieties about retirement. Korean mission agencies are not well prepared in planning for the retirement of their missionary members. They do not have enough housing, funding, and resources to care for returning missionaries. Missionaries' fear and anxiety cause them to depend on properties and other resources that were dedicated to other purposes. By preparing infrastructures and systems for retirement wisely, we can supply missionaries with a sense of security. This task, however, is not easy for mission agencies to approach on their own. Megachurches need to help the agencies in planning and preparing a good retirement for missionaries.

Accountability is part of leadership development. In order to build sound accountability structures, leadership development is needed at multiple levels. The need is significant, requiring strategic investment of resources. To address this need, mission agencies and seminaries should partner with each other. The doctor of missiology program of the Korea Global Leadership Institute (KGLI) provides a good example of a partnership between the Global Missionary Fellowship (GMF) and Malaysia Baptist Theological Seminary. Leaders are needed not just as supervisors of ministry, but also as providers of member care. Accountable member care requires the presence of good team leaders, country coordinators, area directors, and field directors. Strategic investment is urgently needed to redress deficiencies in this significant area. Though not a visible area of investment, leadership development is more important than any visible infrastructure for ministry. Investments in producing visible artifacts should be reconsidered and redirected to be used for leadership development, which is invisible but crucial.

CONCLUSION

Although accountability as a term or concept is not totally foreign to Korea, discussions of it are countercultural to a significant degree. Mission leaders' main concern has been to find appropriate methods for achieving accountability. To do missions well we need to reinforce our systems, operations, and perceptions. The relational aspect of Korean culture sometimes hinders putting in place a set of best practices for organizations and systems. This problem, however, cannot be addressed linear-logically by imposing a top-down style of communication. Mission executives and missiologists have begun to discuss these issues; further discussions should be begun at the grassroots level among missionaries in the field. This process can be viewed as a painful part of self-recognition; ultimately, it will be health giving, strengthening and reinforcing to the missionary movement.

In today's culture of individualism and postmodernity, the pursuit of accountability is also countercultural. Also, the psychological dynamics of the younger generation may not fit well with the normative dimension of accountability, but for the sake of our values, we need to overcome current trends in public outlook. Accountability helps us to avoid the idolatry of ego. Accountability is inseparable from integrity, which is indispensible for Christian ministry. Accountability builds up integrity, and vice versa. Accountability is an expression of true

Christian spirituality. We believe that nobody is immune to error, and thus we need one another and a spirit of togetherness. This humble spirit works as an antidote against the subtle poison of worshiping the leader.[18] To merit respect leadership requires accountability to the laity.

Accountability is not solely a practical issue of dollars and cents. Do we need accountability also in doing theology? Some have considered doing theology to be a private matter, but can we understand theologizing as communal work? Theology is truncated if its does not interact with real churches and real people where they live. The practice of accountability can help us to focus our task of theologizing within real contexts. What has been said applies to the concept of contextualization as well. If we are accountable, we will most likely also contextualize well. Therefore, we can say that the issue of accountability is not a totally new agenda, but is a newly caught old problem.

One implication of current discussion of accountability is that it is a voluntary effort undertaken for the maturation of the Korean missionary movement. Passionate mission leaders had a sufficient sense of their own vulnerability to lead them to bring the issue out into the open. They expressed teachability and were humble enough to discuss the problems involved. They were not quickly satisfied with impressive success stories. In some sense, the two forums discussed above marked a large paradigm shift in Korean missions from focus on quantitative growth to concern for qualitative growth. Korean participants in KGLMF 2011 especially showed true courage by admitting to and sharing openly about areas of weakness in being Korean. Again, this step was countercultural since it overcame the mentality of saving face within ourselves which is a characteristic of Korean culture.

KGMLF 2011 marked the first major missiological period of reflection on the topic of accountability within the Korean missions circle since 2005. The Second Bangkok Forum, in 2005, showed that Korean missioners could discuss and resolve practical problems through missiological reflection by way of self-theologizing.[19] KGMLF is evidence that Korean missioners can reflect and discuss at the global level.

---

18. Hiebert, *Anthropological Reflections*, 130.
19. Ibid., 96–97.

Their missiological reflection actively dealt with real issues and problems. Missiological reflection and argumentation focused on critical issues in Korean missions seems to be very timely in the sovereignty of God. Checking up on and improving missions accountability can prevent possible future missions fatigue among Korean churches. The survey and key informant interviews reported here provide evidence that Korean missionaries and mission leaders sometimes have different perspectives, yet they are grounded on a common basis and seem to believe solutions are possible for the problems they face.

As a new missions force which experienced explosive growth over the past twenty-five years, Korean missions are now striving for maturation. Indeed, maturation seems to be a condition for future growth both numerically and qualitatively. The King of Glory, the Lord of Heaven's Armies, reigns and guides the course of history for the mission work from Korea (Psalm 24:10). Amen.

17
THE PROMISE, LIMITATION, AND FUTURE OF EMPIRICAL RESEARCH IN MISSIONS

Empirical research holds promise for missions. The Korean missionary movement needs to recognize its importance for strategic ministries in many parts of the world. Still empirical research has limitations; it cannot resolve every problem. We need to find a balance between the promise and the limitations of empirical research as we envision its future within missiology. This chapter is devoted to the articulation of the promises, limitations, and developmental issues of field-based empirical research in missions.

THE PROMISE OF EMPIRICAL RESEARCH

Missions take place in real contexts; therefore, missiology is a field-oriented theological discipline. Both the field orientation of missions and of missiology justify empirical field research which, in fact, is essential for the development of missionary practice.

This perspective is clarified when we look at it from a biblical perspective. Numbers 13:1 shows us a research expedition prompted by a mandate from God. God wants his people to be active in approaching the land of promise, not remaining passive. Bold hope and trials are desired. Entry into the land is something to be accomplished rather than given. God orders an empirical research project to be followed up under Moses' leadership.

The promises of empirical research are summarized in seven points below.

Originally published in *Korean Missions Quarterly*, English ed. (2012): 144–51, this chapter has been edited and is reprinted by permission.

First, empirical research clarifies the purpose of ministry. Without concrete contextual understanding, the purpose of ministry can be blurred. Conceptual planning based on abstract norms may lead to setting unrealistic goals. Empirical research enables concrete and realistic goal setting. Missionaries experience disappointment and frustration when they set unrealistic and excessive goals that cannot be obtained. Empirical research facilitates goal setting that encourages realistic and relevant efforts and approaches to ministry.

Second, empirical research helps identify relevant methods of ministry. Research serves creative functions; empirical research does so to an even greater degree. Clear ministry goals do not guarantee identification of ministry methods. Concrete approaches to ministry can be identified through empirical research. Solid research helps us to foresee possible breakthroughs in missionary service. Missiological reflection needs to focus on methodological articulation rather than development of abstract norms. Abstract theoretical discussion without contextual and methodological consideration is not worthy of attention in this fast-moving age. We need to discuss how to accomplish goals effectively. Consciousness of this need leads us to attempt field-based empirical research in various ministry contexts.

Third, empirical research stimulates innovation in ministry. An easygoing outlook has been a missional problem in every age of mission history. Faithfulness in our ministry contexts leads us to pursue innovation so as to overcome an easygoing outlook. Innovation is needed more urgently in missionary service than in the business world. True innovation requires a creative mind. I believe true creativity is derived from a researcher mindset. Empirical research stimulates creative yet realistic consciousness which drives the course of innovation.

Fourth, empirical research promotes team ministry by showing how to apportion the various tasks. We can look into the details of ministry tasks for a deeper understanding of them in order to assign different roles to relevant workers. This will enhance team ministry. By using a research mindset in making decisions about role assignments, mission leaders will be more objective and be more able to guard against subjective judgments. Empirical research also equips leaders with a big-picture mindset, strengthens strategic coordination, and enhances managerial apportionment of tasks according to team members' gifts and expertise. Engaging a researcher's mindset is an important part of strategizing missionary endeavors.

Fifth, empirical research lays a foundation for contextualization. Our message and approach have many transcultural principles in common, but some needs differ from context to context. To "become all things to all people" is an incarnational mindset we should seek to have in order to be like Christ (1 Cor. 9:22). Contextualized ministries overcome ethnocentrism and communicate the Gospel in relevant ways. Contextualization is God's strategy, God's methodology, and God's wisdom. Such an important mandate demands an empirical approach because real people live within real cultural constraints; therefore, again an emphasis on empirical research is needed.

Sixth, empirical research increases effectiveness and efficiency in ministry. Empirical explorations not only suggest relevant means and skills for ministry, but also indicate the right ways toward best practices. Effectiveness toward achieving goals and efficient use of resources are reasonably pursued through the process of empirical research. The pursuit of effectiveness and efficiency is nothing but the modern expression of biblical stewardship. Missionaries need to be aware of the importance of effectiveness and efficiency in ministry in terms of doing their best and utmost. By doing empirical research, we can figure out how to work wisely in a given situation.

Seventh, empirical research prevents the repetition of trial and error. Many cases of trial and error in different contexts are caused by a lack of historical understanding. Empirical research, in contrast, considers historical cases of mistakes in order to prevent the repetition of the same errors in later generations. In this sense, historical data can be analyzed as part of ethnographic research in a particular cultural context. Understanding of the past provides the light of wisdom and offers insight into present issues. Present research bears fruit in improvement for the future. Research with past, present, and future perspectives stimulates and catalyzes progress in ministry.

This emphasis on the importance of empirical research does not deny the limitations of research. Honest researchers always clearly recognize the limitations of any particular approach. Empirical research itself does have limitations.

THE LIMITATION OF EMPIRICAL RESEARCH

Human experience is limited. As humans encounter the world, they process information received through the senses, interpreting that information through cultural prisms and thereby augmenting the accumulation of human knowledge. Epistemologically, human beings are like neither a photograph nor a collage. Human knowing is more like a montage.[20] Human epistemological limitations set limits for empirical research. The question of limits is not an abstract issue, but a realistic matter. The case of the twelve people who explored the land of Canaan in Numbers 13 shows the need to think, analyze, interpret, and judge in light of the covenant of God. The seven points that follow summarize the limitations of empirical research in twenty-first-century missional contexts.

First, empirical research cannot study the transcendental spiritual world directly. The biblical worldview revealed in Scripture provides necessary access to supernatural dimensions. No matter how reasonable a social scientific study may sound, biblical truth has priority. When empirical findings clash with biblical teaching, biblical truth is our ultimate authority. This view, in my opinion, is the foundation of the evangelical understanding of cultures and phenomena. We must base empirical research on biblical principles.

Second, empirical research cannot study extrasensory historical realities directly. People rely on historical records, which are always incomplete, and they are biased by particular historical viewpoints. Limited records and therefore limited access to the facts of history leads empirical research to concentrate on synchronic analysis of presently available data. Historians and historical research are better equipped to deal with such historical issues, though historical knowledge is always imperfect. Interdisciplinary studies complement each other and

---

20. Paul G. Hiebert, *Anthropological Reflections on Missiological Issues* (Grand Rapids: Baker, 1994), 23, 40.

therefore can address many issues more effectively than can any single discipline by itself.

Third, empirical research is not free from methodological limitations. Any research method has limitations that affect its validity and reliability. No research method is free of limitations. The problem is how to identify and reduce the limitations. For quantitative studies the issue is how to analyze correlations in a systematic yet realistic way. In qualitative studies the issues of neutral and objective analysis and interpretation of data stand out. We need to be aware of each research method's possible strengths and weaknesses, coupled with wise and educated effort, if we are to reduce the limitations inherent in any particular research approach.

Fourth, empirical research does not completely reflect an emic view. Even qualitative research approaches do not guarantee a completely emic view, that is, a view uncontaminated by outside perspectives. Intercultural studies, therefore, are not free from biases introduced by outsiders' viewpoints. It would probably be idealistic to expect missionaries to achieve a fully insider perspective, but that is required for deeper cultural exegesis. The point here is to acknowledge that the outsider's perspective interferes with authentic cultural hermeneutics.

Fifth, empirical research faces time limitations. Even though it takes a significant amount of time for a researcher to attain an emic view, most intercultural researchers spend only limited amounts of time in the field. Short stays allow only superficial analyses and understandings. Because the number of expatriate experts present in the field is insufficient, flaws in research findings often fail to come to light. For in-depth analysis of data, intercultural researchers need to stay in the field for at least six months; staying a few years would be much better. Significant research findings and theoretical suggestions cannot be generated from one week of fieldwork.

Sixth, empirical research is not free from linguistic limitations. Short periods of fieldwork, in many cases, do not provide sufficient time for advanced language acquisition capable of nuanced communication. Too often interviews are conducted in an international language, such as English. This limitation often is true even for researchers who are familiar with the host culture. Sometimes learning a local language is essential, but in many contexts the alternative of interviewing through a translator is necessary. This linguistic issue is increasingly a constraint that must be accepted, however much one could wish otherwise.

Seventh, empirical research often faces sampling problems. In many intercultural situations, a probability sampling is impossible to obtain. Sometimes research populations are too small or too complex to draw a probability sample. This sampling limitation inhibits empirical missiological research, and thus, solid academic research is not easily found in mission circles. Sampling problems are even more serious in quantitative approaches. Too many inaccurate statistical reports have been drawn from unscientific research procedures. Constraints on sampling in qualitative research are less rigid, but a sound rationale must be given that relates the process of theoretical sampling to the overall research design. Honest researchers will acknowledge this limitation.

Empirical research does have limitations, as we have seen. These limitations, however, do not cancel out the promises or possibilities it has to offer. The realities of research call us to find a balance between the positive and negative sides. From this balance we can pursue further development, and we can identify developmental issues to be faced. These steps are important to the mission enterprise; therefore, they are also in themselves important *missionary* tasks.

THE FUTURE OF EMPIRICAL RESEARCH

The limitations of empirical research, as in the case of failure recorded in Numbers 13, should not be allowed to obscure its necessity in ministry. Rather, solid research based on covenantal faith is all the more needed in our ministry. Considering both the promise and the limitations of empirical research, we need to pursue wisdom realistically. We need to focus on how to improve the practice of empirical research. The following suggestions are drawn both from other researchers' suggestions and from my own experience.

First, missionaries need to consider empirical research as a valid form of ministry. Missionaries' long-term experience in an intercultural setting is a good foundation for empirical research, but long-term experience alone does not, in and of itself, bear tangible research fruit.

The reason is that most missionaries neither prioritize research nor learn research methods. Mission agencies need to guide selected members by designing proper training in research methods and developing relevant policies. Missionary training centers also need to strengthen area studies and intercultural research.

Second, seminaries need to encourage their students to base their theses, projects, and dissertations on empirical research. Korean seminaries are still weak in harnessing empirical research for their theological and missiological studies. Missiological writings need to be based on empirical field research. For this reason, mission professors need to master empirical research methods themselves. Professors of mission theology and mission history tend to be especially unfamiliar with empirical research; therefore, they need reinforcement in this field. Missiologists and researchers in mission anthropology need to keep up-to-date with the development of research methods in their fields.

Third, international research networks should extend their scope to include empirical research. The present research institutes in missions are mostly information centers serving simple functions such as information gathering and dissemination. Globally, only a limited number of mission research centers are capable of designing and performing independent academic empirical research. In light of these limitations, research institutes and centers need to cooperate with one another by doing joint projects that cross cultural and organizational boundaries. Domestically, Korean mission agencies need to emphasize empirical research, support research projects, and apply research findings in their policy-making. As research becomes a common concern used for strategic planning and evaluation, Korean missions will be able to accumulate expertise and competency for long-term development.

Fourth, constraints on the mission field, more often than not, make evident the need for qualitative research approaches. The research designs and strategies used for data gathering and analysis, however, need to be made more rigorous so as to enhance the development of qualitative research. To optimize intercultural research, researchers need to critically evaluate the methods they use and to adopt new approaches in ethnographic research when appropriate. Training is important, for the danger of subjectivity is high if researchers lack proper grounding in ethnographic research methods. Training programs for both mission practitioners and students of mission are presently available.

Fifth, researchers and research institutes need to master both qualitative and quantitative research methods and approaches.[21] Quantitative research demands a thorough understanding of statistically based analytic models. Regardless of the limitations inherent to research conducted in an international setting, such as weakness in the representativeness of samples, use of probability sampling needs to be optimized. Missiological research needs committed experts in statistical analysis, which, in turn, requires that churches and mission organizations support them by providing relevant working environments. This area will demand long-term investment.

Sixth, expatriate researchers need to work with national researchers in empirical research. Even missionaries resident in the field have only a limited sense of the emic view. Therefore, national researchers need to be recruited and trained to work as members of research teams. At times, national researchers should take the lead in conducting intercultural research projects. Today the quality of empirical research is increasingly dependent on the presence of the emic view that is provided by national researchers. In today's complex world it is essential that diverse cultural perspectives be involved throughout the entire research process. For this to happen, international missions circles need to invest in training researchers within the younger missionary sending countries.

Seventh, research grants need to be established to foster empirical research in missions. The environments for missional research institutes in the majority world are not stable and secure. Only a small number of researchers engage in and continue in this ministry because of a sense of calling. Through support of strategic research projects, research grants can facilitate long-term and macro developments in missions. Such efforts are concrete and productive investments for cultivating missional know-how. Too often funds go only to visible assets such as buildings and facilities. We must recognize the enormous need for investment in nonvisible assets such as knowledge of the future.

---

21. Paul G. Hiebert, *The Gospel in Human Contexts: Anthropological Explorations for Contemporary Missions* (Grand Rapids: Baker Academic, 2009), 162–64.

CONCLUSION

Empirical research has both promise and limitations. The question is how to harness its potential in creative ways. A creative mind does not separate ministry and research, but integrates them. Research and ministry must go together! Research must serve ministry! There are too many cases of ministry without research as well as too many cases of research without ministry. Research and ministry must be done in a reciprocal fashion, guided by the ideal of "reflective practitioners."[22] Missions require deep thinking if transformation at the worldview level is to occur.[23] Commitment to a particular missional task calls for investment in research to accomplish it.[24] Strategizing based on empirical research can be useful for revitalizing the Korean missionary movement in many parts of the world.

---

22. William D. Taylor, "From Iguassu to the Reflective Practitioners of the Global Family of Christ," in *Global Missiology for the 21st Century: The Iguassu Dialogue*, ed. William D. Taylor (Grand Rapids: Baker Academic, 2000), 5–6.

23. Paul G. Hiebert, *Transforming Worldviews: An Anthropological Understanding of How People Change* (Grand Rapids: Baker Academic, 2008), 89–104.

24. Stan Nussbaum, *Breakthrough! Steps to Research and Resolve the Mysteries in Your Ministry* (Colorado Springs, Colo.: GMI Research Services, 2007), 148–49.

18

MISSIONARY FAMILIES AND KOREAN MISSION FINANCE: Realities and Concerns

In a face-saving culture, people do not talk openly about money. In Korea, finances are considered an internal concern of families and organizations, which is the case also for Korean churches and Korean mission agencies. Financial matters are critical, however, to ministry at home and abroad, for they significantly impact missionary families across the board. A more open and candid consideration of finances would therefore benefit both the organizations and the individuals who have committed themselves to advance the mission of God worldwide.

The discussion that follows provides detailed analysis of the financial realities and issues facing Korean missions. This analysis is based on a quantitative survey and a qualitative research project, both conducted by the Korea Research Institute for Mission (KRIM). These efforts tackle for the first time the realities of finance in Korean missions. The quantitative data was gathered with the assistance of KRIM's staff during December 2012, when twenty-two mission agencies responded to a survey. The qualitative data has been drawn from individual interviews carried out during February 2013; thirty-five missionaries representing nine mission agencies were interviewed. Of the thirty-five interviews, twenty-two were conducted with missionaries on furlough, nine with mission executives, and four with members of the home staff.[1]

Originally published as "Missionary Families and Korean Mission Finance: Realities and Concerns," in *Family Accountability in Missions: Korean and Western Case Studies*, ed. Jonathan J. Bonk (New Haven, Conn.: OMSC Publications, 2013), 138–48, this chapter is reprinted by permission.

1. Unless stated otherwise, the information given below is based on these survey and interview projects. The interview records are on file at the KRIM office.

FINANCING KOREAN MISSIONS: AN OVERVIEW

A statistical analysis of microtrends within Korean missions and of the missions' financial status was published in the April 2013 issue of the *International Bulletin of Missionary Research*.[2] As the report outlines, in 2012 a total of $363 million was channeled through mission agencies for 19,798 Korean missionaries. (All figures throughout are in U.S. dollars.) In the period 2009–12 mission finance increased annually by 4.3 percent, while the annual increase in personnel was only 2.4 percent.

Sources of financial support for missions are local churches (41.6 percent), individual supporters (34.9 percent), organizations (9.8 percent), and others (13.7 percent). Mission finances were expended for missionaries' living costs (41.9 percent), field ministry (23.9 percent), home administrative office costs (13.2 percent), organizational projects (2.8 percent), and other general purposes (18.2 percent).

The average monthly expenditure for living costs for a four-person missionary family was $1,518, ranging from a minimum of $376 to a maximum of $2,352. The average monthly cost for the education of two children in a four-person family was $556, ranging from a low of $188 to a high of $941. The average ministry fund, that is, money allocated to cover ministry-related expenses, was $812, with a spread extending from $282 to $1,881.

When the size of the Korean missionary force is considered, we can see that the funds available to Korean mission agencies are not large. Most of these financial resources are used to support missionaries' life and work in the field, and they are not sufficient to support adding new missionaries while still caring for those who are already on the field. Mission agencies have neither the financial surplus in current income nor the reserves to cover missionaries' future needs, such as support in retirement.

Disparity in the size of the monthly allowances paid to Korean missionaries is a particular problem. Mission agencies' financial policies and the ways they make use of missionaries focus on individuals rather than

---

2. Steve Sang-Cheol Moon, "Missions from Korea 2013: Microtrends and Finance," *International Bulletin of Missionary Research* 37, no. 2 (April 2013): 96–97.

on their total missionary community. Voluntary sharing could overcome the disparity in missionaries' financial support, alleviating the suffering of many missionary families whose support level is low. A more fundamental way of solving the problem of the uneven distribution of funds would be to treat separately the additional income needed to cover the costs of educating missionary children and perhaps other specific financial needs.

EXPERIENCES OF FINANCIAL SUPPORT

In general, the Korean missionaries interviewed expressed positive opinions about the financial support they receive for their personal living costs and ministry in the field. For the majority, their financial support has been neither too low nor too high. In past years their financial needs have been met appropriately. Almost all of the thirty-five interviewees exhibited a firm belief that the living God, using various channels, had provided providentially for their needs, and they endorse a faith mission approach as providing a viable ethos and financial policy for modern missions.

Most of the interviewees were positive about financial support, not because their monthly allowance has been large, but because they have been able to adjust their living standard and expenses to match their income. The majority, however, have never received the full allowance set by the field team or home administration for their living expenses and the costs of their ministry. Rather, they have found ways to limit their expenditures to necessities such as housing, food, education of their children, and transportation. A few of those interviewed said that they have managed to survive though they were receiving only 60 percent of their designated monthly support amount. A representative of one mission agency reported that only 10 family units, out of 380 families supported, received over $47,000 annually, and that 40 units had required special additional support, for they received less than $11,300 annually.

One missionary to a Central Asian country said that the support his family received was a half or a third of that received by a typical Western missionary family in the same area. It made no sense to him that a Western missionary family had left the field because they felt that the $4,000 they received per month was insufficient, while a Korean missionary family in the same area could easily live on this amount. The experience of the Western missionary family may have been exceptional, but Korean missions must seek to ensure that it is not replicated among Korean missionaries. The financial realities and living standards of Korean missionaries do not reflect the ideal amount set for their support. Many of the missionaries interviewed said that they had lived within the amount of support they received, although some others had been unable to do so. Many missionaries' accounts with mission agencies are overdrawn.

Assistance from the families of missionaries often serves to fill the gap left by agency support. The parents and siblings of missionaries often provide support, covering the costs of their (grand)children's education and meeting other personal family needs. This funding is either channeled through the official missionary account or sent directly to the missionary's private account. This situation is sometimes reversed, as some missionaries provide financial support for elderly parents in Korea who do not have an income source other than their children. In many ways, family ties are often an important element in the financial lives of missionaries.

Personal relationships are key to raising financial support from churches and individuals. Mission agencies honor this reality insofar as they work to introduce missionaries to churches and potential supporters. In almost all links between missionaries and supporters, direct personal acquaintance is primary. Relationship is not the only factor, but without good relational ties, missionaries will not be able to raise support based solely on their missionary vision.

According to the missionaries interviewed, support from Korean churches and individual Christians is generally consistent only as long as relations between supporter and missionary remain relatively unchanged. New financial commitments and new personnel at the supporting church can have an impact on that relationship. Many Korean churches stop financial support for missionaries temporarily or permanently in order to cover some of the costs for construction of new buildings. New senior pastors may reduce financial support or even end it completely for missionaries with whom they are unfamiliar. A change in the missionary's situation or ministry role can also affect the relationship with a supporting church. Most of the mission executives interviewed had been disadvantaged by returning home to take up leadership roles in mission agencies. Missionaries pursuing higher degrees while on furlough or study leave have found their support from churches reduced. Low esteem for, or lack of awareness of, the significance of leadership roles within mission agencies inhibits the development of leadership within mission agencies.

God's own provision has come to Korean missionaries through various channels, and many churches and individual supporters have been faithful in their support. Lack of consistency in the support offered by many other local churches, however, produces instability and creates severe problems.

FINANCIAL EXPECTATIONS

Estimations of the future financial needs of Korean missions have increased drastically. Three principal factors have shaped this changed outlook: new missionaries are finding it hard to raise support; the cost of university education for missionary kids (MKs) is growing larger; and increased funding is needed to underwrite the development of field ministry. The future of Korean mission finance does not look bright.

Research carried out by KRIM suggests a net growth in the missionary force of 425 persons in 2012. Together these missionaries will require approximately $7.8 million per year in added financial support.[3] Raising such support for overseas ministries, however, has become increasingly challenging. Many churches find that their income is stagnating and that they are therefore unable to support any new missionaries. Only a fairly small number of megachurches are in a position to expand their missionary support. Many new missionaries depart for the field despite lacking sufficient support, with vague hopes that

---

3. This figure is calculated on the basis of the figures cited above, which show the average annual costs for a missionary to be $18,335 ($363 million divided by 19,798).

additional backing will be forthcoming once they are in place. Mission administrators are unwilling and powerless to rigidly require full support before these missionaries are able to leave for the field.

Currently, the average monthly educational cost for a Korean MK is approximately $278. Many mission executives and field missionaries predict that this figure will increase sharply because many MKs will begin university in the near future. Korean parents normally pay for their children's education through university, a burden for which Korean missionaries are not prepared. Most of the interviewees stated that, like many other Korean missionaries they know, they are not prepared for the additional costs of their children's education. My calculations suggest that within ten years over 7,000 Korean MKs will be of university age.[4] Only one missionary couple among those interviewed said that they have means in place, through funding given by their siblings, to cover the future educational costs of their children.

My analysis of the missionary population by age group makes evident the need for retirement planning. In 2012 Korean missionaries aged fifty or older formed 35.6 percent of all Korean missionaries, up from 24.4 percent in 2008. Retirement is perceived as a distant reality by many Korean missionaries, but in fact over 1,400 Korean missionaries will face that reality within the next ten years, and over 7,000 within the next twenty years.[5] The interviewees expressed their conviction

---

4. As of December 2012, there were 8,346 Korean missionaries in their forties. Research I conducted in 2004 suggested that the number of MKs could be calculated as 86.59 percent of missionaries; see Steve Sang-Cheol Moon, "The Spiritual Halryu: The Status and Issues of Korean Missions" (in Korean), 2004, http://krim.org/zbbs/zboard.php?id=openpds&page=2&sn1=&divpage=1&sn= off&ss=on&sc=on&select_arrange=headnum&desc=asc&no=62, an unpublished report on the Korean missionary movement posted on the KRIM website. I have therefore calculated that these Korean missionaries in their forties have 7,226 children, who will be of an age to go to university within in the next ten years.

5. Retirement age varies from agency to agency, and mission agencies in Korea are increasingly extending the retirement age from sixty-five to seventy. For my calculations I have used seventy as the age of retirement. My research suggests that 7.2 percent of Korean missionaries were in their sixties and 28.3 percent were in their fifties in December 2012. My estimation of the number of retiring missionaries is conservative.

that God would care for them in their old age. Such trust is appropriate, yet it is sobering that only a small number of churches have any specific plans to support their missionaries in retirement.

The ministries of Korean missionaries are developing rapidly and will therefore need to draw on additional means in the future. The list is long: church planters need outside assistance, educators need infrastructure and facilities, humanitarian endeavors need systematic and regular aid, business-related projects need seed money and investment, and so forth. When local communities and teams become self-supporting, these needs will decrease, but at present new projects depend largely on support garnered by Korean missionaries from Korean churches.

Moving in step with the Holy Spirit, we must plan and prepare for the future of our ministries and our missionaries. In so doing, we will prevent future suffering on the part of Korean missionaries and their children.

IMPROVING FINANCIAL SUPPORT

The research carried out at KRIM has sounded an early warning. Its results enable us to map out paths to provide adequate financial support for Korean missionaries. Individual missionaries, mission agencies, and supporting churches can all take steps to this end.

What Can Missionaries Do?

Korean missionaries need to become more involved in tentmaking, or bivocational, ministries, which would not only cover part of their costs but also create opportunities for relationship building with local people at the grassroots level. Over the years the Korean missionary movement has produced various models of tentmaking ministry. Almost all the missionaries who are part of Campus Ministry International (CMI) are able to support their families through their secular jobs, for example, as diplomats or embassy staff, employees of Korean companies, engineers, nurses, and factory or restaurant workers.[6] According to Jung Sik Lee,

---

6. CMI is a campus ministry that grew out of University Bible Fellowship in 2003. It has 628 missionaries in 138 countries.

president of CMI, 90 percent of CMI's member missionaries are financially independent. They have other concerns about their ministry such as prefield training, member care, and cooperation and partnership with other mission agencies, but many of their ministries, like those of Stephen Kang in Lithuania and Gideon Kim in Estonia, are bearing fruit. Other Korean mission agencies and missionaries should introduce upgraded tentmaking ministries in new contexts, looking to the new missiological concept of Business As Mission.

Korean missionaries need to use project funds more effectively and more efficiently and to be wary of large-scale and expensive projects. Attempts to establish schools and hospitals in the field are often poorly understood at home and receive limited support from Korean churches and organizations because such projects become unrealistic in scale. All too often a needs assessment is omitted from the planning process, and not infrequently no allowance is made for ongoing institutional costs.

Korean overseas missionaries need to teach and apply the three-self principle of John Nevius—that new churches planted should move in the direction of becoming self-governing, self-supporting, and self-propagating—even as they shape this concept to fit this new, global age. In their own history, Korean churches have witnessed and cherished the fruits of the three-self principle, but many Korean missionaries seem to forget it in their own overseas ministries. Field ministries and projects should be sustainable after missionaries have left the field.

Korean missionaries need to give more attention to avoiding duplication of effort. They need to pursue cooperation and partnership with other teams in the field, which will allow them to save resources and to use their financial reserves more strategically. An increasing number of supporting churches and organizations look favorably on joint projects carried out by more than one missionary team.

Korean missionaries need to plan for their children's university education more realistically. Many MKs have vague expectations of financial support from colleges and universities in the United States. Some who do receive scholarships covering their tuition find the cost of living to be dauntingly high. It is part of Korean culture to place a high value on education, but Korean missionaries need to plan astutely and realistically for their children's education.

What Can Mission Agencies Do?

Korean mission agencies need to determine their optimal size on the basis of their ability to care for their members rather than in competition with other agencies. Member-care systems are still in the development stage, and there are insufficient specialists to provide support for the increasing number of scarred and wounded missionaries who require their care. If Korean mission agencies feel a need to compete with one another, that contest should focus on the quality of their member services.

Korean mission agencies need to screen missionary candidates carefully, including looking carefully at their finances. Too many applicants cannot find a church with the financial means to support them in the field. The mission agency itself may not be able to provide the necessary member care. When screening standards are too low, field ministry, team unity, and the soundness of the mission agency itself are undermined. The Korean missionary movement as a whole needs greater maturation.[7] The mission agencies must be selective when admitting candidates to their communities, recognizing that the resources of the churches are limited.

Korean mission agencies need to cooperate with one another, partnering in their common vision and purpose. Over the last two decades the Korean World Mission Association has played an important role in facilitating networking, cooperation, and partnership, and as a result awareness has grown among its member agencies of the need for joint labors. The efforts of mission agencies need to become more voluntary, radical, and functional, however, if they are to produce tangible results.

Mission agencies need to adopt a long-term perspective and apply strategic thinking to their ministries. Planning for the future must include issues such as housing for missionary families on furlough or home assignment and for after retirement. Mission executives have seemed too busy with routine management and too involved in the issues of the moment to give adequate attention to these important long-range tasks. Field missionaries also need to work on strategic planning, envisioning

---

7. Steve Sang-Cheol Moon, "Missions from Korea 2012: Slowdown and Maturation," *International Bulletin of Missionary Research* 36, no. 2 (April 2012): 84–85.

the possible future of their individual and team ministries, even though field situations may be unstable, especially in creative-access areas.

Korea's faith mission agencies need to redefine their methods of raising funds in light of the new cultural climate of the global age. NGOs in Korea have demonstrated far greater expertise in fund-raising than have mission agencies, which seek to keep a low profile so as to avoid accusations that they are contravening faith mission principles by soliciting funds. NGOs are more proactive, openly sharing their specific needs in stimulating informational material.

What Can Supporting Churches Do?

Korean churches need to be more consistent in their support for missionaries. The financial costs of mission support must be prioritized, with mission budgets protected, managed separately, and not diverted to other purposes. This sense of priority is the touchstone for a truly missional church.

Supporting churches need to sponsor mission-awareness programs that inform their members about the current realities of missionary life. Korean Christians need to improve their understanding of God's global mission and abandon stereotypes that have been shaped by hagiographies of missionaries from the past.

Korean churches need to exert more effort in caring for their missionaries. Many missionaries and MKs suffer from physical and mental illnesses but feel that they cannot tell the leaders and donors in their supporting churches about their problems. The cultural background in which shame is a stigma hinders honest reporting and thus aggravates problems. Korean churches need to become more aware of the need for, and value of, missionary care.

The churches need to recognize the importance of properly caring for mission leaders. When mission leaders are well cared for, then they in turn can properly care for other missionaries. At present, missionaries who return home to take up leadership roles do not feel well received by their supporting churches. For this reason many mission agencies find it hard to form quality leadership teams.

Korean churches need to work in partnership with mission agencies. Megachurches in particular need to appreciate the complexities and sensitivities present as they engage with mission agencies and missionaries. They need to overcome the temptation to act as though they were self-sufficient and to practice the biblical ethos of interdependency, utilizing the expertise of mission agencies to shape their strategic involvement with and for missionaries.

CONCLUSION

Korean missionaries engaged in overseas ministries have made many sacrifices. Family life is significantly affected by the amount and form of financial support given by local churches, organizations, and individual Christians in Korea. High-quality support and care for missionary families is a product of the joint efforts of supporting churches, mission agencies, and the missionaries themselves. If missionaries are content and feel cared for, more volunteers will seek to become missionaries, and the future of Korean missions will be bright. Support for a missionary family's well-being is a worthy investment and is of great value for many souls.

REFLECTION QUESTIONS

1. How can we overcome the current disparity in financial distribution among missionaries?
2. How can we encourage, equip, and support missionaries to engage in tent-making ministries creatively?
3. How can we redefine the financial policies of faith missions properly without undermining their core values?

19

THE KOREAN HOSTAGE INCIDENT:
Seven Lessons Learned
David Tai Woong Lee and Steve Sang-Cheol Moon

On July 13, 2007, twenty short-term workers from Sammool Church left Incheon International Airport for Afghanistan; they were similar to many other teams leaving the country to serve in different parts of the world. Since Sammool Church had already taken a number of short-term mission trips, what they planned to do seemed to be no different from prior ventures. A number of other short-term teams representing different parties were operating within Afghanistan, and no danger seemed imminent. A single female worker sent from the same church had been situated in a region of Afghanistan for almost a year, and a number of other NGO workers had been there for some time. Not many could blame them if they had a false sense of security. Nonetheless, it is necessary to revisit the event to assess what lessons can be learned from each stage of the incident: the pre-hostage stage, the hostage-taking stage, and finally, the post-hostage stage.

SUMMARY OF THE HOSTAGE CASE

The following paragraphs briefly summarize the three stages of the hostage incident. They are followed by missiological reflections on lessons learned from this incident.

Originally published in *Sorrow and Blood: Christian Mission in Contexts of Suffering, Persecution, and Martyrdom*, ed. William D. Taylor, Antonia van der Meer, and Reg Reimer (Pasadena, Calif.: William Carey Library, 2012), 303–8, this chapter has been edited and is reprinted by permission.

Pre-Hostage Stage

Sammool Church belongs to the Koshin Presbyterian denomination that was formed following Korean liberation from Japanese annexation after World War II. During the occupation, Korean Christians had been forced to take part in so-called "emperor worship" (of the Japanese emperor). Some, however, resisted—at the risk of their lives—refusing to bow to the emperor. Koshin was formed among those who refused to bow to the emperor's image. As one of the leading churches in that denomination, Sammool Church has been well known for social service both within and outside the country. Many consider Pastor Un-Jo Park, a staunch evangelical, to be one of the preeminent pastors in Korea. Sending out short-term workers has been an expression of the church's philosophy of ministry which places emphasis on both evangelism and social service.

The Hostage-Taking

As noted, the twenty-member team left Incheon International Airport on July 13, 2007, arriving in Kabul the following day. According to reports, the team successfully carried out their educational and medical service July 14–18 in the northern region of Afghanistan, where it was comparatively safe. On July 19 they were joined by three medical team members who had already been in Afghanistan and moved from Kabul to Kandahar. The three medical personnel were supposed to act as guides. During this journey they were taken hostage.

They should have become suspicious when the bus driver exchanged places with a new driver, and more suspicious when the bus driver picked up a stranger on the road. The rest we already know. The twenty-three were taken as hostages, and it was not until forty-two days later that the final hostages were released. Two persons died; twenty-one returned home safely, but not without physical and mental scars that are bound to haunt some of them for a long time to come.

On July 21, the president of Korea, Mr. Moo Hyun Noh, publicly pleaded through CNN, a global news network, for the Taliban to release the hostages as soon as possible. By then, the matter was out of the church's control and had become a national affair. The entire Korean cabinet, including the president, acted as a sort of contingency committee. The whole nation was in suspense and terror as the news alternated from bad to worse. On July 21 the Korean government banned all travel to Afghanistan. After long hours and days of negotiation, the Taliban finally agreed to release the rest of the hostages on two conditions: one, that the noncombat Korean troops stationed in Afghanistan would be withdrawn by the end of 2007; two, that all Korean expatriates, including missionaries and NGO personnel, would leave Afghanistan as soon as possible. Rumors circulated that the Korean government negotiation team paid a large ransom in exchange for the hostages. There is, however, no way to confirm this. The Korean government has denied these allegations.

Let us turn our attention to the responses of various factions during and after the hostage situation. Following the hostage crisis, many persons have expressed an opinion about the way mission should or should not now be conducted by the Korean church. At one end of the continuum are the secularists; at the other end stand those who are conservative in theology but radical in their mode of mission. The secularists have launched severe attacks against Christian mission and the church. Sammool Church has suffered from harsh criticism that has not yet completely abated. The following paragraphs indicate the range of reactions both toward Sammool Church and the Korean church in general expressed by different groups following the hostage incident.

Almost unanimous agreement exists all across the spectrum that this hostage situation has affected future hostage negotiations, both nationally and internationally. The loss is almost incalculable. Existing rules governing past hostage negotiations were violated, raising the specter that hostage-taking by terrorists around the globe may become more frequent. The Korean church must take responsibility for such an outcome. It must back off from confrontational or aggressive mission and from mobilizing mass demonstrations, particularly in sensitive and dangerous countries such as Afghanistan.

The leaders of Yong Dong Presbyterian Church and like-minded progressive pastors have declared that the days of sending mission workers are over. This is not a view with which the majority of the Korean church would identify.

The declaration made by Han Hum Ok (recently deceased), the former pastor of Love Church, and Myung Hyuck Kim, chairman of the Korea Evangelical Alliance, among others, seems to state the position held by the majority of the evangelical Korean church. They protest against aggressive and confrontational mission methods while at the same time affirming evangelism and social responsibility as the core of mission. Their description of the situation has been quite accurate. They renounced a few radical groups that have staged massive demonstrations involving thousands of people in spite of strong protests by the local authorities, in major daily media, and even from local mission workers.

Post-Hostage Stage

Nineteen hostages finally arrived at Incheon International Airport on September 2, 2007. Two had arrived previously. Of twenty-three hostages, two were killed and twenty-one released. The released hostages were taken to Sam Hospital in An Yang, a satellite city adjacent to Seoul, where a debriefing team was ready to meet them. They spent ten days in a safe environment, being debriefed and counseled. Subsequently, they were taken to a remote town in Kang Won Province for a week of group therapy. Most of them have now returned to normal life, but not without scars. For some of them, the scars will remain for a long time. At least two couples among them have married. Several have changed jobs. Eight family members have become Christians. The families of the two members who were killed were the hardest hit.

MISSIOLOGICAL LESSONS OF THE HOSTAGE CASE

This hostage case provides us with important lessons in the midst of suffering and damage. We must remember that the incident happened in God's providence, and we must find lessons from it to improve the practice of world mission, especially mission from the Majority World.

Lesson one. We learned that passion and pure-mindedness are not sufficient for good practice of missions. The abducted team members and the involved churches and agencies were all pure-minded and passionate, reflecting the zealous mission mind of the Korean church. A pure passion, however, is not enough for missions. We need wisdom, too. What we lack in cross-cultural missions is more often wisdom rather than purity. We assume that knowledge we have gained through our local experience and within our own culture will work in another cultural context, but that is not necessarily true. We need to be wise as serpents in God's work, especially when we cross cultures for the Gospel. Korean Christians are known for their passion and zealousness for the cause of the kingdom of God, but we must learn what it means to be wise and strategic in cross-cultural ministries. Older missionary sending countries need to help younger missionary sending countries, sharing wisdom and expertise they have gained for ministry, especially ministry in security-sensitive locations.

Lesson two. We learned that understanding the local cultural context is a prerequisite for missionary activity. Knowledge of the context is necessary for cross-cultural ministry. Accurate information and in-depth research on the local situation and environment are needed before we embark on serious engagement in the mission field. Pure missionary motivation should lead to in-depth research on the cultural characteristics, social changes, and potential risks in areas being considered. Activism and excessive optimism may lead to neglect of this need. Over the years the service that research can provide to missions has not received enough emphasis among Korean churches and missions. Korean missionaries' desire to pursue visible ministry outcomes and their activistic tendencies stand in the way of strategic development of the missionary movement. Churches and missions need to create an environment of corporate learning for mature missionary engagement across cultures.

Lesson three. We learned that we need to pursue qualitative growth instead of quantitative increase in this developmental stage of the Korean missionary movement. Over the past thirty years, the Korean missionary movement experienced phenomenal quantitative growth, but it did not grow qualitatively as much as was required. Here the matter is not one of either/or, but of both/and. At this stage of development, however, things are imbalanced and qualitative growth seems to be more urgent. The simple number of missionaries and short-termers cannot be a reason for self-content; proper systems for member care and training are needed as well. Qualitative growth means that the Korean church must pursue global standards in missions. National cultural traits are reflected in national missionary movements, but we need to pursue true globalism as well as localism for the sake of glocalization of the missionary movement.

In this global age, partnership and networking across cultural and organizational boundaries are desirable for qualitative growth. Many Korean churches and missions are not connected enough with other mission entities. We can make better decisions when we are connected properly. In that way, we can avoid many unnecessary dangers, particularly in hostile situations such as Afghanistan.

Lesson four. We learned that we need to invest in development of expertise for the maturation of the missionary movement. Approximately twenty thousand Korean missionaries serve in over one hundred seventy countries around the globe, but more missionary experts are needed if a repeat of this crisis is to be avoided. We need expertise in information networks, research and development, strategic coordination, mobilization, member care (including counseling services), missionary training, and administration. For balanced development, local churches in Korea need to recognize this need and invest in the development of expertise among mission agencies. Sharing of expertise is also needed. Limited but substantial sources of expertise are available within the various Korean mission communities, but self-centeredness on the part of large local churches stymies wide sharing of this expertise.

Lesson five. We learned that massive rallies in the field can have serious negative side effects. The hostage crisis in 2007 had something to do with the massive rallies with missionary purpose held in Kabul in 2006. The big mission events were planned and performed with good intentions, but without due regard to the opposition expressed by Korean missionaries already serving in Afghanistan. In sensitive Islamic contexts, massive events of such a nature can be seen as alien religious demonstrations staged by foreigners. A rally can raise the level of tension rapidly, so much wisdom is needed when missioners plan such a program. For missioners to think they should hastily drive out demons and evil spirits so as to facilitate and guarantee the fruitfulness of missionary activities in specific countries is an example of spiritual myopia. A long-term perspective is needed to carry out spiritual warfare well. We are concerned about the short-term mentality of some massive rallies, particularly in hostile countries such as Afghanistan. We wonder if they are based on an erroneous worldview perspective. We need to recover the biblical balance between the extremes.

Lesson six. We learned that short-term "vision" trips need to focus on educating participants rather than on direct evangelism in creative access areas. Wide agreement exists that we cannot expect too much from a vision trip, especially in a creative access area. Fewer and fewer countries permit direct evangelistic activities by foreigners. We need to be realistic in setting the goals of short-term trips to sensitive areas. We need first to learn before engaging in any serious mission activities. We can think and pray about what to do and how to serve the local people from a missional perspective as we gather information and learn more about the local people. One temptation on the part of sending churches and short-term visitors is to leave some visible result of their activities. Too many unwanted buildings and facilities stand as evidence that they were not initiated from a thorough needs assessment. Physical artifacts not based on actual needs may serve to self-satisfy the sending churches and short-termers, but may not serve the local people well. Short-term visitors should focus on learning what it means to live as Christians in this ever-globalizing world. They can learn to pray, give, and do more in this way for reaching the unreached in God's salvific will.

Lesson seven. We learned that we need to expend more effort toward caring well for missionaries. Missionary activities involve dangers and risks, both long-term and short-term. Missionaries are more vulnerable than ever before to various kinds of potential dangers and risks. Through high quality member care, Korean churches and missions need to emphasize establishing a balance between a sacrificial life and personal well-being. Pastors of sending churches and mission leaders have an obligation to care well for their members. Sometimes people overemphasize martyrdom and neglect their obligation to care for members. As pastors, fellow missionaries, mission leaders, and supporters, our part is to do our best in caring for missionaries. According to a survey by the

Korean Research Institute for Mission that was directed to Korean mission executives, member care is regarded as one of the weakest points of Korean missions. We need nationwide awareness and orchestrated efforts in promoting member care.

Whether in long-term or short-term ministries, we need incarnational approaches which highlight unity in the midst of diversity, humility and self-emptying, contextualization, soft power, and the presence of the Holy Spirit. The hostage crisis of August 2007 may turn out to be a disguised blessing for the maturation and development of Korean missions as we commit to incarnational ministry.

QUESTIONS FOR REFLECTION

1. This chapter contains the refreshingly frank reflections of two Korean missionary leaders. Discuss the statement, "Almost unanimous agreement exists all across the spectrum that this hostage situation has affected future hostage negotiations, both nationally and internationally. The loss is almost incalculable."
2. Discuss the wider implications of the statement that "national cultural traits are reflected in national missionary movements."
3. In what specific ways might "older missionary sending countries" help "younger missionary sending countries"? What would be required for this to work?
4. In what ways might more "incarnational approaches" mentioned in the final paragraph mitigate potential future crises?

20

THE PLACE AND FUNCTION OF RESEARCH IN CONTEXTS OF SUFFERING, PERSECUTION, AND MARTYRDOM

The notion of "reflective practitioner" assumes the importance of combining reflection and practice in missions.[1] Reflection without practice is irresponsible abstraction. Practice without reflection is naive activism. Putting reflection and practice together requires research; research enables practice and reflection to be combined.

Reflective practitioners in the contexts of suffering, persecution, and martyrdom need to delve into what it means to be faithful and accountable in their contexts. Research certainly has a place and a function in such ministerial situations. In fact, reflective practitioners need even more urgently to invest time and energy in research and development in such contexts.

In this chapter we attempt to clarify the place and function of research in the uneasy ministerial contexts of suffering, persecution, and martyrdom. Through research, purity and wisdom of mind are combined.

THE PLACE OF RESEARCH

Not only is research integral to ministries carried out in contexts of hardship, but it also plays important roles in every ministerial context.[2]

Originally published in *Sorrow and Blood: Christian Mission in Contexts of Suffering, Persecution, and Martyrdom*, ed. William D. Taylor, Antonia van der Meer, and Reg Reimer (Pasadena, Calif.: William Carey Library, 2012), 469–73, this chapter has been edited and is reprinted by permission.

1. William D. Taylor, "From Iguassu to the Reflective Practitioners of the Global Family of Christ," in *Global Missiology for the Twenty-First Century*, ed. William D. Taylor (Grand Rapids: Baker Academic, 2000), 5–6.

2. Stan Nussbaum, *Breakthrough! Steps to Research and Resolve the Mysteries in Your Ministry* (Colorado Springs, Colo.: GMI Research Services, 2007), 148–49.

In normal situations, research aims at promoting the effectiveness and efficiency of ministries. In difficult situations, research may also contribute to alleviating tensions and coping with hardships.

The nature of missiology as a discipline betwixt and between text and context suggests the necessity of empirical research, which is a good foundation for down-to-earth approaches in incarnational ministries.[3] This research reinforces a humble attitude toward the cultural contexts in which ministries occur. Missional theologies should naturally draw on empirical findings in seeking to reflect on and address context-specific issues and problems. The empirical dimension of missiology should highlight the wholistic needs of humankind, one of which is related to human suffering. Studying the context, that is, conducting an environment scan, in this kind of situation is not a matter of choice, but of necessity.

The task of contextualization presupposes contextual research, without which, contextualization is merely an abstract process. Contextual research sharpens the focus of contextualization, and when it includes a future perspective it is "envisioning." Envisioning is beginning with the end in mind, that is, beginning a ministry with the very end purpose of the ministry efforts and activities in mind.[4] Contextualization of churches, theologies, worship styles, leadership structures, organizational cultures, or other artifacts of faith is possible with envisioning or imagineering (or reimagineering) based on contextual research. This research requires both historical and cultural understanding, both of which should be combined with biblical understanding.

The core of contextual research is cultural exegesis, which enables systematic cultural understanding at a deeper level. Cultural exegesis also makes it possible for cross-cultural workers to do needs assessment in preparation for their ministries. It lays the foundation for contingency planning, which is an important ministry obligation, even more so in sensitive areas of the world. Cultural exegesis, in this sense, is not a

---

3. Paul G. Hiebert, *Transforming Worldviews: An Anthropological Understanding of How People Change* (Grand Rapids: Baker Academic 2008), 89–104.

4. Shane Bennett and Kim Felder, *Exploring the Land* (Littleton, Colo.: Caleb Project, 1995), 35–39.

task of purely theoretical research, but one of applied research. In this sense cultural exegesis is a process that is to be continued and renewed for up-to-date and relevant situational understanding. This process is a spiral one, dynamically driven by ministry foci, purposes, approaches, and methods.

The limitations of empirical research are clear and evident in the sense that we cannot fathom the depth of the transcendental world in our experience through our senses. In the same way, we acquire knowledge and expertise but we cannot thereby control the environment of our ministry world. We must humbly acknowledge our finiteness and limitations as human beings. We must confess that we cannot control the course of history. We must accept the historical givens that might lead to suffering, persecution, and sometimes even martyrdom. Research supplies input into whether we will accept, resist, or flee from such situations; changing the course of given conditions lies outside its scope. Nevertheless, the limitations of research do not prove that research is worthless, for research only claims to offer suggestions to assist us in selecting the best possible way to serve the Lord faithfully and wisely. For this reason, empirical research should be integrated with biblical and theological insights. The reference points are the biblical norms, which should precede theological or cultural guidelines.

Today's global age has made the clash of worldviews more serious than before. This phenomenon has given rise to more cases of religious persecution, which makes cultural research more complex. A local perspective is not enough. We need a global perspective in our research, one that is not just emic or etic, but glocal. A glocal view can subtly differentiate and yet connect local and global understandings at the same time. Ministry under hardship is both a local and a global problem for the global church. Missional cultural exegesis or environmental scans should address this problem. In today's global age, empirical research should be thoroughly up-to-date, for to be relevant, understanding needs to be updated frequently. Many area studies and ethnographies are outdated. We need to address new issues and research problems in this rapidly changing world. In order to do such research more efficiently and effectively, we need to focus on information that is strategic for understanding contexts of suffering. We need to summarize the stories, not just the numbers, of persecuted Christians and churches and share them with the global church so that all parts of the body of Christ can share in the suffering, paying the price for being Christian.

Contexts of suffering, persecution, and martyrdom make the need for empirical research even more pressing. They call for a sense of urgency in sharing real-life stories rather than engaging in abstract discussion or idle collection of basic data. We need to gather strategic information for our decision making. Regardless of the limitations of empirical research, we need to invest in field-based research projects. We need to obtain the prize of the right information, for the quality of resources available on the Internet is too often weak, monographs are too outdated, and journals are overly selective.

THE FUNCTION OF RESEARCH

Research is not magic, but it plays an important role. The promise of research can be summarized in seven points. First of all, field-based empirical research clarifies the purpose of ministry. Second, it helps identify appropriate ministry methods. Third, it facilitates innovation in ministry. Fourth, it makes the allotment of tasks possible for team ministries. Fifth, it lays the foundation for contextualization. Sixth, it raises the levels of effectiveness and efficiency of ministry. Seventh, it helps avoid repeating the same mistakes in ministry. Well-done field-based research brings about the overall improvement of ministry performance. This observation also holds true for contexts of extreme hardship.

In order for research to perform these important functions, the researcher should utilize relevant research methods, such as research design, data gathering, and data analysis. Research design should be realistic enough to be executed in missional contexts. A research design that is too rigorous hinders the actual execution of research by ordinary missionaries, who need to understand such basic issues as validity and reliability. Simple methods that can lead to profound findings are the wisest strategy in research design for real missional contexts, especially in sensitive areas. Data gathering strategies should also be flexible and able to adjust to missional conditions. Often questionnaire surveys are not feasible in creative access countries, which guides us to consider qualitative approaches. Participant observation and ethnographic interviews are two important means for gathering data in qualitative research. Even the interview questions should remain descriptive and open-ended instead of focusing immediately on a specific point. Building rapport is critical for use of this approach, something that is all the more true in sensitive areas. In qualitative research, data analysis techniques have developed enormously over the past thirty years. The whole body of cognitive anthropological theory seeks to overcome the traditional limitations of qualitative data analysis. Missionary researchers do not have to follow all the discussions surrounding the analysis of qualitative data; it will suffice to say that we need to focus our analytic attention toward worldview exegesis. Semiotic analysis can help us to do this in a more systematic way.[5] Another recent strategy, schema analysis, can also be helpful.

The activistic orientation of missioners might not suggest a bright future for research. Over the course of mission history, certain stereotypes have accumulated, but the increasing globalization of the world requires that some of them be challenged. Following are several developmental issues that are important for the future of field-based empirical research. First, missionaries must understand the role of research as a foundation of ministry. Second, seminaries and missionary training centers need to equip their students to write field-based reports, projects, theses, and dissertations. Third, international research networks should be strengthened so that they can function as strategic alliances. Fourth, qualitative research methods need to be developed further and to be incorporated more extensively in mission studies. Fifth, missionary researchers need to update their understanding of both quantitative and qualitative research approaches.[6] Sixth, in order to elevate the level of empirical research, good teamwork between national and expatriate workers is necessary. Seventh, research grants should be established to encourage researchers not only in the younger missionary sending coun-

---

5. Steve Sang-Cheol Moon, "A Hermeneutical Model of Urban Religious Symbols: The Case of Konya, Turkey" (Ph.D. diss., Trinity International University, 1998), 308–13; Hiebert, *Transforming Worldviews*, 97.

6. Paul G. Hiebert, *The Gospel in Human Contexts: Anthropological Explorations for Contemporary Missions* (Grand Rapids: Baker Academic, 2009), 162–64.

tries but also in the older ones. With these conditions met, the quality of research will be solidified, and breakthroughs in mission will be visible.

In contexts of suffering, persecution, and martyrdom, the process of mission research should be sensitive enough to reflect those realities. The function of research in such situations should be preventive and proactive rather than reactive. The tasks of environmental scan, or surveying the context, and of envisioning should themselves lay a foundation for preventive and proactive mission thinking. In many contexts, the need for knowledge workers with expertise is great.[7] The global missions community needs to seek out such experts and make the best use of research networks. Expertise is needed in contingency planning, as it is in crisis counseling, an area often neglected among the churches. Missionary sending countries urgently need to develop expertise in missionary deployment. A definite need is expertise in the trends of world religions at both formal and folk levels. The global missions community needs to accumulate expertise and to develop a knowledge base at the country, regional, and global levels.

CONCLUSION

Research is related to both reflection and practice. It can facilitate a happy coexistence and combination of the two. Metaphorically, a traditional understanding of the place of research would be the root from which the tree grows or the foundation upon which a building is erected. But in this globally contingent world, the place of research is not fixed in one part; it is more or less ubiquitous. Research is really multifunctional. The value of research cannot be overemphasized, considering the orientation toward activism among missioners, especially in the younger missionary sending countries. Activism is a sign of immaturity in a missionary movement. In contexts of hardship, adopting a mind-set of critical realism entails adopting a learning attitude, which will lead to the growth of research.

---

7. Peter F. Drucker, *Management Challenges for the Twenty-First Century* (New York: HarperBusiness, 1999), 143–48.

QUESTIONS FOR REFLECTION

1. How can we integrate theological insights and empirical findings in missiological research?
2. How can missiologists and mission researchers cooperate with field missionaries for empirical research?
3. How can the global missions circle raise the level of quality for international research projects?

21
KOREAN MISSIONARY CHILDREN AND THEIR EDUCATIONAL NEEDS

The education of missionary children is an important responsibility for all who are involved in mission. If their overseas ministry is to be successful, missionaries must have access to a reasonable educational option for their children. Educational support systems have not kept pace, however, with the remarkable increase in the number of Korean missionaries. Although Korean mission agencies recognize their obligation in relation to the education of missionary kids (MKs) and in the past two decades have taken steps to improve their education, Korean churches and individuals show little awareness of the issue.

The information presented here is based on empirical research of two sorts: first, a quantitative survey I designed that was processed by staff at the Korea Research Institute for Mission (KRIM) in late December 2012; second, qualitative research involving field-based interviews carried out in nine countries in which 176 members of the Korean mission community took part—missionaries (70 persons), MKs (76 persons), and MK educators (30 persons)—during the period of October 2012 through April 2013.[1] The quantitative data were analyzed using SPSS

Originally published as "Korean Missionary Children and Their Educational Needs," in *Family Accountability in Missions: Korean and Western Case Studies*, ed. Jonathan J. Bonk (New Haven, Conn.: OMSC Publications, 2013), 243–58, this chapter is reprinted by permission.

1. SaRang Community Church, Seoul, Korea (pastor: Jung Hyum Oh), supported this research project financially. EunYong Cindy Kim carried out the interviews in the Philippines and Thailand. The remainder of the interviews in seven countries were carried out by Steve Moon with the assistance of Hee-Joo (Yoo) Moon and Jung Joo Lee. All are on the KRIM staff. In all but four instances

statistical analysis software, and the qualitative data were analyzed after transcription and manual coding according to the model developed by Vincent Faherty.[2] Unless noted otherwise, the information presented in this article is based on this research.

Three research questions helped to determine the project's research design, the gathering and analyzing of data, and the shape of this report. (1) How do the educational realities for the children of Korean missionary families differ in various contexts? (2) What problems do Korean missionary families face related to the education of their children? (3) In practice, how can the education of Korean MKs be improved?

THE REALITIES OF KOREAN MK EDUCATION

Statistics, along with careful, personal listening, help us in understanding the educational realities of Korean MKs. In the following, statistical analysis is accompanied by in-depth qualitative analysis, allowing a balance to be maintained between etic and emic approaches.

---

the interviews were of individuals rather than group interviews. The 176 interviews generated over 800 pages of field notes, which are now kept, along with recordings of the interviews, at KRIM.

The schools covered by our research are Manila Hankuk (Korean) Academy, Manila, Philippines (principal: Segi Hong, www.mha.or.kr); Grace International School, Chiang Mai, Thailand (superintendent: Jennie Garcia, www.gisthailand.org); Black Forest Academy, Kandern, Germany (principal: Robert Shuman, www.bfacademy.com); Hanal Korean School in GDQ International Christian School, Tirana, Albania (director: Roger Pearce, www.gdqschool.org); Dakar Academy, Dakar, Senegal (director: Joseph Rosa, www.dakar-academy.org), and Bourofaye Christian School, Dakar, Senegal (www.bcs-senegal.org); International Gateway Academy, Istanbul, Turkey (www.int-gateway.com); Glovill High School, Busan, Korea (principal: Kiyoung Shin, www.glovillhigh.hs.kr); Sejong Global School, Cheonan, Korea (director: EunHwa Chai, www.runkorea.org); and home schools in China and Myanmar. The preceding list of schools is in the order of the interviewing. Two separate group interview sessions with a total of eight university students were added later. The cooperation of these schools and students with this project is greatly appreciated.

2. Vincent E. Faherty, *Wordcraft: Applied Qualitative Data Analysis (QDA)* (Los Angeles: SAGE, 2010), 43–91.

A Statistical Overview

The results of the questionnaire administered by KRIM staff in late December 2012 show that 19,798 Korean missionaries were working with 167 mission agencies in 175 countries.[3] These missionaries had a total of 17,432 children,[4] with the percentage of children at each educational level as follows: preschool (16.8), elementary school (22.9), middle school (13.4), high school (12.9), college or university (29.1), and employed or employable adults (4.9). For Korean missionary parents with children of the age for primary or secondary education, the type of schooling selected, by percentage, was as follows: local schools (35.9), international schools (28.6), schools in Korea (14.6), homeschooling (9.0), MK schools (8.9),[5] and other options (3.0).

Mission leaders are often curious to know how many Korean MKs become missionaries as adults. According to this survey, only 2.3 percent of the total Korean MKs have become involved in an intercultural ministry on completion of their education.[6] Interpretation of this figure must take into account, however, that the majority of Korean MKs are still in school or university.

Of the 7,044 MKs identified in this survey, 61 (or 0.9 percent of the total) were reported to have had serious problems adjusting to a school environment, of whom 14 (about one-quarter) attended MK schools.[7] According to mission executives, 0.6 percent of Korean MKs need professional counseling and/or mental health treatment.

---

3. Steve Sang-Cheol Moon, "Missions from Korea 2013: Microtrends and Finance," *International Bulletin of Missionary Research* 37 (April 2013): 96–97.

4. The statistical analysis that follows is based on survey data collected from forty-four mission agencies. These agencies are representative of Korean mission agencies in terms of size, denominational affiliation, area of focus, and ministry type.

5. This figure of 8.9 percent includes students at both international MK schools and Korean MK schools.

6. This figure does not reflect age groups or job seekers but simply tells of the proportion of our total number of MKs who are in intercultural ministry.

7. Adjustment problems seem to be more common than these figures suggest. It is probable that mission executives and even staffers assisting in MK education lack detailed information about the experiences of individual missionary families.

Options for MK Education

Six types of schooling are available to Korean missionary kids. Field studies suggest that each option has both advantages and disadvantages.

Korean overseas schools. Schools established by Koreans or Korean organizations, sometimes specifically for the education of MKs, are one important option. At least eight Korean schools specifically for Korean MKs have been established in six countries, with at least eight more Korean schools in seven countries receiving the children of Korean expatriates, including MKs. Altogether, a minimum of sixteen Korean overseas schools are presently available for the education of Korean MKs.

The majority of overseas Korean schools are still at a formative stage, for they have been recently established and have only a small endowment. Instruction is primarily in Korean, although many schools also have an emphasis on English. The strength of this type of schooling is in furthering children's Korean heritage, both linguistically and culturally. Membership in a community of students who share a common ethnolinguistic background provides a stepping-stone for Korean MKs when (or if) they reenter Korea. Overall, the expense to parents for this option is much lower than the cost of international schools or international MK schools. The Manila Hankuk (Korean) Academy in the Philippines provides a good example of an institution with a clear educational vision and a philosophy that emphasizes the Christian, Korean, and global dimensions of its ministry.

Korean schools in the field, especially those dedicated to MK education, tend to struggle to tap the resources needed to maintain staffing levels and facilities, lack a knowledge base that is current, and have little long-term strategic planning in place. These schools are defined in particular by the presence of MKs who live in a dormitory during the school term, separated from their parents, who work in another country. The attention and holistic care required by these MKs is a demanding challenge for teachers and dorm parents/assistants. Long-term commitment to such schools by qualified Korean teachers requires a significant sacrifice. The teachers must raise funds to cover their living expenses and to support their ministry, and Korean churches are generally unaware of the value of supporting this need.

International MK schools. Missionary schools founded by American or European organizations provide an educational option that benefits increasing numbers of Korean MKs. Over twenty schools of this kind in nineteen countries welcome Korean MKs, including Black Forest Academy (Germany), Bourofaye Christian School (Senegal), Dakar Academy (Senegal), GDQ International Christian School (Albania), and Grace International School (Thailand). Korean membership of the total student body at such institutions ranges between 7.2 and 18.0 percent. The international MK schools provide Korean MKs with a Christian worldview and a vision of mission that reaches across generations and cultures. The internationality of the student body helps MKs feel comfortable in a multicultural environment. Teachers and dorm parents/assistants provide a sense of security for MKs who are away from home.

International MK schools struggle, however, to support a specifically Korean cultural identity and need outside assistance if they are to provide systematic instruction in Korean language, history, and culture. Korean MKs often find it hard to prepare for entrance examinations for Korean universities and for the transfer into the Korean workplace that may follow. The cost of international MK schools is much higher than the cost of Korean schools either abroad or at home, and as a result Korean missionaries often do not see such schools as an option for their children.

Other international schools. International schools not devoted strictly to MKs welcome any expatriate children and even local children, and therefore the composition of the student body is more complex. The distinction between international MK schools and other international schools is becoming blurred as many MK schools have changed their policies to include non-MKs in their community. Also, although they were not established solely for MKs, a large majority of the international schools have a Christian background. Korean MKs are found in numerous international schools throughout the world. The figure of 28.6 percent of school-age children who are attending international schools includes students attending local schools whose education is in either English or French.

Many international schools have a long history, but others are still at a developmental stage and are seeking to improve the quality of their education. International schools tend to be diverse, and MKs who attend such schools are exposed to varied worldviews, religions, and cultures. The plurality of this setting can prepare MKs well for their subsequent education and social engagement in a secular and heterogeneous world.

Many international schools are too expensive for missionary families to consider. In most cases the standard of living of the missionary children is far lower than that of other expatriate children, which can cause the MKs discomfort. The educational philosophy of an international school is not always compatible with a Christian worldview or values, and Korean MKs seeking to enter a Korean university may find that their schooling has lacked critical elements.

Local schools in the field. The most common educational choice for MKs is local schools, which provide education in the official language of the host country. Curricula are largely in line with the educational policies of the government of the host country. The quality and relevance of local schooling vary from country to country.

Advantages of local schools include accessibility—missionary children can live with their family while attending nearby schools—and costs that are much lower than other forms of schooling. Additionally, missionary children can mingle with local children, allowing them to develop meaningful relationships based on a mutual understanding, an opportunity that is lacking in other educational options. Increasing demand for area-specific expertise in the business sector and other parts of Korean society makes local schooling an increasingly viable option for Korean MKs.

Although for many Korean missionary families local schooling is in practice the only affordable option, it has certain disadvantages. Problems include a clash of worldviews, in particular in Islamic and Communist countries, the often low quality of education provided, and a lack of educational infrastructure. Additionally, such schools do not prepare MKs for the transition to the home country or to a third country, and there are examples of MKs, as members of a minority group, being bullied.

Schools in Korea. Another option for MK education is attending school in Korea. Many MKs experience Korean schools during their parents' furlough, and if an appropriate option is not available in the field, schooling in Korea is worth considering. In addition to regular local schools, there are estimated to be over 230 alternative schools in Korea,[8] and almost half of these alternative schools appear to have a Christian background.[9] Both Glovill High School, in Busan, and Sejong Global School, in Cheonan, were founded with a particular vision for MK education. Other types of schools in Korea could also accommodate missionary children well if their principles and their practices are in keeping with the values of missionary families.

Attendance at a Korean school is a realistic alternative in particular for children who have completed their elementary education. They are older now and thus can more easily live apart from their parents. The experience allows MKs to begin a program of Korean education at an early stage and avoid the difficulties of transferring into that system when older; children who have attended school in Korea will face fewer challenges later in reintegrating into Korean society. If schooled in Korea, MKs can benefit from maintaining family ties and kinship networks, which can also be significant for their long-term future in Korea.

The principal disadvantage of schooling in Korea is that missionary children are separated from their immediate family. Additionally, Korean schools are not always well prepared to respond to the particular needs of MKs. They require dormitories and other relevant facilities, as well as effective systems of care and teachers and staff with intercultural experience and understanding. The financial strain can be great, especially if a child attends an alternative school, for such schools tend to be

---

8. Hae Joang Cho, *A Study of Ways to Develop Comprehensive Alternative Education* (in Korean) (Seoul: Ministry of Education, Science, and Technology, 2011), 5, 63. In crosschecking these figures, I identified only 170 such schools, but this figure is likely conservative and may no longer be current. The *Hankyoreh* reported that, as of July 2010, there were more than 179 alternative schools in Korea; see www.hani.co.kr/arti/society/schooling/428740.html. It is often difficult to characterize the nature of these schools.

9. Sang-Jin Park estimates that there are approximately one hundred Christian alternative schools in Korea ("A Study on Types of Christian Alternative Schools" [in Korean], *Korea Presbyterian Journal of Theology* 37 [2010]: 156, 186). The existence of at least seventy Christian alternative schools has been verified; see Tae-Gyu Lim, "The Status of Christian Alternative Schools in Korea" (in Korean), 2009, www.casak.org.

more expensive than regular local schools. If educated in Korea, MKs may lose their ties to their parents' ministry, including the intercultural experience that comes with presence in the field.

Homeschooling. The final option for MK education is homeschooling, which for many missionary families may be the only realistic option, particularly in light of the high cost of international schools and of the possibly inferior quality of local schooling. Currently 9.0 percent of Korean MKs are homeschooled, a figure that we expect will only grow higher. The homeschooling of MKs in the field should be supported by home churches, organizations, and individuals in Korea.

A significant advantage of homeschooling is its flexibility. With their own educational philosophy shaping their approach, parents, with their children, can make decisions about content, deadlines, resource materials, and learning media. Increasing numbers of parents in Korea, including many missionaries, are gaining confidence in this model of schooling. Parents' values can be transmitted to their children effectively and intensely through concentrated effort. Parents may be able to invest financial resources in their children's future that might otherwise have been spent on sending their children to school outside the home. If an MK plans to enter a Korean university, he or she can work toward this goal through a focused individual plan.

This alternative educational model can be greatly strengthened by external support, but at present homeschoolers and their parents can rarely access such assistance. A team of experts could, for example, select suitable materials and send them to the family, and up-to-date information is essential when decisions are being made about university applications. Homeschoolers can gain a sense of their progress by objective assessment. A fellowship network of homeschoolers can provide a peer group with whom children who are being homeschooled can spend time regularly—for example, on a retreat or trip relevant to missionary concerns.

PROBLEMS IN THE EDUCATION OF KOREAN MKS

Each child has a unique set of educational needs, and the specific needs of MKs are complex. We look here in turn at spiritual, linguistic, emotional, psychological, cultural, physical, financial, and systematic issues that have been identified from the interview data.

Many missionary children struggle spiritually and carry inner spiritual burdens that may have to do with their relationship with their parents. Korean missionary parents often fail to spend the time and effort needed to prepare their children for departure from Korea, including explaining what the children might expect and engaging them as much as possible in the decision to go. Many MKs feel that, as a result of a decision made by their parents, they had to leave Korea suddenly and without the opportunity to prepare. MKs who are unhappy in the field may begin to question God's goodness. If missionaries become so task-oriented that they fail to give time to their family responsibilities, their children's image of God can become negative, perhaps unconsciously so. Healthy spiritual relationships with God and parents should be consolidated before MKs reach adolescence.

Linguistic challenges are a hurdle in the education of MKs, especially during the first years in a new field. In the long term, MKs may benefit from being bilingual, but the processes that give them this advantage can be quite stressful. When MKs return to Korea on furlough, their Korean language abilities are routinely tested by their grandparents and church members, and all too often the children are made to feel shame for their deficiencies. Yet at the same time teachers at international schools think that many Korean MKs need to give more effort to improving their English. Also, many Korean MKs feel they should have greater competency in the local language of their parents' country of service. Conflicting expectations can leave Korean missionary children very unsettled.

The emotional and psychological challenges for MKs are also substantial. MKs who attend boarding school may miss their parents and siblings. Those who attend local schools often lack close friendships. An absence of peer bonding is particularly marked for children who are homeschooled. On all fronts, relational satisfaction seems very low, which can cause severe loneliness and depression.[10] Such loneliness,

---

10. Esther Schubert, "Keeping Third-Culture Kids Emotionally Healthy: Depression and Suicide among MKs," in *International Conference on Missionary*

I have observed, can lead MKs to marry early. Schools with a communal atmosphere are best placed to meet this subtle yet significant need. The answer does not necessarily lie in the creation of a wide circle of friends and acquaintances, but rather in membership in a network of MKs in a communal atmosphere.[11]

MKs often struggle with their cultural identity, which is vitally related to one's sense of self and one's pattern of behavior.[12] The quest for a singular cultural identity is increasingly challenging in this acceleratingly globalizing world. Identities are always "in the process of becoming rather than being."[13] MKs' multiple cultural identities surface especially on their reentry to the home country. Some MKs suffer from bullying and are alienated from peer groups in schools that have the characteristics of a collective monoculture. Cases of acute discomfort upon entering the home culture need to be understood as trauma that must be acknowledged and treated wisely.[14] Turning traumatic experience into a creative process of social becoming is an eloquent missional message in itself.[15]

Kids (November 5–9, 1984, Manila, Philippines) (Pasadena, Calif.: William Carey Library, 1986), 96–102.

11. One characteristic of a communal atmosphere is multiplex relationships within the community as contrasted with simplex relationships in urban societies. See Max Gluckman, *The Judicial Process among the Barotse of Northern Rhodesia* (Manchester: Manchester Univ. Press, 1955), 18–19. Note also Paul G. Hiebert and Eloise Hiebert Meneses, *Incarnational Ministry: Planting Churches in Band, Tribal, Peasant, and Urban Societies* (Grand Rapids: Baker, 1995), 274.

12. Dorothy Holland, William Lachicotte Jr., Debra Skinner, and Carole Cain, *Identity and Agency in Cultural Worlds* (Cambridge, Mass.: Harvard Univ. Press, 1998), 8.

13. Stuart Hall, "Introduction: Who Needs 'Identity'?," in *Questions of Cultural Identity*, ed. Stuart Hall and Paul du Gay (Los Angeles: SAGE, 1996), 4.

14. Jeffrey C. Alexander, "Toward a Theory of Cultural Trauma," in *Cultural Trauma and Collective Identity*, ed. Jeffrey C. Alexander, Ron Eyerman, Bernhard Giesen, Neil J. Smelser, and Piotr Sztompka (Berkeley: Univ. of California Press, 2004), 10, 15. Alexander rightly warns, "If the trauma process unfolds inside the religious arena, its concern will be to link trauma to theodicy" (15).

15. Addressing collective cultural trauma, Piotr Sztompka has observed, "In spite of the disruption and disarray of cultural order that trauma brings about, in a different time scale it may be seen as the seed of a new cultural system" ("The

Korean missionary children may find the food in dormitories and hostels unfamiliar and of poor quality, which raises concerns about their nutrition. Occasional Korean meals served by Korean staff serve to good purpose. Good facilities in some international (MK) schools support physical fitness and provide a source of fellowship for MKs. Vision-trip programs—as offered, for example, by Black Forest Academy—provide not only a break from school but also valuable intercultural exposure.

Financial problems are experienced by almost all Korean missionary families. Tuition and other expenses can be a determining factor when they are deciding how their children will be educated. Only a small number of Korean missionaries have been able to afford education insurance or other plans that help parents prepare early for the high cost of a university education. Some Korean high school students earn pocket money by working part-time, and many Korean MKs who attend American universities endeavor to cover their living costs on their own.[16] The large majority of MKs whom we interviewed hoped to earn well in the future, seeing such income as providing the opportunity to support their parents and contribute to the world. Only a small number of MKs showed any interest in following in their parents' footsteps by becoming missionaries. Interviews have led me to hypothesize that children of missionaries who have been securely supported by churches, fruitful in ministry, and respected by local Christians are more likely to see missionary service as a positive career path that they themselves might follow.[17]

In addition to issues such as spiritual support, peer-group relationships, and identity formation, MK education needs stronger practical foundations. Existing schools would benefit from improved facilities.

Trauma of Social Change," A Case of Postcommunist Societies," in *Cultural Trauma and Collective Identity*, by Alexander et al., 194).

16. In general the financial pressure is heavier when an MK chooses to attend a university in the United States, which is leading more MKs to consider enrolling in a Korean university for financial reasons.

17. In an interview carried out for this project, Ruth Insook Baek, founding director of MK Nest, Seoul, Korea, observed that after graduation from university some MKs see service as a missionary in a more positive light. Interviews with university students confirm this tendency among young adult MKs.

Even international MK schools with a long history need more buildings and space and improved organization. With an increased number of Korean MKs attending international mission schools, Korean churches and organizations should be open to requests for support from such schools. Qualified individuals with awareness of Korean-specific needs could serve as teachers, dorm parents/assistants, and administrators. Another advance would be an improved provision of information by Korean MK educators, again tailored to specific Korean needs.[18]

RECOMMENDATIONS FOR IMPROVEMENT OF MK EDUCATION

Stakeholders in MK education need to define and refine their educational philosophy. Taking into account both biblical ideals and realities on the ground, they should reconsider the role of educational institutions, mission agencies, and local churches. Glocal changes that might affect MK education must be acknowledged. Consideration must be given to how spiritual, ethnic, and cultural identities are shaped. The MKs considered by this study are spiritually God's children, ethnically Korean, and culturally global citizens.

We must restore optimism that the complex goals of MK education can be achieved. Currently, MKs may sense that they belong to neither the home culture "A" nor the host culture "B," but only to a third culture "C." When coined in the early 1950s, the term "third-culture kid" lacked its current positive connotations that stress the child's intercultural

---

18. Twenty years after the 1993 MK seminar with David C. Pollock in Seoul, I hope that Korean missionaries will continue to accumulate, and share globally, their expertise on MK education. The potential of such shared knowledge can be recognized in the proceedings of the 1994 Manila conference, published as *International Conference on Missionary Kids*, and the more recent *Raising Resilient MKs: Resources for Caregivers, Parents, and Teachers*, ed. Joyce M. Bowers (Colorado Springs, Colo.: Association of Christian Schools International, 1998). As Ted Ward has argued, empirical research through "intercultural collaboration" will build expertise for MK education ("Doing Research Together," in *Raising Resilient MKs*, ed. Bowers, 445–55).

adaptability and competence.¹⁹ Successful educational missionaries can help ensure that MKs belong to both the home culture "A" and the host culture "B," and thus in practice to a hybrid culture "AB." I suggest that such processes would allow us to replace the term "third-culture kid" with "hybrid-culture kid." Our understanding of the nature and mission of MK education should be updated along these lines.

Korean missionaries need to plan their children's education wisely by making informed decisions. A vague fideism among some Korean missionaries has been seen to hinder appropriate planning, effective preparation, and practical support for their children's education. An approach based on trial and error has meant that some Korean MKs have had to withdraw from American universities because estimations of the costs involved had been unrealistic. An increasing number of church leaders and individual supporters are critical of missionaries who choose an educational path for their children that is determined by prestige or prospects rather than by affordability. Affordable best practice should guide decisions about MK education, which should be tailored to the situation of individual missionary families.

Missionary children need to understand and accept the realities of their lives and education and appreciate what is available to them. There are both advantages and disadvantages to being an MK. An MK's spiritual heritage, cultural capital, and personal relationships are very rich and will provide him or her with opportunities later in life. In overcoming difficulties earlier in life, MKs will build up inner strengths. Frequent moves and the accompanying transitions may be difficult at the time, but they will cultivate adaptability. Loneliness, ideally, can feed deep thinking and creativity. Insofar as MKs internalize their identities and develop coping strategies, they develop psychological strengths and an emotional stability that will serve them well in unfamiliar situations.

A more nuanced approach will overcome the stereotypes of an idealized missionary life and will encourage Korean churches to upgrade

---

19. David C. Pollock notes that the term "third-culture kid" was coined by Ruth Useem, a sociologist at Michigan State University, to describe the children of American expatriates who shared a common set of distinguishing characteristics ("Being a Third-Culture Kid: A Profile," in *Raising Resilient MKs*, ed. Bowers, 45).

their mission programs to take into account the details of missionary life, including the realities for MKs. Their attitude toward MKs should be sympathetic and encouraging, with support that might include short-term trips to meet the MKs themselves.[20] When a home church forms a supportive missional community, its care for missionary families becomes easier.[21] An MK who feels at home in his or her home church has additional stabilizing roots. Local churches should set aside a portion of their mission giving as support for lay missionaries who work with MKs, for missionaries who lack a denominational background often find it hard to raise financial support. Many supporters assume that MK educators live on salaries paid by the school in which they work, which is not the case. MKs attending university in Korea need more hostels and scholarships available for them while they are away from their parents.[22]

Developing the skills of MK educators is essential. Education in an intercultural setting has particular challenges. Because of factors often beyond their control, teachers, dorm parents/assistants, and administrators tend not to stay in this ministry for a long period of time, which inhibits the development and accumulation of expertise. School leadership teams need to find creative ways of furthering corporate learning, recruiting, fund-raising, and planning. At present, few MKs show an interest in becoming MK teachers and staffers, but many MKs are concerned about MK education, which would be strengthened if adult former MKs fed their experience and resources back into the MK system.[23]

---

20. Woncheon Baptist Church, Suwon, Korea, has been active in sending teachers for Korean MKs, including to Hanal School, which is part of GDQ International Christian School, Tirana, Albania.

21. One MK in Senegal was notably proud and appreciative of the support of his home church, Chuncheon Onnuri Church, in Chuncheon, Korea.

22. Many MKs who attend Korean universities have to move frequently, especially during school breaks when they must move out of university dormitories and find alternative lodging which is a cause of anxiety. Many also must earn their living expenses during the breaks.

23. Encouragingly, an increasing number of young adult MKs are volunteering to assist younger MKs during camp programs specifically designed for them.

Mission agencies need to reinforce systems for MK care. Mission agencies should recruit education specialists who can provide MKs with up-to-date information about university admission and career counselors who can guide job seekers creatively. MKs in general, and isolated homeschoolers in particular, would greatly benefit from the assistance of itinerant teachers. Short-term volunteers can play a significant part in improving the performance of students. Mission mobilizers should bear in mind the specific needs of MKs and think creatively about how to encourage participation in MK care. Mission strategists need to overcome a tendency to think only of the work of the missionary and need also to bear in mind the needs of the children of the missionary. As they form policies and make decisions, mission executives need to balance between extremes and harmonize the differing perspectives of work and family.

CONCLUSION

Those who have participated in MK education are aware of its problems, and future good practice must address their spiritual, linguistic, emotional, psychological, cultural, physical, financial, and organizational concerns. It is only right that we clarify for MKs what is expected of them and that we teach them to have confidence in what they do, to cope with uncertainties, and to appreciate what they are given. We must not sideline their needs but rather stay with them as they grow to adulthood, and we must work together to maximize their opportunities.

Korean missionary children are part of God's kingdom. The sovereign hand of God is working in their lives. People who accept the lordship of God and desire the progress of his kingdom need to pay close attention to this often marginalized yet auspicious group of people. We need to address urgent needs astutely and deal with long-term issues faithfully. God's mission is both cross-cultural and cross-generational. Korean MKs are God's covenantal people, but they are vulnerable as they stand with their parents on the front lines of the *missio Dei*.

22
KOREA AND THE MIDDLE EAST:
Religious Encounters

On the surface, common ground is difficult to identify between the religious heritage of Korea and that of the Middle East. The major religions of Korea are shamanism, Buddhism, Confucianism, and Christianity, while Islam predominates in the Middle East. Rapid globalization and the increased frequency of exchange between Koreans and the peoples of the Middle East, however, are beginning to challenge common assumptions about the religious composition of each region. This chapter describes the history and current status of Islamic expansion in Korea as well as Korean Christian missions in the Middle East.

ISLAMIC EXPANSION IN KOREA

The influx of migrant workers and students with Islamic backgrounds is slowly changing the religious composition of the Korean population. According to Jung-Gook Ahn's estimates, there were 137,000 Muslims living in Korea in 2011.[1] Of these, 45,000 were permanent residents, including

---

Originally published online as an essay in the Middle East Institute's series on Korea and the Middle East (2014), www.mei.edu/content/map/korea-and-middle-east-religious-encounters, this chapter has been edited and is reprinted by permission.

1. Jung-Gook Ahn, "Hankukeui Muslim Eolmana Doena?" [How many Muslims are in Korea?], 2011, www.hani.co.kr/arti/SERIES/298/478232.html. Ahn's estimate draws on a statistical report on foreigners in Korea published by the Ministry of Law. He uses the number of foreigners by nationality and the percentage of the population that is Muslim in each country of origin to arrive at his estimated total.

35,000 ethnic Koreans.² Although Muslims account for only 0.08 percent of the total Korean population, 8.1 percent of foreigners in Korea are Muslims.

Contact between Korea and the Islamic world dates back many centuries. Between 723 and 727 C.E., a Buddhist monk named Hye Cho traveling to Persia and the Eastern Roman Empire became the first Korean to visit Islamic lands and leave behind written records.³ Scholars believe that Cheo-Yong, the first Arab Muslim to settle in Korea, arrived sometime in the ninth century.⁴ Evidence is insufficient, however, to support the existence of an indigenous Muslim community in Korea prior to the Korean War (June 25, 1950–July 27, 1953). At that time Turkish soldiers serving under the United Nations command attracted some Koreans to Islam.

Turkish soldiers formed the largest foreign division after U.S. troops, and they were known both for their bravery and for their efforts to assist war orphans and poor children. Their admirable reputation impressed some Koreans, which created opportunities for Islamic missions to Korea. By the end of 1953, Turkish commanders had decided to allow Koreans to attend Friday services, and in 1955 the Korean Muslim Federation was founded. The Federation later introduced doctrinal education and established a secondary school. The Korean Muslim community reached 1,500 members in 1960; in 1967, the Ministry of Culture and Communication formally registered the Korean Islamic Foundation.

The next decade saw an increase in exchanges between Korean Muslims and Islamic organizations in other countries. The first mosque in Korea was constructed in Seoul in May 1976. While the Korean government donated the land, a few Middle Eastern governments and

---

2. Ministry of Foreign Affairs and Trade, August 2, 2013, www.cdnews.co.kr/blog/blogOpenView.html?idxno=182255. The Korea Muslim Federation asserts that the number of ethnic Korean Muslims reached 40,000 in 2005. See Abdul Hamid Hyun-Cheol Kim, www.islamkorea.com/islamkorea_2.html.

3. Hee Soo Lee, *Islam Kwa Hankuk Munhwa* [Islam and Korean culture] (Seoul: Chung-A Book, 2012), 66.

4. Hee Soo Lee concludes that one of the first Muslims to emigrate and live in Korea was Cheo-Yong during the Silla Dynasty in the ninth century. Different interpretations of the historical records surrounding Cheo-Yong exist, but some historical materials support Lee's contention that Cheo-Yong was an Arab/Persian Muslim.

private organizations paid for the mosque's construction. From 1976 to 1979, the Korean Muslim population grew from 3,700 to 15,000.[5] Most converts were inspired by education in Islamic educational institutions abroad, intermarriage with Muslims, and business relationships.

Starting in March 1978, Korean Muslims began efforts to convert Korean workers who had been dispatched to the Middle East. These outreach projects, which were conducted through established liaison offices in countries such as Saudi Arabia, Kuwait, and Indonesia, successfully converted thousands of Korean workers to Islam. The return home of these workers prompted the establishment of new mosques in several cities. In 2014 there were a total of twelve mosques in Korea.[6]

Though the general Korean public has shown more suspicion of Islam since the September 11, 2001, attacks, the Korean media have recently shown increased willingness to describe Islam and Muslims positively. They explain the origins and current practices of Islam with an emic approach that is often neutral and sometimes favorable to Muslims; this perspective frequently differs from the stance adopted by many Middle Eastern media outlets toward Korean Christian missions in the Middle East.

KOREAN CHRISTIAN MISSIONS IN THE MIDDLE EAST

The Korean Presbyterian Church began sending missionaries abroad in the early twentieth century.[7] Ki-poong Lee, one of the pastors ordained at the first presbytery in 1907, was sent to Jeju Island as a missionary,

---

5. Abdul Hamid Hyun-Cheol Kim, "Hankuk Islam Hyunhwang" [The status of Korean Islam], (2006), www.islamkorea.com/islamkorea_2.html.

6. Though the governments of Korea and Saudi Arabia formed an agreement to establish an Islamic university in Korea in 1980, Saudi Arabia ultimately did not fund the project. See Sung-Taek Lee, "Hankuk Islamdae Sullipdo . . ." [Korean Islamic University frustrated . . .], December 27, 2012, Hankooki.com, http://news.hankooki.com/service/print/Print.php?po=news.hankooki.com/lpage/society/201212/h2012122702365021950.htm.

7. Yong Kyu Park, "Historical Overview of Korean Missions," in *Accountability in Missions: Korean and Western Case Studies*, ed. Jonathan J. Bonk (Eugene, Ore.: Wipf & Stock, 2011), 6.

after which other missionaries were sent to neighboring countries. In the 1950s, the Korean church began to send missionaries to more distant countries, such as Thailand and Pakistan.[8] Pakistan was not only geographically distant, but also very different in religious background from Korea. The missionaries sent there were the first from Korea to travel to an Islamic country.

The *Directory of Korean Missionaries and Mission Societies* was first published in 1979. Edited by Marlin L. Nelson, an American missionary who studied Christian missions in Korea for forty years, the report lists ninety-three Korean Christian missionary units (singles and families). Four were working in the Middle East and another fifteen in Islamic countries outside the region.[9] In 1979, nearly one of twenty-three Korean missionaries (4.3 percent) were working in the Middle East. The proportion dropped to 1.7 percent in the 1986 report and increased to 3.6 percent in the 1989 edition.[10]

According to the 1992 *Korean Mission Handbook*, 3.0 percent of the 2,576 Korean missionaries were reportedly working in Middle Eastern countries.[11] This figure grew to 4.3 percent in 1994 and reached 6.0 percent in 1996; however, it dropped to 4.4 percent in 1998.[12] Since then, identifying and counting the number of Korean missionaries who work in the Middle East and other regions that restrict or regulate Christian missionary activities has become increasingly difficult. So as to protect their members and to continue operating, Korean mission agencies do not openly share the details of their activities. From 2000 to 2013, the percentage of Korean missionaries working in the Middle East ranged from 1.2 percent to 5.4 percent.[13]

---

8. Park, "Historical Overview of Korean Missions," 9.

9. Marlin L. Nelson, *Directory of Korean Missionaries and Mission Societies* (Seoul: Asian Center for Theological Studies and Mission, 1979), 44.

10. Nelson, *Directory of Korean Missionaries*, 1986, 26–27, and 1989, 201–3.

11. Steve Sang-Cheol Moon, ed., *Korean Mission Handbook* (Seoul: Global Missionary Press, 1992), 6.

12. Moon, *Korean Mission Handbook*, 1994, 350–51; 1996, 328–29; 1998, 482–84.

13. Steve Sang-Cheol Moon, *Reports on the Korean Missionary Movement* (Seoul: Korea Research Institute for Mission, 2000–2013).

Korean missionaries have faced government restrictions on as well as social opposition to their activities in the region. Most of them have tried to maintain a low profile, but many have been expelled from countries in accordance with laws that prohibit missionary activities. Securing visa extensions has been a concern for many of them.

One reason Korean missionaries continue to go to the Middle East despite these challenges is the frontier mission movement, which emphasizes the importance of spreading the Gospel message to groups who are least familiar with Christianity. Although the movement originated in the United States, many Korean mission circles have taken up its goal and believe that the Gospel will move westward from East Asia until the second coming of Jesus.

Official missionaries affiliated with churches and Christian organizations have not been the only ones involved in missionary activities in Islamic areas. During the 1970s and 1980s, Korean construction workers in the Middle East established roughly 40 Korean diaspora churches and 150 workplace churches that catered to one million Christians per year.[14] In 1984 some of the workers who returned to Korea after their projects were completed took the initiative to form the Middle East Team, a mission agency that now has eighty-two members in nineteen countries.

PEACEFUL COEXISTENCE AND TOLERANCE

As a minority group, Muslims who live in Korea face some degree of social alienation and cultural prejudice. The general public needs to separate the image of radical, violent Islamists from that of ordinary Muslims who pursue peaceful coexistence and religious tolerance. In Korea, religious freedom is normative and protected by law; but as a relatively new religion to the country, Islam is at times misunderstood, and Muslims may find themselves isolated in society. Korean religious

---

14. Sang-Mok Shin, "Choongdongseonkyohei hongkeyhyun bonbujang . . ." [Hong Gye Hyun, director of Middle East Team, looking for . . .], *The Kukmin Daily*, March 21, 2014, http://m.missionlife.co.kr/view.asp?arcid=0008155690&code=23111111.

leaders, therefore, should encourage interreligious dialogue and discussion so as to overcome the presence of Islamophobia.

Korean Christians living in the Middle East face certain religious restrictions, the degree of which varies, depending on the constitution and religious laws of each country. Korean missionaries who work in the Middle East often feel that their religious freedom and human rights are in jeopardy,[15] and they question whether Shariah law is compatible with a Western democratic system that locates religion in the private domain. They believe that their missionary activities offer an alternative way of life that should be made available for people to choose.

CONCLUSION

Both the history of Islam in Korea and the history of Korean Christian missions in the Middle East are longer than most would imagine. Both religions have attracted adherents within the local populace through humanitarian works and other peaceful means. The two groups' missionary endeavors must be understood in light of the innate missionary nature of both Christianity and Islam. Missionary activities are also an important part of religious freedom, and tolerance for them should be protected.

---

15. Ho Jin Jun, *Junhwanjume Sun Jungdongkwa Islam* [The Middle East and Islam at the turning point] (Seoul: SFC Publishing, 2005), 197–99.

23
THE EDUCATIONAL MINISTRIES OF KOREAN MISSIONARIES

The most recent survey of Korean missions, conducted by the Korea Research Institute for Mission (KRIM) at the end of 2013, showed a total of 20,085 Korean missionaries working in 171 countries through 166 mission agencies.[1] During 2013 the total number of Korean missionaries increased by 287, for an annual growth rate of 1.43 percent.[2] Although the rate of growth in the number of missionaries being sent is slowing down, the data show that the churches of Korea are still sending many missionaries.

A sizeable proportion of Korean missionaries in the field (10.4 percent) are involved in running mission schools, universities, and institutes (hereafter collectively referred to as "mission schools"), and an additional 6.6 percent are providing theological education. In total, 17.0 percent of Korean missionaries are involved in educational ministries, through which they seek to evangelize a certain region or area.[3]

The research project on which this report is based was driven by three questions, all of which concern the educational institutions established overseas by Korean missionaries.

Originally published in *Korean Church, God's Mission, Global Christianity*, ed. Wonsuk Ma and Kyo Seong Ahn (Oxford: Regnum Books International, 2015), 270–84, this chapter has been edited and reprinted by permission.

1. The research project was sponsored by Asian Mission, a ministry of the E-Land Company group.

2. Steve Sang-Cheol Moon, "Missions from Korea 2014: Missionary Children," *International Bulletin of Missionary Research* 38, no. 2 (April 2014): 84–85.

3. Steve Sang-Cheol Moon, "Missions from Korea 2013: Microtrends and Finance," *International Bulletin of Missionary Research* 37, no. 2 (2013): 96–97.

- What are the realities of the mission schools?
- What are the needs of the mission schools?
- How can the effectiveness and efficiency of the mission schools be increased?

RESEARCH DESIGN AND METHODS

This examination of the educational ministries of Korean missionaries was launched as a research project in March 2013. The research design, which was complete by the end of April, drew in part upon a number of suggestions for ways of evaluating nonprofit organizations.[4] It included a survey questionnaire, interviews, and on-site observation. Recommendations from mission agencies played a significant part in a screening process that identified educational institutions offering positive models, a process that was complete by the end of June, and by the end of August additional recommendations received from senior missionaries had been reviewed as well.

Beginning in September 2013, the research team visited six countries—Mongolia, Bangladesh, Nepal, Indonesia, Cambodia, and Cameroon (in the order the team visited them)—to conduct on-site interviews and to carry out direct observation. Altogether, the research team visited fourteen educational institutions and interviewed 112 persons (71 students, 20 educators, and 21 administrators), ending up with recordings and transcribed interview notes totaling 269 pages (A4, single spaced). The questionnaire survey, conducted from December 2013

---

4. Peter K. Drucker, *The Drucker Foundation Self-Assessment Tool: Participant Workbook* (New York: Peter F. Drucker Foundation for Nonprofit Management, 1999); Peter K. Drucker, Max De Pree, and Frances Hesselbein, *Excellence in Nonprofit Leadership: Facilitator's Guide* (New York: Drucker Foundation, 1998); Scott Johnson and James D. Ludema, eds., *Partnering to Build and Measure Organizational Capacity: Lessons from NGOs around the World* (Grand Rapids: Christian Reformed World Relief Committee, 1997); Suresh Srivastva and Frank J. Barrett, "Appreciative Organizing: Implications for Executive Functioning," in *Appreciative Management and Leadership: The Power of Positive Thought and Action in Organization*, ed. Suresh Srivastva and David L. Cooperrider (Euclid, Ohio: Williams Custom Publishing, 1999), 381–400.

through February 2014, sought to establish the overall profile of schools established by Korean missionaries.

Data gathering for this research project proceeded from a pilot project to a qualitative field study and then to the quantitative questionnaire survey. Quantitative data were gathered primarily online through QuestionPro, but additional means such as telephone calls were used to complement the process. Quantitative data analysis was done using SPSS, and qualitative data analysis was done through the processes of manual coding, concept mapping, and pattern analysis.[5]

THE REALITIES OF EDUCATIONAL MINISTRIES

A statistical overview will help to clarify the kinds and scope of the educational ministries in which Korean missions are engaged. Further identification of the fourteen schools selected for on-site visits, in-depth interviews, and direct observation follows the statistical overview.

Statistical Overview

The questionnaire showed that Korean missionaries have established a total of 810 mission schools overseas. This total is based on reports provided by fifty major mission agencies and denominations. Possibly some schools were not officially identified and reported, so the actual number of mission schools could well exceed 900.

The 810 known educational institutions comprise 389 seminaries/theological colleges, 183 after-school learning centers, 104 primary schools, 55 secondary schools, 44 universities/colleges, and 35 vocational training centers. The institutions are located in Asia (62.4 percent), Africa (18.0 percent), Latin America (13.0 percent), Europe (3.3 percent), former USSR (1.9 percent), and Oceania (1.4 percent).

The schools in Asia form 62.4 percent of the total, considerably above the proportion of Korean missionaries working in Asia (52.9 percent).[6]

---

5. Vincent E. Faherty, *Wordcraft: Applied Qualitative Data Analysis (QDA); Tools for Public and Voluntary Services* (Los Angeles: SAGE, 2010).

6. Steve Sang-Cheol Moon, "Missions from Korea 2013: Microtrends and Finance," *International Bulletin of Missionary Research* 37, no. 2 (April 2013): 97.

A majority of the after-school learning centers are also located in Asia (65.0 percent). Though much lower in number, the percentage of mission schools located in Africa (18.0 percent) is much higher than the percentage of Korean missionaries (7.3 percent) serving on that continent (see table 23.1).

	Asia	Africa	Latin America	Europe	Former USSR	Oceania	Insufficient Information[A]	Total
Primary	31	18	8	1	1	0	45	104
Secondary	21	6	6	1	0	2	19	55
University/College	10	3	2	1	1	0	27	44
Seminaries	60	5	12	9	3	4	296	389
Vocational Training	23	9	2	1	0	0	0	35
Learning Centers	119	35	25	1	3	0	0	183
Total	264	76	55	14	8	6	387	810

[A] For many schools the mission agencies provided only limited information, including in 387 cases omission of the location of schools established by their members. The problem seems to be one of documentation.

Table 23.1. Mission schools established by Korean missionaries[7]

Selected Schools

Six primary and secondary schools were selected for field study and analysis: Bright Future Global Academy, Ulaanbaatar, Mongolia; Mongolia International School, Ulaanbaatar, Mongolia; Livingstone Academy, Kathmandu, Nepal; Covenant Academy, Kathmandu, Nepal; Antioch

---

7. Unfortunately, for many schools represented in this table the mission agencies provided only limited information, including omission of the schools' location for 387 of the schools established by their members. This problem seems to be a problem of documentation.

High School, Ketapang, Indonesia; and All Nations School, Yaounde, Cameroon. See table 23.2.

Name	Location	Year Opened	Principal	Students	Staff	Budget (US$)
Bright Future Global Academy	Ulaanbaatar Mongolia	1997	Sung Hye Heo	80	20	200,000
Mongolia International School	Ulaanbaatar Mongolia	2010	Young Jun Tak	33	12	140,000
Livingstone Academy	Kathmandu Nepal	2001	Geum Rae Kim	535	60	200,000
Covenant Academy	Kathmandu Nepal	2002	Tae Hoon Jin	364	30	60,000
Antioch High School	Ketapang Indonesia	1987	Saltdnce Mel Nesimnasi	59	16	Not Available
All Nations School	Yaounde Cameroon	2009	Sung Hee Choi	152	30	50,000

Table 23.2. Primary and secondary schools

Field studies were conducted at two universities, both in Ulaanbaatar, Mongolia: Mongolia International University and Mongol Huree University. See table 23.3.

Name	Location	Year Opened	President	Students	Staff	Budget (US$)
Mongolia International University	Ulaanbaatar Mongolia	2002	Oh-Moon Kwon	1,040	60	2,500,000
Mongol Huree University	Ulaanbaatar Mongolia	2002	Sun Hoon Jung	1,450	45	Not available

Table 23.3. Universities

Four seminaries were visited for on-site study: Mongolia Presbyterian Seminary, Ulaanbaatar, Mongolia; Cameroon Faculty of Evangelical

Theology, Yaounde, Cameroon; Cambodia Presbyterian Theological Institute, Phnom Penh, Cambodia; and ATI (Sekolah Tinggi Theologia "Abdi Tuhan Injili"), Pontiakak, Indonesia. See table 23.4.

Name	Location	Year Opened	President/ Dean	Students	Staff	Budget (US$)
Mongolia Presbyterian Seminary	Ulaanbaatar Mongolia	2005	Byung Il Roh	39	17	30,000
Cameroon Faculty of Evangelical Theology	Yaounde Cameroon	1997	Sameul Yeo Kyung Kwak	91	24	85,000
Cambodia Presbyterian Theological Institute	Phnom Penh Cambodia	2004	Ho Jin Jun	122	13	120,000
ATI (Sekolah Tinggi Theologia "Abdi Tuhan Injili")	Pontiakak Indonesia	1985	Moris Takaliwang	122	16	126,00

Table 23.4. Seminaries

Researchers visited one vocational training center and one after-school learning center. They were the Institute of Sustainable Agriculture and Community Development, also known as ISAC School, Ta Keo, Cambodia; and Wing Wing Center, Dhaka, Bangladesh. See table 23.5.

Name	Location	Year Opened	President	Students	Staff	Budget (US$)
ISAC School	Ta Keo Cambodia	2003	Ki Dae Kim	27	17	Not available
Wing Wing Center	Dhaka Bangladesh	2007	Seok Bong Lee	500	3	36,000

Table 23.5. Other institutions

The following analysis of educational ministries' needs is based on interviews and on-site observation conducted at the above institutions.

NEEDS OF EDUCATIONAL MINISTRIES

For convenience, the needs of educational ministries can be divided into common needs and particular needs in particular areas. Also, for clarity in discussion, it is helpful to differentiate between felt needs and real needs. Felt needs are immediate and are needs of which people are aware. They often require an urgent respone. Real needs may lie beneath the surface and be harder to discern but it is important that they be addressed from a long-term perspective.

Common Needs

Mission schools in the field have certain needs in common regardless of location or type of school. For example, they should recruit good educators as professors and teachers and obtain competent and resourceful administrative staff. Frequent changes in the composition of the staff undermine the quality of education offered. Librarians and webmasters are also priority needs.

Mission schools must have proper buildings and facilities, with many schools needing to own their own buildings. The character and quality of dormitory buildings are important because much community interaction occurs there. Provision of proper housing for faculty is important because of the effect it has on the amount of support that expatriate faculty members need to raise. For the development of an educational institution, adequate library space is essential.

Building up the institution's library collection is an important need that all mission schools have in common. As books are expensive, schools have difficulty purchasing all that may be desired or required. In many places, using an online library service is a solution for students who commute from distant locations. In today's globalizing age, access to good information services is essential for the development of mission schools.

Facilities and equipment are important needs as well. For example, mission schools require furniture, computers, digital projectors, copiers, musical instruments, laboratory equipment, and other equipment. Some mission universities receive used equipment from Korean universities when those institutions upgrade their equipment.

Mission schools have significant financial needs. The schools the research team visited are more stable financially than many schools, but they still have significant financial needs that must be met from external sources. Construction projects and scholarship funds need to be subsidized by outsiders.

For mission schools to exist, they need students. The schools our research team visited were all successful in recruiting students, but many other schools experience difficulty in this area. School administrators need to give thought to the optimal size of the student body and to recruit students effectively.

For mutual benefit, mission schools need to establish ties with other schools. Reciprocal exchanges with other educational institutions, in Korea and elsewhere, have much to do with the success of mission schools. More attention needs to be given to promoting programs of student and faculty exchange.

Providing opportunities for advanced education for teachers and professors is critical to educational quality. For the sake of the future success of educational ministries, deliberate effort and long-range investment need to be channeled into this area. Some of the selected schools are to be commended for setting a good example in this respect. Also to be commended are the experts from Korea who at times volunteer to come to the mission schools to lead seminars for their teachers or professors.

Though not easy, educating the parents of students about the educational philosophy of the school is an important and necessary part of a holistic Christian education. Most mission schools undertake this task, but how to do so in a foreign country where the major religious or ideological backdrop is Hinduism, Islam, or Communism poses challenges.

Software development is another significant need of mission schools. Although it may be difficult to do in the field, for the future of Christian education on the mission field, mission schools should consciously invest effort in this area. Experts in Korea can assist mission schools in developing software programs effectively and efficiently.

Another area too often neglected is the food in the dormitories. Students, especially in seminary dormitories, are not satisfied with the quality of the food. Misunderstandings between managers and students are caused primarily by the hard financial realities facing the schools.

The manner in which schools cooperate with their local communities is an important factor in their success. When a mission school is well received in the local community, it will not only survive but also thrive and influence that community. Cooperation with the government and local authorities is important, too.

Particular Needs in Particular Contexts

Some needs are specific to particular contexts. Although this discussion now moves beyond needs that all mission schools have in common, the issues raised here are significant and must be addressed within particular ministry settings.

Mission schools need to pursue specialization in the type of education they offer for then they will stand out as distinctive or as having special strength. It is not enough to have a Christian educational philosophy and background. A school's whole curriculum should have a focus or be specialized on one area. Specialization as an international university or a university of science and technology are good examples.

At certain kinds of schools, more attention must be paid to the faculty's academic qualifications. For example, seminaries in Indonesia urgently need qualified faculty members so as to meet government requirements. Many universities need faculty with doctoral degrees.

Mission schools need to strengthen their expertise related to the area where they are located. Seminaries in Africa, for example, need to develop expertise in youth education, HIV/AIDS-related ministry, and refugee ministry.

Denominational ties are important for seminaries. Seminary leaders need to maintain good relations with denominations in their countries of service, for both personnel and financial support can come through networking with denominations. In many contexts, solid denominational relationships will contribute to the successful indigenization of a seminary.

High on the agenda for many mission schools in Africa is securing quality water and electricity supplies. Needs of this type relate directly to the quality of the living conditions and education on campus. Korean churches must be attentive to such significant needs and support mission schools in this area.

Seminaries in francophone Africa definitely need theological books in French, yet, unfortunately, Korean churches seem to have little awareness of this need. Meeting needs such as this requires that a group of committed people work together continuously.

Personnel of mission schools in remote areas find it hard to meet supporters and spend time with them. School leaders have difficulty traveling back to and returning from the places where current and potential supporters live. They need others as advocates who can represent them.

Vocational training centers need not only technical expertise but also marketing expertise. They need specialized equipment for practical workshops, and also advice on how to make a profit out of their technologies and skills.

After-school learning centers need committed teachers who are devoted to the education of children and to evangelism. In running a learning center in an Islamic cultural background, cultural sensitivity is a must, and much flexibility is required in terms of the systems and methods used.

Real Needs or Visionary Needs

The needs just mentioned are felt needs; that is, they are present in the minds of educators as urgent concerns that should be addressed directly. Real needs differ in being deeper and longer-term concerns that lie beneath the surface. Distinguishing conceptually between the two kinds of needs can be helpful.

A real need of significance in educational ministry is for an educator to build up relationships of trust with students and fellow educators. Just as evangelism implies a relationship or a friendship, successful educational ministry presupposes good relationships and a close network. Educators can influence students spiritually only on the basis of sound and healthy personal relationships.

Developing curricula for holistic education is another real need in educational missions. Educational leaders must be more specific in explaining their vision of holistic education, for then they will design curricula that are forthrightly based on their vision. In understanding the educational task before them, teachers and students must be enabled to operate from the same perspective.

Another significant need lies in developing a communal atmosphere within a school's environment. Personal interaction in a community setting is an important element of holistic education. Communities provide people with a sense of belonging.

From the outset educational missions should have the preparation of local educational leaders as an explicit long-term goal. Without leadership development, educational missions cannot be indigenized or engage initiatives undertaken by local people. School administrators often focus on finding teachers and staff who can serve immediately, but a long-term perspective demands the identification of potential leaders who can sustain the mission into the next generation.

Building and maintaining a knowledge base is essential to the health of the endeavor. This task includes integrating knowledge that currently is compartmentalized and sharing this knowledge widely to create synergy. The know-how of educational missions must be accumulated systematically.

The ultimate purpose of these educational ministries is to transmit a Christian worldview. The essence of Christian education is to help students to internalize the Christian worldview and embody it in their lives. This understanding of the nature of Christian education is fundamental and must be in place before any discussion of specific issues concerning attitudes and directions in concrete situations.

EFFECTIVENESS AND EFFICIENCY OF EDUCATIONAL MINISTRIES

The educational ministries carried out by Korean missionaries can be evaluated in two ways. The first approach, using quantitative methodology, calls upon mission executives to evaluate the mission schools.

The second approach, using the methods of qualitative research, asks for students, as insiders, to evaluate the schools.

Opinions of Mission Executives

As a quantitative survey 124 mission executives representing major Korean missionary sending agencies were asked to respond to a ten-item questionnaire. Altogether 60 survey forms were filled out and returned by the mission executives.

The first question asked the executives to rank on a Likert scale the effectiveness of Korean missionaries' educational ministries. More than half (58.2 percent) of the respondents evaluated the ministries positively. More than one in five (21.8 percent) evaluated the ministries as very positive, while 16.4 percent scored the schools' contribution as average. Only 3.6 percent gave a negative response, and no one characterized the ministries as being very negative.

The second question asked the executives to select among suggested possible answers the most positive aspect of the educational ministries of Korean missionaries. The majority of respondents (62.5 percent) highlighted the fact that the mission schools seek to provide students with limited financial means an opportunity to learn. Another 12.5 percent of the respondents indicated specialized education in at least one area as a special strength. Only 5.4 percent of the respondents identified the educational ministries as being worthwhile because they seek to offer elite education, and a further 5.4 percent chose provision of Korean-style education. A number of respondents (14.3 percent) found other aspects to be important in their evaluation.

The third question asked the respondents to identify the most negative aspect of the educational ministries of Korean missionaries. Almost half of the respondents (46.4 percent) marked the answer that mission schools' financial dependency is a negative aspect. One in five (19.6 percent) pointed to schools' lack of stability because of the fluctuating sociopolitical situations where they are located. Another 12.5 percent indicated the educational ministries' lack of cost efficiency. One in ten (10.7 percent) pointed to competition with local schools as a negative aspect. Another 10.7 percent identified various other concerns.

The fourth question asked respondents to identify important points of improvement that would enable the educational ministries of Korean missionaries to advance. Half (50.9 percent) marked assessing each field's educational needs so that schools could be run at an optimal size. Slightly more than one in five (22.6 percent) emphasized cooperation with local schools and avoiding duplication. Participation in the global trend of establishing international exchange programs was pointed out by 13.2 percent of the respondents. Supplying the Korean educational experience in the field received minimal support (1.9 percent). A significant number of respondents (11.3 percent) were not specific, but marked the category "Other."

The fifth question addressed financial self-support. More than half of the respondents (56.0 percent) emphasized the need for flexibility in applying self-support policies to schools. Another important block was formed by the 20.0 percent of respondents who held the opinion that schools should be self-supporting within ten years of start-up. The idea that educational ministries need to be supported by Korean churches and organizations on a long-term basis received less support (12.0 percent). Least support was garnered by the idea that schools should be self-supporting through tuition payments and internal income from the beginning (4.0 percent). Other ideas came to 8.0 percent.

The sixth question sought for desirable ways to carrying out leadership transition. The suggestion with greatest support (37.7 percent) was that local educators be recruited onto the faculty from the outset and then developed as leaders step by step. Receiving less support (28.3 percent), but still important, was the proposal that leadership transition be planned from the beginning and be completed within ten years. Another realistic opinion (26.4 percent) was to be flexible in considering different educational environments in different countries. Least support (1.9 percent) was expressed for the option of having the founder of the school remain in charge until retirement. The remaining opinions totaled 5.7 percent.

The seventh question concerned property ownership. The majority opinion (53.7 percent) was to be flexible in applying policies regarding property ownership. Another significant opinion (33.3 percent) was to register the school as a legal body from the beginning and then acquire property;

otherwise the school should not purchase real estate. Neither registering property through co-ownership by multiple local individuals (1.9 percent) nor ownership by a missionary when permitted legally (1.9 percent) received much support. Unspecified answers totaled 9.3 percent.

The eighth question addressed educational missionaries' qualifications. The majority of respondents (67.3 percent) pointed to the importance of missionaries' educational philosophy and beliefs. Passion for student care took second place (19.2 percent), while administrative experience ranked third (7.7 percent) and teaching experience fourth (3.8 percent). The remainder was only 1.9 percent.

The ninth question looked to the future prospects of educational ministries. The majority outlook (69.2 percent) was that as a result of the impact of globalization on the educational market, educational ministries will need to grow. Significant support (19.2 percent) was expressed for the view that in the future, educational missions will be limited to certain areas and will need to be limited to small-scale projects. Some respondents (7.7 percent) believed that as indigenous educational initiatives gain momentum in many countries, educational missions will no longer be needed. A few (3.8 percent) did not answer or offered responses not specified in the questionnaire form.

The tenth question sought to examine niches in educational ministry. A significant number of respondents (32.7 percent) replied that various levels of regular mission schools are still needed. An equal number (32.7 percent) felt that vocational training centers are much needed for poor children. A smaller number (15.4 percent) supported specialization of regular schools. After-school learning centers were seen as a niche by some respondents (11.5 percent). Other opinions were 7.7 percent.

The above analyses show that Korean mission administrators are well aware of the issues and concerns related to educational missions. Their varied choices on specific issues provide an important etic, or outsider's, view of the complex reality of mission schools.

Student Response

The research team sought to evaluate the quality of education mission schools offer by interviewing students enrolled in them. In this analysis from an emic, or insider's, view, a distinction was made between the academic quality and the religious educational quality of students' school experience.

Our interviews showed that school administrators and educators were not alone in evaluating the academic quality of the mission schools as superior to that of most of the other educational institutions in the six countries; the schools' students did so as well. Administrators and teachers, especially of schools that pursued specialization in education, emphasized that their schools perform better than the local schools in their neighborhoods and cities, although they still had concerns about school facilities, equipment, and the need to enhance their schools' educational programs. Students' responses to the interview questions supported this observation.

Most of the seventy-one students interviewed expressed gratitude to both the school leaders and the Korean churches for the benefits they receive through the mission schools, although they also mentioned problematic areas where improvement is needed. The students' optimistic attitude may be partly a carryover of their cultural heritage, but their positive evaluation resonated with the servant attitude of the missionaries.

Schools that showed a comparative advantage in their contexts typically had well-qualified leadership teams. The missionaries were recognized for their spiritual leadership and educational expertise, and for the intercultural competence they showed in carrying out their ministries. The strengths possessed by members of the leadership team complemented each other. When a top leader was not well equipped in one area, other members of the team were able to compensate for that individual weakness.

Most of the mission schools sought to be holistic in their approach to Christian education, with religious education as an important part of their purpose and curricula. Therefore, evaluation of their performance needed to cover the religious as well as the academic aspects of the education they were providing. The brevity of our visits was an obstacle to such extensive investigation, but use of a narrative analytical approach offered some results. The students expressed satisfaction and gratitude for the religious education offered in the schools. They showed trust in the teachers and the staff. Many of those interviewed, especially among the middle school students, confessed that their faith in God began while they were attending the schools.

Both in interviews of the students and in analysis of the data, the theme of value transmission from educators to students was selected as a focus. Overall, the interviews showed that values emphasized by school leaders are being effectively transmitted to the students. For example, in Yaounde, Cameroon, Sung Hee Choi's emphasis on the lordship of Christ was naturally expressed in her repeated use of "God said," "God led," "God willed," and similar phrases (twenty-four times in a forty-six-minute interview session). Another key word she used was "love" (four times). These words connected with her students' repeated use of words such as "disciple" and "obedience."

Choi's faith in God's sovereignty and Christ's love appear to have influenced the formation of her students' values, and the students' application of these values showed itself in a disciplined and obedient life in a school context where harmonious relations with fellow students are important. When asked about their future, students often expressed a vision for serving the countries and regions where they lived or were in school, practicing God's *agape* love. Many said that their vision was to serve poor people as a doctor. Won Roh Yoon, Sung Hee Choi's husband, recently started a medical college in Yaounde to advance medical service in Africa, and a number of the high school students are highly interested in entering the college after they graduate.

Additional values of importance that were transmitted from the educators to the students in these educational institutions were "worshiping God," "Christian worldview," "community," "optimal technology," "evangelicalism," "Reformed theology," and "saving lost souls." Many students confessed that their dreams had changed from worldly achievement to a missional vision or from the prosperity of their own family to commitment to the kingdom of God.

The mission schools showed a sense of balance between academic excellence and religious faithfulness in their educational task. Many mission schools—though none of those we visited—lean toward elite education, placing great emphasis on academics at the expense of a balanced Christian education. Therefore, over time they are losing the focus supplied by their founding vision, as have many mission schools established years ago in Korea by American missionaries. The schools we visited are working, each in its own way, to maintain a balance.

Both the quantitative evaluation by the mission executives and the qualitative evaluation by the students are positive about the performance level of the mission schools the research team visited. This evaluation, however, does not mean that the schools perform well in all aspects of their practice, for problems and weaknesses were encountered in some areas. One school's strength is another school's deficiency. The goal must be to look to models of excellence and achievement in order to maximize strengths and counter weaknesses by learning from one another.

OBSERVATIONS AND RECOMMENDATIONS

To prevent repeating past mistakes, schools and teachers need to share their experience—and lessons learned in educational ministry—with one another. Issues of attitude and know-how are fleshed out now, with recommendations for future development following.

Seven Desirable Attitudes

The following seven attitudes, desirable in themselves but required in missionaries involved in educational ministries, are necessary:

- To be filled with unconditional love so as to care for students well
- To be able to see the students' potential
- To wait patiently
- To make listening a disciplined habit
- To cooperate and collaborate well with other people
- To have a creative mind
- To possess the power to motivate and influence people

Shareable Know-How

The following seven forms of accumulated know-how are essential for missionaries working in educational ministries:

- Extensive understanding of the educational policies of the country of service before an educational ministry is planned
- Identification of niches of educational need even in countries where the educational environment is stable and with specific planning to meet a particular need
- Consideration of the geographical conditions when developing a ministry strategy
- Establishment of a strategic information system with other educational institutions, especially with Korean institutions, to recruit faculty members and to receive consideration for donated equipment.
- Cooperation with NGOs to obtain subsidies for low-income students
- Thorough familiarity with host countries' educational ministries for the sake of marketing and to draw upon existing skills and resources
- Monitoring of changes in Korean society, especially changes in the educational sector, to keep the field ministries up-to-date

Recommendations for Future Development

Supporting churches, mission agencies, and NGOs and companies in Korea all have a role to play. Seven recommendations for each follow.

Supporting churches in Korea need to

- Show more interest and loving concern for educational ministries. In unreached areas, educational ministries are as important as church-planting ministries.
- Encourage young mission volunteers to consider educational ministries overseas.
- Provide information and support to retired professionals so that they can serve in mission schools.
- Support mission schools' construction projects, especially in the churches' countries of special interest. Mega-churches need to pay greater attention to such needs.

- Upgrade vision trip programs to include assisting mission schools.
- Sponsor scholarship programs for mission schools.
- Provide continuous support for seminaries and theological colleges established by Korean missionaries.

Korean mission agencies need to
- Show more concern and care for their missionaries in educational ministries.
- Conduct a needs assessment before their members attempt an educational project.
- Evaluate their mission schools at each developmental stage.
- Recruit support groups for their educational ministries. Sometimes each project will need a separate support group.
- Help their missionaries to extend their networks.
- Show more concern and care for students who live in Korea and attend a university as part of an exchange program.
- Maintain a database to support recruitment of school faculty and administrative staff.

NGOs and companies with a Christian background need to
- Show more interest and concern for the educational ministries of Korean missionaries.
- Support the construction projects of mission schools and universities.
- Increase sponsorship of scholarship programs for mission schools and universities.
- Contribute to the advancement of educational ministries in their countries of special interest and in their areas of specialization.
- Support socially less-privileged children in poor countries.
- Support social enterprises in partnership with mission universities.
- Assist in member care for missionaries in educational ministries.

CONCLUSION

Our research has shown that exemplary institutions and models of good practice that can be used as benchmarks exist among the educational ministries of the Korean church. Such achievement should be made widely known. Not all mission schools are positive cases, the positive cases are not perfect, and more effort needs to be invested in organizational learning. But Korean educational missions are rich in accumulated knowledge and skills. This wealth must be shared across boundaries and generations so that educational ministries can advance their practices.

CONCLUSION

The striking dimension in Korea's experience of global missions is the country's swift turn from being a missionary-receiving country to being one of the foremost missionary-sending countries. As recently as the end of the 1970s, the number of foreign missionaries working in Korea was greater than the number of Korean missionaries working abroad. By the late 1980s that paradigm had been reversed.

The Korean church has cherished a missional DNA from its beginning. That spiritual heritage was an important factor in the phenomenal growth in the number of missionaries sent from Korea beginning in the 1980s. The sociocultural conditions that moved the globalization of the country forward also played a vital role in advancing the Korean missionary movement. Another contributing factor was the structural development of Korean mission agencies. Each factor was orchestrated under God's providence. God is the originator, initiator, driving force, sustaining dynamic, and developer of the Korean missionary movement.

Korean mission leaders have exercised their responsibility for missional leadership well. In Korean missions' early years, many things were uncertain and unpredictable, and preparation was lacking. Leaders did not have the depth of experience to know what it takes to do missions well; they simply obeyed the call to mission leadership and did the best they could. These leaders led sacrificial lives for the sake of their ministries. Even though they did not have enough time for reflection or to prepare for the future—the rapid growth of the missions movement always kept them stretched to their limits—they addressed emerging issues wisely. Korean missionaries have been fortunate to have had good leaders.

Korean mission agencies have shown excellence in organizational learning. They evaluated new mission strategies critically and applied them in their ministries. They were receptive to new paradigms for missions. Mission agencies have offered many training programs and seminars, and as a result ordinary people in Korea have had no problem learning about missions. In the quarter century from 1988 to 2013, active learning became a dominant trait in the organizational culture within the Korean missions circle.

As its missional spirituality, leadership, and learning are consolidated, the Korean dimension of global missions will surely play an even stronger role in the future. Relying on God's sovereignty and grace, we can expect yet deeper maturation of the movement in the years ahead. *Soli Deo Gloria*!

BIBLIOGRAPHY

Ahn, Jung-Gook. 2011. "Hankukeui Muslim Eolmana Doena?" [How many Muslims are in Korea?]. www.hani.co.kr/arti/SERIES/298/478232.html.

Ashkenas, Ron. "The Organization's New Clothes." In Hesselbein, Goldsmith, and Beckhard, *Organization of the Future*, 99–108.

Alexander, Jeffrey C. "Toward a Theory of Cultural Trauma." In *Cultural Trauma and Collective Identity*, edited by Jeffrey C. Alexander, Ron Eyerman, Bernhard Giesen, Neil J. Smelser, and Piotr Sztompka, 1–30. Berkeley: Univ. of California Press, 2004.

Bangkok Mission Forum Steering Committee, ed. *Mission and Accountability* (in Korean). Chunan, Korea: Hebon, 2005.

Bennett, Shane, and Kim Felder. *Exploring the Land*. Littleton, Colo.: Caleb Project, 1995.

Bonk, Jonathan J., ed. *Accountability in Missions: Korean and Western Case Studies*. Eugene, Ore.: Wipf & Stock, 2011.

———, ed. *Family Accountability in Missions: Korean and Western Case Studies*. New Haven, Conn.: OMSC Publications, 2013.

———. "Mission by the Numbers." *International Bulletin of Missionary Research* 35, no. 1 (January 2011): 1–2.

———. *Missions and Money: Affluence as a Missionary Problem*. Rev. ed. Maryknoll, N.Y.: Orbis Books, 2006.

Bowers, Joyce M., ed. *Raising Resilient MKs: Resources for Caregivers, Parents, and Teachers*. Colorado Springs, Colo.: Association of Christian Schools International, 1998.

Cho, David Dong Jin. "Nacu Somyeong, Naeu Seonkyohaengjeon" [My calling, my mission acts]. In *Somyeong: Naega Yeogi Itnaida*,

Nareul Bonesoseo [Calling: Here I am! Send me!], edited by Timothy Kiho Park and Wonsuk Ma, 40–60. Seoul: Qumran, 2010.

Cho, Hae Joang. *Daean gyoyuk jonghapbaljun banganeh gwanhan yongu* [A study of ways to develop comprehensive alternative education]. Seoul: Ministry of Education, Science, and Technology, 2011.

Choi, Chan Young. *Choi Chan Young Iyagi* [The story of Choi Chan Young]. Seoul: Joy Press, 1995.

Choi, Hyung-Keun. "Preparing Korean Missionaries for Cross-Cultural Effectiveness." Ph.D. diss., Asbury Theological Seminary, 2000.

Drucker, Peter F. *The Drucker Foundation Self-Assessment Tool: Participant Workbook*. New York: Peter F. Drucker Foundation for Nonprofit Management, 1999.

———. "Introduction: Toward the New Organization." In Hesselbein, Goldsmith, and Beckhard, *Organization of the Future*, 1–5.

———. *Management Challenges for the Twenty-First Century*. New York: HarperBusiness, 1977, 1999.

Drucker, Peter F., Max De Pree, and Frances Hesselbein. *Excellence in Nonprofit Leadership: Facilitator's Guide*. New York: The Drucker Foundation, 1998.

Duques, Ric, and Paul Gaske. "The 'Big' Organization of the Future." In Hesselbein, Goldsmith, and Beckhard, *Organization of the Future*, 33–42.

Faherty, Vincent E. *Wordcraft: Applied Qualitative Data Analysis (QDA): Tools for Public and Voluntary Services*. Los Angeles: SAGE, 2010.

Farrell, B. Hunter. "Broken Trust: Sexual Abuse in the Mission Community: A Case Study in Mission Accountability." In Bonk, *Accountability in Missions*, 206–15.

Foster, George M. "Peasant Society and the Image of Limited Good." *American Anthropologist* 67, no. 2 (1965): 293–315.

Fullerton, Larry. "Accountability in Mission: Black Rock Congregational Church as a Case Study." In Bonk, *Accountability in Missions*, 149–76.

Geertz, Clifford. *The Interpretation of Cultures*. New York: Basic Books, 1973.

George, Sherron Kay. "Local-Global Mission: The Cutting Edge." *Missiology: An International Review* 28, no. 2 (April 2000): 187–97.

Glanz, Jeffrey. *Finding Your Leadership Style: A Guide for Educators.* Alexandria, Va.: Association for Supervision and Curriculum Development, 2002.

Gluckman, Max. *The Judicial Process among the Barotse of Northern Rhodesia* (Manchester, U.K.: Manchester Univ. Press, 1955).

Green, Stanley W. "Mission, Missionary, and Church Accountability That Counts: Implications for Integrity, Strategy, and Dynamic Continuity." In Bonk, *Accountability in Missions*, 71–82.

Greenlee, David. "Cookbooks, Firemen, Jazz Musicians, and Dairy Farmers: Strategy and Research for Twenty-first Century Missions." In *Global Passion: Marking George Verwer's Contribution to World Mission*, edited by David Greenlee, 163–70. Carlisle, Eng.: Authentic Lifestyle, 2003.

Hahn, Geoffrey W. "Response to Kiho (Timothy) Park, 'The Big Picture.'" In Bonk, *Accountability in Missions*, 66–70.

Hall, Stuart. "Introduction: Who Needs 'Identity'?" In *Questions of Cultural Identity*, edited by Stuart Hall and Paul du Gay, 1–17. Los Angeles: SAGE, 1996.

Hesselbein, Frances, Marshall Goldsmith, and Richard Beckhard, eds. *The Organization of the Future.* San Francisco: Jossey-Bass, 1997.

Hiebert, Paul G. *Anthropological Reflections on Missiological Issues.* Grand Rapids: Baker Books, 1994.

———. *Cultural Anthropology.* Grand Rapids: Baker Books, 1976.

———. *The Gospel in Human Contexts: Anthropological Explorations for Contemporary Missions.* Grand Rapids: Baker Academic, 2009.

———. *Transforming Worldviews: An Anthropological Understanding of How People Change.* Grand Rapids: Baker Academic, 2008.

Hiebert, Paul G., and Eloise Hiebert Meneses. *Incarnational Ministry: Planting Churches in Band, Tribal, Peasant, and Urban Societies.* Grand Rapids: Baker, 1995.

Holland, Dorothy, William Lachicotte Jr., Debra Skinner, and Carole Cain. *Identity and Agency in Cultural Worlds.* Cambridge, Mass.: Harvard Univ. Press, 1998.

International Conference on Missionary Kids. *Compendium of the International Conference on Missionary Kids: New Directions in Missions, Implications for MKs, Manila, Philippines, November 5–9, 1984*. Pasadena, Calif.: William Carey Library, 1986.
Jang, In Sik. 2005. "Seonkyohyunji Haengjeong System: Response to 'Receiving Entity System'" [Administration system in mission fields: Response to "Receiving Entity System"]. In Bangkok Mission Forum Steering Committee, *Mission and Accountability*, 243–52.
Johnson, Scott, and James D. Ludema, eds. *Partnering to Build and Measure Organizational Capacity: Lessons from NGOs around the World*. Grand Rapids: Christian Reformed World Relief Committee, 1997.
Johnstone, Patrick. *Operation World*. Grand Rapids, Mich.: Zondervan, 1993.
Johnstone, Patrick, and Jason Mandryk. *Operation World: When We Pray God Works*. Carlisle, Eng.: Paternoster Lifestyle, 2001.
Johnstone, Patrick, and Jason Mandryk, with Robyn Johnstone. *Operation World. Twenty-First Century Edition*. Carlisle, Cumbria: Paternoster Publishing, 2001.
Jun, Ho Jin. *Junhwanjume Sun Jungdongkwa Islam* [The Middle East and Islam at the turning point]. Seoul: SFC Publishing, 2005.
Jung, Min-Young. "Seonkyowa Chaekmu" [Mission and accountability]. In Bangkok Mission Forum Steering Committee, *Mission and Accountability*, 19–35.
———. "Strategic Accountability: God's Mission in God's Way." In Bonk, *Accountability in Missions*, 267–79.
Kim, Abdul Hamid Hyun-Cheol. "Hankuk Islam Hyunhwang" [The status of Korean Islam]. 2006. www.islamkorea.com/islamkorea_2.html.
Kim, Hark Yoo. "The Retention Factors among Korean Missionaries to Japan." Ph.D. diss., Trinity International University, 2001.
Kim, Soo Jung. "Seonkyosaeu Seongkongjeokin Sayeok Yoine Daehan Yeonku: Egypt Seonkyosareul Jungsimeuro" [A study of the factors for successful ministries: The case of Korean missionaries

in Egypt]. M.Div. thesis, Hapdong Theological Seminary, 2003.
Lee, Ban Seok (Peter). "Accountability Issues among Korean Missions Organizations." In Bonk, *Accountability in Missions*, 181–200.
Lee, David Taiwoong, and Steve Sang-Cheol Moon, eds. *Directory of Korean Missionaries and Mission Societies*. Seoul: Basilae, 1990.
———. "The Korean Hostage Incident: Seven Lessons Learned." In Taylor, *Sorrow and Blood*, 303–8.
Lee, Hee Soo. *Islam Kwa Hankuk Munhwa* [Islam and Korean culture]. Seoul: Chung-A Book, 2012.
Lee, Shin Chul. "Accountability in Mission: A Case Study of Korean Presbyterian Mission (Kosin)." In Bonk, *Accountability in Missions*, 222–39.
Lee, Sung-Taek. "Hankuk Islamdae Sullipdo . . ." [Korean Islamic university frustrated . . .]. December 27, 2012. http://news.hankooki.com/service/print/Print.php?po=news.hankooki.com/lpage/society/201212/h2012122702365021950.htm.
Lim, Tae-Gyu. "The Status of Christian Alternative Schools in Korea" (in Korean). 2009. www.casak.org.
Moon, Steve Sang-Cheol. "Acts of the Koreans: Status and Current Trends of the Missionary Movement in Korea." In Moon, *Korean Mission Handbook*, i–v. 1996.
———. "The Educational Ministries of Korean Missionaries." In *Korean Church, God's Mission, Global Christianity*, edited by Wonsuk Ma and Kyo Seong Ahn, 270–84. Oxford: Regnum Books International, 2015.
———. *Hankook Kyohoeeu Koyukseonkyo Hyonhwangkwa Baljeonbangan* [The status of the educational ministries of Korean missionaries and agendas for development]. Seoul: GMF Press, 2014.
———. "Hankuk Gidokgyo Seonkyowoondongeu Donghyangkwa Kwaje" [The trends and tasks of the Korean Christian missionary movement]. Pabalma 192 (September 10, 2007).
———. *Hankuk Kyohoeeu Kyoyukseonkyoeu Hyeonhwangkwa Baljeonbangan* [The status of educational missions of the Korean church and suggestions for development]. Seoul: GMF Press, 2014.

———. "Hankuk Seonkyo Hyeonhwangkwa Kwaje" [The status and tasks of Korean missions]. In Moon, *Korean Mission Handbook*, 21–32. 1996.

———. *Hankuk Seonkyosa Janeodeuleu Kyoyukjeok Pilyo* [The educational needs of Korean missionary children]. Seoul: GMF Press, 2013.

———. "A Hermeneutical Model of Urban Religious Symbols: The Case of Konya, Turkey." Ph.D. diss., Trinity International University, 1998.

———. "Korea and the Middle East: Religious Encounters," 2014. www.mei.edu/content/map/korea-and-the-middle-east-religious-encounters.

———. "The Korea Research Institute for Missions." In *Church Partnerships in Asia: A Singapore Conversation*, edited by Michael Nai-Chiu Poon, 154–67. Singapore: Genesis and Trinity Theological College, 2011.

———. "The Korean Hostage Incident: Seven Lessons Learned." In *Sorrow and Blood: Christian Mission in Contexts of Suffering, Persecution, and Martyrdom*, edited by William D. Taylor, Antonia van der Meer, and Reg Reimer, 303–8. Pasadena, Calif.: William Carey Library, 2012.

———, ed. *Korean Mission Handbook*. Seoul, Korea: Global Missionary Press, 1992, 1994, 1996, 1998.

———. "Korean Missionary Children and Their Educational Needs." In Bonk, *Family Accountability in Missions: Korean and Western Case Studies*, 243–58.

———. "The Korean Missionary Movement and Leadership Issues (2000–2020)." Unpublished paper, 2009.

———. "Missional Accountability in Korean Contexts." *Hapshin Theological Review* no. 1 (November 2012): 137–49.

———. "Missionary Attrition in Korea: Opinions of Mission Executives." In Taylor, *Too Valuable to Lose*, 129–42.

———. "Missionary Families and Korean Mission Finance: Realities and Concerns." In Bonk, *Family Accountability in Missions*, 138–48.

———. "Missions from Korea 2012: Slowdown and Maturation." *International Bulletin of Missionary Research* 36, no. 2 (April 2012): 84–85.

———. "Missions from Korea 2013: Microtrends and Finance." *International Bulletin of Missionary Research* 37, no. 2 (April 2013): 96–97.

———. "Missions from Korea 2014: Missionary Children." *International Bulletin of Missionary Research* 38, no. 2 (April 2014): 84–85.

———. "The Place and Function of Research in Contexts of Suffering, Persecution, and Martyrdom." In Taylor, *Sorrow and Blood*, 469–73.

———. "The Promise, Limitation, and Future of Empirical Research in Missions." *Korean Missions Quarterly*, English ed. (2012): 144–51.

———. "The Protestant Missionary Movement in Korea: Current Growth and Development." *International Bulletin of Missionary Research* 32, no. 2 (April 2008): 59–64.

———. "The Recent Korean Missionary Movement: A Record of Growth, and More Growth Needed." *International Bulletin of Missionary Research* 27, no. 1 (January 2003): 11–17.

———, ed. Reports on the Korean missionary movement. Seoul: Korea Research Institute for Mission, 2000–2013.

———. "The Spiritual Halryu: The Status and Issues of Korean Missions" (in Korean), 2004, unpublished report, www.krim.org.

———. "Who Are the Korean Missionaries?" In Moon, *Korean Mission Handbook*, 1–7. 1994.

Nelson, Marlin L., ed. *Directory of Korean Missionaries and Mission Societies*. Seoul: Asian Center for Theological Studies and Mission, 1979, 1982, 1986.

———, ed. *Directory of Korean Mission Societies, Mission Training Institutes, and Missionaries*. Seoul: Basilae, 1989.

Nussbaum, Stan. *Breakthrough! Steps to Research and Resolve the Mysteries in Your Ministry*. Colorado Springs, Colo.: GMI Research Services, 2007.

Park, Sang-Jin. "A Study on Types of Christian Alternative Schools" [in Korean]. *Korea Presbyterian Journal of Theology* 37 (2010): 153–87.
Park, Yong Kyu. "Historical Overview of Korean Missions." In Bonk, *Accountability in Missions*, 1–18.
Pate, Larry D. "The Changing Balance in Global Mission." *International Bulletin of Missionary Research* 15, no. 2 (April 1991): 56–61.
Pollock, David C. "Being a Third-Culture Kid: A Profile." In Bowers, *Raising Resilient MKs*, 40–49.
Ro, Bong Rin. "Sunkyosaro bureombateun chukbok" [The blessing of being called as a missionary]. In *Somyeong: Naega Yeogi Itnaida, Nareul Bonesoseo* [Calling: Here I am! Send me!], edited by Timothy Kiho Park and Wonsuk Ma, 86–97. Seoul: Qumran, 2010.
Robert, Dana L. "Shifting Southward: Global Christianity since 1945." *International Bulletin of Missionary Research* 24, no. 2 (April 2000): 50–58.
Robertson, Rolland. *Globalization: Social Theory and Global Culture*. London: SAGE Publications, 1992.
Schreiter, Robert. *The New Catholicity: Theology between the Global and the Local*. Maryknoll, N.Y.: Orbis Books, 1999.
Schubert, Esther. "Keeping Third-Culture Kids Emotionally Healthy: Depression and Suicide among MKs." In *Compendium of the International Conference on Missionary Kids: New Directions in Missions, Implications for MKs, Manila, Philippines, November 5–9, 1984*, 96–102. Pasadena, Calif.: William Carey Library, 1986.
Shin, Caleb. "Mogeum Wonchikkwa Huwon Guideline: Seonkyodanche Ipjang" [Principles of fund-raising and guidelines for support: A mission agency perspective]. In Bangkok Mission Forum Steering Committee, *Mission and Accountability*, 159–80.
Shin, Sang-Mok. "Choongdongseonkyohei hongkeyhyun bonbujang ..." [Hong Gye Hyun, director of the Middle East Team, looking for . . .]. *Kukmin Daily*. March 21, 2014. http://m.missionlife.co.kr/view.asp?arcid=0008155690&code=23111111.

Siewert, John A., ed. *Mission Handbook 1998–2000: U.S. and Canadian Christian Ministries Overseas*. 17th ed. Monrovia, Calif.: MARC, 1997.

Sohn, Chang-Nam. "Seonkyo Danche Jaejung System: Hyegye Gijun" [The financial system of mission agencies: Accounting standard]. In Bangkok Mission Forum Steering Committee, *Mission and Accountability*, 91–101.

Srivastva, Suresh, and Frank J. Barrett. "Appreciative Organizing: Implications for Executive Functioning." In *Appreciative Management and Leadership: The Power of Positive Thought and Action in Organization*, edited by Suresh Srivastva and David L. Cooperrider, 381–400. Euclid, Ohio: Williams Custom Publishing, 1999.

Sztompka, Piotr. "The Trauma of Social Change: A Case of Postcommunist Societies." In *Cultural Trauma and Collective Identity*, edited by Jeffrey C. Alexander, Ron Eyerman, Bernhard Giesen, Neil J. Smelser, and Piotr Sztompka, 155–95. Berkeley: Univ. of California Press, 2004.

Sung, Nam Yong. "Response to Stanley W. Green, 'Mission, Missionary, and Church Accountability as a Case Study.'" In Bonk, *Accountability in Missions*, 83–87.

Taylor, William D. "From Iguassu to the Reflective Practitioners of the Global Family of Christ." In Taylor, *Global Missiology for the Twenty-First Century*, 3–13.

———, ed. *Global Missiology for the Twenty-First Century: The Iguassu Dialogue*. Grand Rapids: Baker, 2000.

———, ed. *Kingdom Partnerships for Synergy in Missions*. Pasadena, Calif.: William Carey Library, 1994.

———, ed. *Too Valuable to Lose: Exploring the Causes and Cures of Missionary Attrition*. Pasadena, Calif.: William Carey Library, 1997.

Taylor, William D., Antonia van der Meer, and Reg Reimer, eds. *Sorrow and Blood: Christian Mission in Contexts of Suffering, Persecution, and Martyrdom*. Pasadena, Calif: William Carey Library, 2012.

Tucker, Ruth. *From Jerusalem to Irian Jaya: A Biographical History of Christian Missions*. Grand Rapids: Zondervan, 1983.

Vanston, John H. *Minitrends: How Innovators and Entrepreneurs Discover and Profit from Business and Technology Trends*. Austin, Tex.: Technology Futures, 2010.
Walls, Andrew F. *The Cross-Cultural Process in Christian History*. Maryknoll, N.Y.: Orbis Books, 2002.
———. *The Missionary Movement in Christian History: Studies in the Transmission of Faith*. Maryknoll, N.Y.: Orbis Books, 2000.
Ward, Ted. "Doing Research Together." In Bowers, *Raising Resilient MKs*, 445–55.
Watanabe, Toshikazu, and Mitsunori Miyake. *Performance Leadership*. Trans. Sin-Il Kang. Seoul: Sigma Insight, 2003 [2002].
Weber, Linda J., and Dotsey Welliver, eds. *Mission Handbook: U.S. and Canadian Protestant Ministries Overseas, 2007–2009*. Wheaton, Ill.: Evangelism and Missions Information Service, 2007.
Yang, Young Ran. "Jungkuk Jujae Hankuk Seonkyosaeu Seongkongjeakin Jangkisayeoke Daehan Yeonku" [A study on the factors of successful ministries of Korean missionaries in China]. Th.M. thesis, Hapdong Theological Seminary, 2006.
Yim, Yun Taek. *Haebang Hu Choechoeu Seonkyosa Cheheomgi* [The biography of the first missionary after independence]. Seoul: Duranno Press, 2009.

INDEX

A
accountability, 24–27, 36, 50, 68–69, 109, 203–15, 217–20
AD2000 and Beyond movement, 179
Adopt-A-People movement, 205
Afghanistan, 8, 16, 86, 109, 243–45, 248–49
Africa, 30–31, 41, 48, 66, 80, 94, 112, 283–84, 289–90, 296
Ahn, Jung-Gook, 275
All-Asia Mission Consultation, 176
All Nations Christian College, 177
All Nations School, 285
American Bible Society, 175
animism, 16, 41, 67, 81, 96, 112
Antioch High School, 284–85
Asbury Theological Seminary, 175
Asia, 4, 8, 30–31, 38, 41, 48, 66, 80, 90, 94, 107, 112, 179, 283–84
 Central Asia, 9, 233
 East Asia, 179, 279
 See also specific countries and regions
Asia Graduate School of Theology (AGST), 179
Asia Pacific region, 174–75
Asia Pacific Bible Society, 174
Asia Theological Association (ATA), 179–80
Asian missionaries, 76

Asian Missions Association, 176
Australia, 124

B
Bangkok, 174
Bangladesh, 282, 286
Barrington College, 175
Bethany Mission College, 175
Bible
 college, 179
 distribution, 174
 stories, 76
 studies, 206–7
 translation, 4, 17, 38, 41, 64, 84, 90, 96, 108
Black Forest Academy, 263, 269
Bourofaye Christian School, 263
Bright Future Global Academy, 284–85
Buddhist contexts, 16, 41, 67, 81, 96, 112, 190
Business As Mission, 10, 19, 238

C
Cambodia, 282, 286
Cameroon, 282, 285–86, 296
Campus Ministry International (CMI), 19, 80, 237–38
Canada, 70, 80–81, 94, 108, 124
Central Asia, 9, 233

China, 13, 49, 66, 80, 89–90, 94, 108, 174, 190
Cho, David Dong Jin, 173, 175–77, 190
Cho, Hye, 276
Choi, Chan Young, 173–75, 190
Choi, Paul Hyung Keun, 154
Choi, Sung Hee, 285, 296
Chongshin Theological University, 180
Chosun Theological Seminary, 175
church
  global, 13, 59, 80, 106, 173, 175, 178–79, 186, 202, 253–54
  indigenous, 17
  local, 6, 16, 19–20, 27, 40–41, 54, 56, 59, 62, 72–75, 87–88, 98–99, 101, 105, 148–49, 188–89, 191–94, 232, 235, 241, 248, 270, 272
  planting, 4, 17, 30, 38, 41, 64, 83, 96, 108, 116, 127, 160, 180, 197–98, 237–38, 298
  revival, 7, 81, 109
  sending, 14, 73, 188, 205, 249
Columbia Bible College, 178
Columbia International University, 180
Communist contexts, 16, 41, 67, 81, 96, 112, 175, 264, 288
Concordia Seminary, 178
Confucianism, 275
contextualization, 55, 101, 103, 145, 201, 219, 223, 250, 252, 254
Covenant Academy, 284–85
Covenant Seminary, 178
cultural exegesis, 225, 252–53

D
Dakar Academy, 263
Dankook University, 179

Darakbang Evangelism Fellowship, 177
David Cho Missiological Institute, 176
diaspora ministry, 83, 44, 96, 127, 279
Directory of Korean Missionaries and Mission Societies, 278
discipleship training, 4, 17, 38, 64, 83, 96, 108, 198

E
East Asia, 179, 279
ethnocentrism, 146, 150, 223
Eurasia (former USSR), 9, 38, 41, 48, 112
Europe, 9, 30–31, 38, 41, 48, 66, 80, 94, 112, 190, 283–84
  Western Europe, 9, 38, 41, 80, 94, 112
evangelicals, evangelicalism, 6, 17, 97, 224, 244, 246, 296
evangelism, 4, 17, 30, 38, 41, 64, 76, 84, 96, 108, 116, 127, 156, 158–60, 244, 246, 249, 290
Ewha Woman's University, 177

F
Farrell, Hunter, 206
field research, 58–59, 88, 114, 221, 227, 262, 285
field strategy, 50, 54–56, 59, 72–73, 101
finances, 27, 37, 54, 69, 71, 72, 86, 115, 121, 138, 140, 192, 194, 204, 208–10, 231–41, 265–66, 272, 288–89, 292–93
frontier missions. *See* missions
Frontiers, 181
Fuller Theological Seminary, 175–77

Fullerton, Larry, 206

G

GDQ International Christian School, 263
GEDA International, 175
Germany, 49, 66, 80–81, 94, 108, 124, 263
Glanz, Jeffrey, 164–65, 167
Global Bible Translators (GBT), 90
Global Mapping International (GMI), 193
Global Missionary Fellowship (GMF), 47, 65, 80, 90, 166, 181, 192, 218
Global Missionary Society (GMS), 46–47, 65, 79, 90, 166, 180
Global Missionary Training Center (GMTC), 177, 181
globalization
  educational ministries and, 32, 34, 287, 294
  increasing, 13, 43, 85, 88, 103, 115, 196, 202, 249, 255, 268, 275
  of Korean missions, 50, 56, 70, 74, 77, 80–81, 84, 101, 143, 145, 175, 186
  of Korean society, 7, 80–81, 301
  localization vs., 143, 150–51
glocal, glocalization, 84–85, 90, 143–51, 181, 187, 192, 248, 253, 270
  Korean missions and. *See* Korea
Glovill High School, 265
Gospel, 10, 38, 48–49, 66, 73–74, 80, 86, 142, 196, 247, 279
Grace International School, 263
Green, Stanley, 206

H

Hahn, Geoffrey, 206

Hahn, Paul, 205
Hanyang University, 181
Hawaii Theological Seminary, 179
Hiebert, Paul, 14, 97, 214
Hindu contexts, 16, 41, 67, 81, 96, 112, 288
homeschooling, 29, 114–15, 117, 261, 266–67, 273
hostage incident, 8, 16, 243–50
hybrid culture kids, 29, 115, 271

I

idolatry, 212, 218
Iguassu Missiological Consultation, 182
imperialism, 55, 73, 194
India, 49, 66, 80–81, 89, 93–95, 108, 124
individualism, 50, 57, 110, 147, 199, 218
Indonesia, 49, 66, 80, 94, 108, 277, 282, 285–86, 289
information technology (IT), 43, 53, 61, 71
Institute of Islamic Studies (Seoul), 177–78
International Association for Mission Studies (IAMS), 178
International Bulletin of Missionary Research (*IBMR*), 193, 232
International Fellowship of Evangelical Students, 178
Islamic contexts, 9, 16, 34, 38, 41, 81, 112, 178, 190, 198, 248, 264, 275–80, 288, 290
Islamophobia, 280

J

Japan, 49, 66, 80–81, 94–95, 108, 179, 244
Jeju Island, 277

Jeon Ju University, 175
Jung, Min-Young, 204, 207

K
Kang, Dae Heung, 205
Kang, Stephen, 238
Kang, Sung-Sam Samuel, 173, 179–80, 185–87, 190, 205
Kim, Gideon, 238
Kim, Hark Yoo, 154
Kim, Myung Hyuck, 246
Kim, Soo Jung, 154
Kim, Tae-Kwon, 75
Kim Il-sung University, 176
Korea, Korean
  hostage incident, 8, 16, 243–50
  missionary
    children, 6, 27–28, 30, 53, 76, 113–14, 116–17, 140, 181, 233, 259–61, 264–65, 267, 269, 271, 273
    educational needs, 28, 75–76, 87–88, 113–15, 140, 214, 233, 236, 238, 259–73, 290
    educational ministries, 4, 17, 20, 32–36, 38, 41, 64, 83, 281–83, 287–88, 290–94, 297–300
    leadership styles, 135, 163–66, 168–71
  movement
    growth, 3, 6–7, 11, 14, 21, 44–45, 50, 61, 74, 76–78, 81, 84, 101–3, 107–8, 111, 215, 247
  missions
    finance, 41, 138, 231
    glocalizing, 84, 90, 143–44, 146, 148, 192, 248
    indigenous, 52, 70, 145, 210, 216

microtrends and finance, 37, 39, 232
minitrends and issues, 8, 15–17, 36
partnership. *See* partnership
strategic agenda, 84
North Korea, 175–76, 178–79
South Korea, 37, 107, 175
War, 276
Korea Evangelical Alliance, 246
Korea Evangelical Fellowship, 177
Korea Evangelical Missiological Association, 177
Korea Evangelistic Inter-Mission Alliance (KEIMA), 175
Korea Global Leadership Institute (KGLI), 218
Korea International Mission (KIM), 175
Korea Interserve, 177
Korea InterVarsity Christian Fellowship, 177
Korea Presbyterian Mission (KPM Kosin), 206–7
Korea Research Institute for Mission (KRIM), 5, 37, 43, 61, 77, 113, 122, 191–92, 208, 210, 231, 250, 259, 281
Korea University of International Studies, 177
Korea World Mission Association (KWMA), 177, 180–81, 239
Korean Global Mission Leadership Forum (KGMLF), 203, 205
Korean Islamic Foundation, 276
Korean Mission Handbook, 3, 7, 124, 128–30, 192, 278
Korean Muslim Federation, 276
Korean Presbyterian Church, 277
Korean War, 276
Kuwait, 277

L

Laos Bible Society, 174
Latin America, 30, 41, 48, 66, 80, 94, 112, 283–84
Lausanne Congress on World Evangelization, 176
leadership
  assessment, 104
  development, 12, 21, 27, 100, 102–6, 109, 170, 182, 187–88, 215, 217–18, 235
  global, 103, 176, 182, 184, 196
  servant, 22, 24, 97
  structure, 23, 97–98, 100, 103, 252
  styles, 135, 163–66, 168–71
Lee, Ban Seok (Peter), 206
Lee, David Taiwoong, 173, 181–83, 187, 190
Lee, Jung Sik, 237
Lee, Ki-poong, 277
Lee, Shin Chul, 206
Livingstone Academy, 284–85
localization, 143, 150–51
London Bible College, 177

M

Majority World, 50, 52, 59, 85, 89–90, 121, 182, 184, 188–89, 194, 196, 246
Malaysia Baptist Theological Seminary, 218
Manila Hankuk (Korean) Academy, 262
martyrdom, 249, 251, 253–54, 256
megachurches, 55, 58, 201, 216–17, 235, 240
member care, 11–12, 20–21, 43, 46–47, 50–51, 57, 59, 61, 68–69, 75, 94, 101–2, 108, 110, 134, 138–40, 146, 182, 184, 188, 205, 218, 238–39, 247–50, 299
  noninterference, 50–51, 68–69
  specialist, 51, 57, 59, 101, 182, 239
  systematic care, 50, 68
microbusiness, 85
Middle East, 41, 48, 66–67, 80, 94, 112, 275–80
Middle East Concern, 193
Midwest Theological Seminary, 178
missiology, missiologists, 13, 88, 101–3, 105, 140, 146–48, 150–51, 175–76, 178–82, 188, 206, 218, 221, 227, 252, 257
missionary
  attrition, 37, 45, 63, 121–24, 129–39, 141–42, 154, 198
  causes of, 123, 131, 134–35, 137, 141
  average monthly living cost, 6, 27, 232
  care, 20, 74–75, 87, 109, 122, 138–39, 141–42, 240–41, 272
  career, 47, 78, 115, 117, 149, 178
  expansion, 124
  families, 11–12, 109–10, 115–17, 131, 231, 233–34, 239, 241, 260, 264–66, 271–72
  married, 41, 44–45, 63, 81–82, 95, 112, 132–33, 166
  overseas, 7, 61–62, 64, 80–81, 101, 113, 201, 235, 238, 241, 259, 281, 298
  retirement, 10, 12, 18, 39, 63, 75, 109, 136, 213, 217, 232, 236–37, 239
  sending structures, 50–51, 59, 68, 70, 79–80
  single, 4, 9, 18, 39, 41, 44–45, 53, 63, 72, 75, 81–82, 95, 112, 129, 131–34, 137, 141, 166, 278
    female, 132–34, 178
    male, 132–34

training, 12, 16, 21, 46, 64, 79, 87–89, 102, 140, 142, 151, 154, 157, 180–81, 189, 199, 227, 248, 255
missionary kids (MKs), 5, 11–12, 20–21, 28–30, 36, 88, 110, 113–17, 140, 235–36, 238, 240, 259–73
  education, 28, 235, 259, 262, 267
  recommendations for improvement, 270
missions
  executives, 11, 20–21, 24, 26, 30, 32–35, 86–90, 97–99, 121–22, 127, 134, 136–37, 140, 208–12, 217, 231, 235–36, 239, 250, 261, 273, 291–92, 297
  frontier, 4, 10, 16–17, 41, 48, 86, 96, 108, 112, 128, 279
  pioneer, 127–28
  short-term, 16, 44, 86, 243–44, 247, 249–50, 272
Miyake, Mitsunori, 164–65, 168
mobilization, 50, 94, 188–89, 193
Mongol Huree University, 285
Mongolia, 282, 284–86
Mongolia International School, 284
Mongolia International University, 285
monocultural background, 58, 66–67, 83, 96, 136, 142, 145–46, 150, 199, 268
Moreau, Scott, 207
multicultural teams and settings, 55, 58, 76, 84, 99, 180, 263
Murree Language School, 177
Muslim, 4, 67, 275–77, 279

N
Nelson, Marlin L., 43–44, 62, 77, 154, 278

Nepal, 282, 284–85
Nevius, John, 238
NGOs, 36, 240, 243, 245, 298–99
Nigeria, 180
Noh, Moo Hyun, 244
North America, 41, 48, 66, 80, 94, 112
North Korea, 175–76, 178–79

O
Oceania, 30–31, 41, 48, 66, 112, 283–84
Ok, Chun Chae, 173, 177–78, 183, 190
Ok, Han Hum, 246
Operation World, 193
Overseas Ministries Study Center (OMSC), 193, 205
Overseas Missionary Fellowship (OMF), 90, 177–79

P
Pakistan, 178, 278
Park, Song-Su, 75
Park, Timothy, 206
Park, Un-Jo, 244
partnership, 13, 52–56, 64, 72, 74–76, 151, 173–74, 177, 180, 182, 185–86, 188–94, 196–97, 202, 205–6
persecution, 251, 253–54, 256
Persia, 276
Philippines, 49, 66, 80, 108, 174, 179, 262
Pittsburgh Theological Seminary, 174
postmodernity, 218
Presbyterian
  General Assembly, 174
  Hapdong, 90, 166
Presbyterian Theological Seminary, 174–76

Protestant, 44, 50, 68, 77–78, 81, 83, 93
Pyongyang Seminary, 176

R
Reducing Missionary Attrition Project (ReMAP), 122, 124, 126–27, 130, 134, 136, 154
research, development, and delivery (RDD), 191
revival, 7, 81, 109
Ro, Bong Rin, 173, 178–79, 184–85, 190
Roman Catholic, 50, 68
Russia, 49, 66, 80–81, 94–95, 108

S
Saudi Arabia, 277
Second Bangkok Mission Forum, 203–5, 219
secular, 18, 23, 96, 99, 110, 149, 198, 210, 237, 245, 264
Sejong Global School, 265
Seoul National University, 178
Seoul Theological Seminary, 176
September 11, 2001, 277
shamanism, 275
Shin, Caleb, 204
Sohn, Chang Nam, 204
Sohn, Ensup, 75
South Korea, 37, 107, 175
South Pacific, 66, 80, 94
Southern Baptist Theological Seminary, 181
spiritual fundamentals, 182, 190
SPSS, 144, 155, 164, 259, 283
suffering, 251–57
Sung, Nam Yong, 206

T
Taliban, 86, 244–45

Taylor, William, 173
Thailand, 49, 66, 80–81, 94–95, 108, 174, 204, 263, 278
Thailand Bible Society, 174
theological
   education, 4, 17, 30, 38–39, 41, 45, 63–64, 83, 96, 108, 142, 150, 157, 176, 179–80, 281
   foundation, 6
   orientation, 6, 17, 23, 47, 84, 96, 99
   principles, 65
   reflection, 101
   training, 45, 140
theology, 83, 88, 179–81, 196, 219, 227, 245, 296
third culture kids, 29, 115, 270–71
   See also hybrid culture kids
Torch Trinity Graduate University, 175, 177–79
Trinity Evangelical Divinity School, 181
Trinity International University, 180
Turkey, 144–47, 149–50, 153, 156, 276
Turkish, 155–56

U
United Bible Societies, 175
United Kingdom, 51, 89, 124, 177
United States of America, 44, 48–49, 51, 61, 66, 70, 80–81, 89–90, 93–94, 108, 124, 175, 180, 238, 279
   American, 89, 263, 269, 271, 278, 297
University Bible Fellowship (UBF), 19, 46–47, 65, 79
University of London, 177
Urbana Mission Convention, 6
U.S. Center for World Mission, 193
Uzbekistan, 49, 66

W
Watanabe, Toshikazu, 164–65, 168
WEC International, 90
WEC Missionary Training Center, 175
Western Seminary, 176
Wheaton College, 178
William Carey International University, 176
World Evangelical Alliance Mission Commission, 154, 176–77, 179–80, 193

Wright, Christopher, 207
Wycliffe Bible Translators (WBT), 90
Wycliffe Global Alliance, 181, 207

Y
Yale Divinity School, 178
Yang, Young Rang, 154
Yoon, Won Roh, 296